A Very Serious Thing

AMERICAN *AC* CULTURE

Edited by Stanley Aronowitz, Sandra M. Gilbert, and Jackson Lears

Nancy A. Walker

A Very Serious Thing

Women's Humor and American Culture

University of Minnesota Press • Minneapolis

Published by the University of Minnesota Press
2037 University Avenue Southeast, Minneapolis MN 55414.
Published simultaneously in Canada
by Fitzhenry & Whiteside Limited, Markham.
Printed in the United States Of America.

Library of Congress Cataloging-in-Publication Data

Walker, Nancy.
    A very serious thing: women's humor and American culture/Nancy
Walker.
        Bibliography: p.
        Includes index.
        ISBN 0-8166-1702-3
        ISBN 0-8166-1703-1 (pbk.)
            1. American wit and humor—Women authors—History and
        criticism.   2. Women and literature—United States.   3. Feminism
        and literature —United States.   4. Women—United States—
        Humor—History.
        I. Title.
        PS430.W3 1988
        817'.009'9287—dc19   88-17143

For my father

Contents

Preface

When I began a formal study of American women's humorous writing in 1979, I felt as though I had ventured into uncharted territory. Studies of American humor abounded, but, as is the case in so much traditional scholarship, the women were left out or relegated to footnotes. Except for an occasional mention of Dorothy Parker, the published sources I consulted made it seem as if those who wrote about American humor lived in a different culture than I. I remembered having read Phyllis McGinley's light verse in the magazines to which my mother subscribed, I knew that Jean Kerr's *Please Don't Eat the Daisies* had been a book before it was a film and then a television series, I had studied and had taught the work of Dorothy Parker, and Erma Bombeck's column, "At Wit's End," was in my daily newspaper. Why weren't these writers part of "American humor"?

At first I assumed that the virtual absence of women's humor from anthologies and critical studies was caused by the same myopic perspective that had made us think for so long that there had been no female composers or scientists. And this is certainly part of it. But as I continued to investigate, I discovered an even more basic reason: women aren't supposed to have a sense of humor. Time and again, in sources from the mid-nineteenth century to very recently, I encountered writers (male) commenting — and sometimes lamenting — that women were incapable of humor, and other writers (female) explaining that they knew women weren't *supposed* to have a sense of humor and then proceeding to be very funny indeed. From Frances Whitcher in the 1840s to Deanne Stillman in the 1970s, America's female humorists have deomonstrated an awareness that they were writing humor in the face of a prevailing opinion that they were not capable of what they were in fact, at that moment, doing.

Explaining the reasons for this fundamental absurdity is one of the major intentions of this book. The other major purpose is to demonstrate how closely tied American women's humor is to the realities of being a woman in this culture during the past 150 years. No matter what form the writers use—light verse, sketches, newspaper columns, fables, jokes—a dominant theme in women's humor is how it feels to be a member of a subordinate group in a culture that prides itself on equality, what it is like to try to meet standards for behavior that are based on stereotypes rather than on human beings. Women have used humor to talk to each other about their common concerns, to survive, and frequently to protest their condition.

The territory I had entered proved not to be entirely uncharted. In fact, two anthologies of women's humor, Kate Sanborn's *The Wit of Women* (1885) and Martha Bensley Bruère and Mary Ritter Beard's *Laughing Their Way: Women's Humor in America* (1934), had been published with the express purpose of refuting the premise that women had no sense of humor. That they had failed to do so is perhaps not surprising in view of the fact that only in the 1970s did feminist scholars begin to undertake revision of the established canon in virtually every field, including American literature and American Studies, attempting not merely to represent women's writing and experience, but to create a new, gender-balanced lens through which to view our common—and uncommon—lives.

At the same time that I began to investigate this interesting territory, Zita Dresner was finishing a dissertation on twentieth-century American women humorists, and Jane Curry and Linda Ann Finton Morris had completed dissertations on selected nineteenth-century humorists. Gloria Kaufman and Mary Kay Blakely were editing *Pulling Our Own Strings: Feminist Humor and Satire* (1980), drawn primarily from contemporary sources. Soon there was a Network, a Field, a Movement, sessions at professional meetings, and a special issue of *Studies in American Humor* devoted to women's expression.

The present study has, as all studies do, some limitations. Although there are occasional references to other media, I have concentrated primarily on women's *written* humor as opposed to that found in cartoons, film, television, and stand-up comedy. There is a wealth of material in these media available for study, and some of that study is now in progress, but each medium presents a different set of issues and problems, including those of production, setting, and audience. There is also the question of the ephemeral nature of some of this humor. The best (most revealing, funniest) humor is probably spoken, but without a Boswell in constant attendance, it gets lost. Written humor stays put, even when the pages get yellow.

Further, the excerpts that I have selected to illustrate my points have had to be brief enough to be manageable in the text, even though sometimes a longer selection might have been more effective. Much humor works by cumulative effect, not by one-liners: Dorothy Parker's verses are pithy and quotable, but Mary Roberts Rinehart's "Tish" stories and Ann Warner French's "Susan Clegg" stories from the turn-of-the-century period are long and droll, the latter stories told in the form of the lengthy conversations between women that are basic to communication among women and thus to women's humor.

Not all of the writers whose work is excerpted or referred to here are known as humorists — e.g., Anne Bradstreet and Emily Dickinson. They have, however, written humorously on occasion about issues of self-definition and cultural constraints: issues that are central concerns of women whose primary mode is humor. Some writers, too, who have been known for wholly serious literature, have turned to the comic for different purposes. Shirley Jackson, for example, is remembered for compelling stories such as "The Lottery," yet her books *Life Among the Savages* (1953) and *Raising Demons* (1957) are squarely within the genre of American women's domestic humor. Still other writers, such as Edna St. Vincent Millay, have used pseudonyms for their humorous work; Millay wrote as "Nancy Boyd" when she wished to go further than the occasional wit of her sonnets.

The use of the terms "humor," "wit," and "comic" inevitably brings up the thorny issue of definition, which I intend to sidestep here as neatly as I can. In doing so, I am in good company. E. B. White, in his preface to *A Subtreasury of American Humor* (1948) provided the most frequently-quoted justification of such an evasion:

> Analysts have had their go at humor, and I have read some of this interpretative literature, but without being greatly instructed. Humor

can be dissected, as a frog can, but the thing dies in the process and the innards are discouraging to any but the pure scientific mind.

Dorothy Parker, in her introduction to *The Most of S. J. Perelman*, emphasizes the exertion of the effort rather than the deadness of the result:

> I had thought, on starting this composition, that I should define what humor means to me. However, every time I tried to, I had to go and lie down with a cold wet cloth on my head.

The terminology associated with humor in its various forms has been endlessly debated, and definitions tend to vary according to disciplinary approach. Thus "comedy" most often refers to theatrical performance, whereas satire and parody are primarily literary forms. Linguist Umberto Eco distinguishes between humor and the "comic"—the latter having a fine disregard for rules and restrictions—in ways that I have found useful in defining two types of feminist humor. Indeed, the variety of disciplines that I have drawn upon in this study—including psychology, history, anthropology, linguistics, and feminist literary theory—makes precise, fixed definitions impossible.

However, some distinctive characteristics of women's humorous writing, while they do not amount to a definition, become apparent to anyone who reads much of this material. First, women tend to be *story*tellers rather than *joke* tellers. Humor functions for them more as a means of communication than as a means of self-presentation, a sharing of experience rather than a demonstration of cleverness. Related to this is the fact that women's humorous expression is almost never purely comic or absurd. Even when, as is frequently the case, it points to the myriad absurdities that women have been forced to endure in this culture, it carries with it not the lighthearted feeling that is the privilege of the powerful, but instead a subtext of anguish and frustration.

When, in the mid-nineteenth century, humorist Frances Whitcher noted that it was "a very serious thing to be a funny woman," she was speaking primarily in terms of the negative cultural reaction to a female humorist, but her statement should also compel us to move women's humor from the footnotes to the center of the text and allow it to illuminate the experience of women in American culture.

Preface

I am indebted to a number of people for their assistance with this project. The staff of the Hugh Stephens Library at Stephens College—especially Joanna Todd—complied promptly and cheerfully with my numerous requests for interlibrary loan materials. My colleague Bertrice Bartlett shared with me her work on irony and introduced me to the newspaper columns of Molly Ivins. Alan Havig and Thomas F. Dillingham were constantly alert to sources that I found useful. For sensitive readings and critiques of parts of the manuscript I am grateful to Dick Caram, Hamilton Cravens, John Lowe, and Kathleen Wells-Morgan. Finally, for his unfailing love and support, my thanks to Burton M. Augst.

A Very Serious Thing

Introduction

I

In 1924 a book titled *Distressing Dialogues*, by Nancy Boyd, was published by Harper & Brothers. The book includes satiric sketches, some in the form of dialogues and monologues, of urban sophisticates or would-be sophisticates. In "No Bigger Than a Man's Hand," a marriage dissolves because the husband continually leaves the cap off the toothpaste. "Knock Wood" features a group of people identified by such names as "the Man with the Wrong Kind of Tie," "the Very Clever Woman," and "the Only Woman in Black," who talk about superstitions at a party. "Cordially Yours" is a series of imaginary letters of the sort that people often wish they had the courage actually to write, including one to "Person who has made you a Proposal of Marriage, Rejecting him," which begins by describing a common female fantasy:

> Sir:
>   Do you take me for an idiot? For four seasons I have parried the advances of the talented, the titled, the handsome-as-Apollo, and the verminous-with-wealth. It was for me Paderewski took up politics, for me D'Annunzio became a soldier. The Grand Duke Michael has begged for my photograph in three languages and Russian, Freud has dreamed of me. . . .[1]

The tone and settings of these sketches are similar to those of Dorothy Parker, and tie the pieces closely to a period in American

3

literary history; but the common theme of women's desire to claim autonomy and power is central to American women's humor.

The preface to *Distressing Dialogues* was written by the poet Edna St. Vincent Millay, who speaks of herself as the author's "earliest admirer," and refers to her "never-failing interest and delight" in the author's work. Appropriately so: "Nancy Boyd" was the pseudonym that Millay used when publishing her humorous pieces, as a means of separating them from her poetry. Millay's "Nancy Boyd" sketches appeared in *Ainslee's* and *Vanity Fair* in the teens and the 1920s, as Millay struggled to make a name for herself as a poet. The income from the Boyd pieces helped to provide vital income during this period. As she wrote to her sister Norma in 1922, "Nancy is going strong in Vanity Fair, isn't she? Isn't she a blessing? Almost two years now the woman has been well nigh supporting me."[2]

Despite the popularity of her "Nancy Boyd" stories, Millay was concerned that her real name be associated only with her poetry, and that her ultimate reputation rest on her serious work rather than on her humor. She regarded Nancy Boyd as a sort of alter ego, and sometimes almost as a naughty child with a mind of her own. When Franklin P. Adams ("F. P. A.") accepted a Nancy Boyd piece for his humorous "Conning Tower" column in the New York *World* and then selected it for his annual award for the best contribution in 1925 (the prize being a watch), Millay wrote to him, "It's to be inscribed to Nancy, isn't it?—Else she'll be mad" (207).

Millay's career as "Nancy Boyd" exemplifies one set of circumstances for a female humorist in America. First, her place in American literature is based not on her humorous writing, but on the sonnets and lyrics for which she preferred to be known. Like Shirley Jackson, Alice Childress, and Jean Kerr, none of whom used pseudonyms, she was a serious writer for whom humor was a sideline, an avocation.[3] Second, although the Nancy Boyd stories were financially important to Millay, she speaks of them and of Nancy as though she is not really in control of them and wishes to be disassociated from them. The Boyd stories, she says in a letter, are "beautifully written, after a flippant fashion" (91); writing to Edmund Wilson, she begs him not to edit anything that is published under her real name, but, "as for Nancy, that's a little different" (160). Whereas many authors have preferred to be known for serious rather than humorous work (assuming that the two can be separated so neatly), the woman writer, facing more of a struggle to be taken seriously, may be even more concerned not to be associated with humor.

In sharp contrast to Millay is Deanne Stillman, co-editor of the 1976 collection of women's humor titled *Titters* and author of *Getting Back at Dad* (1981), a volume of her own humorous essays. From the time she was a teenager, Stillman wanted to be a humorist, but she believed that "writing funny was something girls didn't do," and therefore signed the parodies that she submitted to *Mad* magazine "Dean" rather than "Deanne."[4] Stillman's use of a different name was motivated by reasons entirely different from those prompting Millay to sign her humorous work "Nancy Boyd" — reasons that illustrate yet another central issue in the study of American women's humor: the absence of a visible tradition of such humor, so that women (and men) assume humor to be a male prerogative. Stillman was introduced to the established American humor canon by her father, who "proudly displayed the complete works of S. J. Perelman, Mark Twain, James Thurber" (5). When Stillman and her co-editor Anne Beatts published *Titters* in 1976, they subtitled it "The First Collection of Humor by Women," unaware of two previous collections: Kate Sanborn's *The Wit of Women* in 1885, and Martha Bruère and Mary Beard's *Laughing Their Way: Women's Humor in America* in 1934.

It may seem odd that in the 1920s Edna St. Vincent Millay felt free to write humor (as did Dorothy Parker, Margaret Fishback, and many other women), using a pseudonym only to protect her major ambition to be a poet, whereas Stillman, in the 1960s, felt prohibited by her gender from doing so. But the intervening years had changed women's lives and perspectives dramatically: World War II and its subsequent suburban movement had led women "back to the kitchen" to be fulfilled as wives and mothers, effectively negating those tentative steps toward gender equality that had been made in the early part of the century.

Stillman's impulse to write humor — specifically satire — arose from her perception of the incongruities of her own life. Following her parents' divorce, she was moved abruptly from an affluent life with gardeners and maids to a blue-collar neighborhood populated primarily by Catholic immigrants. The contrast between statues of Christ "nailed up over every kitchen table in town" (7) and her own Jewish upbringing, and between her father's continued affluence and her mother's struggle to pay the rent, developed her keen sense of the ironic: "Dad called to complain about having trouble joining the all-WASP Oakdale country club, and I was so broke I had to beat the tab for a Manner's Big Boy. . . . I had to write all of this stuff down because I couldn't believe it myself" (8). But even more basic to Stillman's motivation was another factor that affects women writers generally and women humorists in particular: the need to be taken seriously as an intellectually capable person, to prove to all the "Dads" of the world that a woman can perceive absurdity and convey it to others.

The career of Erma Bombeck, whose column about the perils of being a mother and homemaker, "At Wit's End," has been syndicated for more than twenty years, illustrates still other significant aspects of women's humor in America. One of these is the centrality of her subject matter to the tradition of women's humorous writing. Because the focus of most women's lives has been the home, it is natural that much of their humor should be located there, but the more important issue is how women perceive their role as homemakers. Bombeck's work typifies a major theme in women's humor: the harder a woman works, the more things go wrong—the washing machine eats socks, the children will not behave, the diet does not work. Bombeck's first book, *At Wit's End* (1967), opens with the following passage:

> It hits on a dull, overcast Monday morning. I awake realizing there is no party in sight for the weekend, I'm out of bread, and I've got a dry skin problem. So I say it aloud to myself, "What's a nice girl like me doing in a dump like this?"
> The draperies are dirty (and will disintegrate if laundered), the arms of the sofa are coming through. There is Christmas tinsel growing out of the carpet. And some clown has written in the dust on the coffee table, YANKEE GO HOME.[5]

Yet as Bombeck and the other writers of domestic humor convey in their work, it is not housewives who are failures, but a social system—including the media—that makes women solely responsible for the functioning of the household and sets impossibly high standards for their performance.

Bombeck also typifies American women's humor in her use of the newspaper column as her primary medium. Since the 1840s, the newspaper or magazine column has been the most common outlet for women's humorous observations. Frances Whitcher wrote for *Neal's Saturday Gazette* and *Godey's Lady's Book* in the 1840s and 1850s; Dorothy Parker for *Vanity Fair* in the 1920s. More recently, Nora Ephron has written a column for *Esquire*, Fran Lebowitz for *Mademoiselle* and *Interview*, Mary Bess Whidden for *Century* and *New Mexico Magazine*, Veronica Geng for *The New Yorker*, Molly Ivins for the Dallas *Times Herald*, and Ellen Goodman for syndication in hundreds of newspapers. With the exception of Ivins, all of these writers have had collections of their columns published in book form, with Bombeck emerging as far and away the most popular: between 1970 and 1980, her books sold more copies than those of any other author on the *New York Times* best-seller list.

It is important also that Bombeck's focus has changed over the years as women's lives have changed. When she started writing "At Wit's End" in 1965, she had taken ten years off from newspaper work to bear and care for three children; in 1981 she campaigned for the Equal Rights Amendment. Her columns have increasingly reflected the fact that the majority of women work outside the home. In February of 1982, for example, she wrote a column about children and the working mother that includes the following paragraph:

> Most mothers entering the labor market outside the home are naive. They stagger home each evening, holding mail in their teeth, the cleaning over their arm, a lamb chop defrosting under each armpit, balancing two gallons of frozen milk between their knees, and expect one of the kids to get the door.[6]

Bombeck's *persona* is also more assertive in more recent columns and books. In *Aunt Erma's Cope Book* (1979), when her husband tells her that one of his shirts has a ring around the collar, she responds, "What a coincidence! It matches the one around your neck!"[7]

As the examples of these three writers suggest, women's humor is an index to women's roles and values, and particularly to their relationship with American cultural realities. Being a female humorist in America has been problematic in a number of ways that are tied closely to other issues in women's history: the tension between intellect and femininity, male and female "separate spheres," women's status as a minority group, and the transforming power of a feminist vision. Seen in this cultural perspective, women's humor is indeed a "serious thing."

II

The history of women's humorous writing in America—and its relationship to conventional cultural formulations of woman's proper "sphere"—partakes of some of the elements of humor itself, chiefly irony. Despite the publication of several anthologies devoted exclusively to humorous verse, stories, essays, and sketches written by women, this remains a largely invisible tradition, even to those who are regarded as scholars of American humor. The reasons why this is true are complex, arising as they do from a number of seemingly unrelated factors in American cultural history: sociological realities such as the emergence of a middle-class, genteel culture in the early nineteenth century and mass migration to the suburbs in the 1950s; political issues such as the prohibition of female suffrage until 1920 and the exclusion of women from most of the professions until very recently; male hegemony in publishing and education; and assumptions about the nature and purpose of humor and the nature and abilities of women.

The central irony emerging from this intricate web of realities and beliefs is that women have been officially denied the possession of— hence the practice of—the sense of humor, and yet for more than 150 years in America they have written and published large amounts of it, often to enthusiastic public reception. Long before Dorothy Parker began writing for *The New Yorker* in 1926, women had written light verse, sketches, and columns for major publications such as *Godey's Lady's Book* as well as for their local newspapers; Anna Cora Mowatt's 1845 comedy *Fashion* had been received enthusiastically by the critics, including Edgar Allan Poe; and Marietta Holley's many books featuring her outspokenly feminist narrator Samantha Allen had rivaled the works of Mark Twain in sales and popularity. And yet, as recently as the 1970s, even female humorists themselves—essayists, script-writers, and stand-up comics—expressed time and again the sense of being pioneers in a field that lacked a female tradition.

To some extent, this is not surprising. Women in many professions have worked without the assurance of knowing that they were building upon a heritage established by generations of women before them—a heritage that would sanction their contributions and allow them to feel that they were participating in an ongoing process of female creativity. Yet literature, far more than most other professional areas, has traditionally been a haven for creative women: even though their work has often been regarded as trivial, or writing itself considered a harmless avocation for women of leisure, the strict prohibitions that have barred women from such professions as law and medicine (and that still persist in the form of discrimination against them in these areas) have not been as strictly applied. Among the educated classes in America, literacy has been a badge of gentility, and the ability to write poetry, in particular, a desirable mark of femininity. The fact that in the seventeenth century Anne Bradstreet became America's first widely recognized poet is something of an anomaly, but Bradstreet was not unique among women of her time, nor was her work "scorned," as she fears in her "Prologue." By the nineteenth century, female authors were sufficiently common to provoke Hawthorne's well-known comment about the "mob of scribbling women." As Fanny Fern's 1855 novel *Ruth Hall* illustrates, an educated woman in the nineteenth century could turn to writing to support herself if need be without giving up those qualities of modesty and decorum that the culture deemed appropriate for her.

But humor is different. The humorist is at odds with the publicly espoused values of the culture, overturning its sacred cows, pointing out the nakedness of not only the Emperor, but also the politician, the pious, and the pompous. For women to adopt this role means that they must break out of the passive, subordinate position mandated for them by centuries of patriarchal tradition and take on the power accruing to those who reveal the shams, hypocrisies, and incongruities of the dominant culture. To be a woman and a humorist is to confront and subvert the very power that keeps women powerless, and at the same time to risk alienating those upon whom women are dependent for economic survival.

This delicate balance between power and powerlessness informs the themes and forms of women's humorous writing. This literature has described myriad aspects of women's lives, employing familiar stereotypes of women for the purpose of mocking those stereotypes and showing their absurdity and even their danger. In the mid-nineteenth century, Frances Whitcher declared an unsuccessful war on the status-seeking inspired in women by the spread of genteel culture; in the 1920s, Margaret Fishback and Dorothy Parker deplored women's emotional dependence on men; in the 1970s, Judith Viorst explored the tension between traditional marriage and motherhood and the enlightenment of the women's movement. Embedded in the humorous writing of American women for more than 150 years is an exploration of powerlessness that constitutes a subversive protest against it.

To document, as this book does, the relationship between women's humorous literature and the culture in which the authors lived and wrote is to reveal yet one more example of women's lack of autonomy. The very invisibility of this significant portion of American humor is one testament to women's exclusion from power, and the messages of the humor itself are frequently eloquent statements of women's subordination. Just as important, a study of the relationship between humor and culture shows how deeply related are a variety of forces within that culture. For example, the rapid urbanization of American society at the turn of the twentieth century, together with the appeal of the assertive "New Woman" and the phenomenon of increased numbers of women pursuing careers, created the impression among many that a new era of freedom for women was indeed dawning. But by the mid-1920s women's humor made it clear that nothing had essentially changed. Florence Guy Seabury noted in *The Delicatessen Husband* (1926) that even in dual-career marriages, housework was still the responsibility of the woman. By the 1950s, the postwar suburban ideal that led many middle-class families out of the cities, the labor-saving devices that merely elevated the expectations for women's performance as homemakers, and the virtual isolation of women from their commuting husbands promoted the subgenre of domestic humor that shows women interacting more often with Girl Scout cookies and mateless socks than with ideas—which led to the frustrations that Betty Friedan described in *The Feminine Mystique* in 1963.

Most studies of American humor, particularly since Constance Rourke's *American Humor: A Study of the National Character* in 1931, have acknowledged the close link between humor and cultural values. Walter Blair's *Native American Humor* (1937) argued that a *true* American humor arose from the widespread frontier experience of Jacksonian America. Jesse Bier's 1968 *The Rise and Fall of American Humor* posited that American humor thrives on the tension between national pride and social criticism. Richard Hauck, in *A Cheerful Nihilism* (1971), found an American preoccupation with absurdity. But none of these studies, or those prior or subsequent to them, has taken into account the perspective of women, a perspective that would modify considerably the various characterizations of American humor that have been offered through the years.

In fact, most assessments of American humor—its themes, its strategies, and its value as an index of attitudes and values—are predicated upon the writing of those whose claim to the role of social critic and commentator (even on the most ephemeral fads and fashions) is secure: white males. Even when the white male humorist adopts for his own purposes the stance of the outsider—the naïve bumpkin who nonetheless sees the follies of the legislature, the "little man" bewildered by bureaucracy or technology—he writes with the authority of the insider, the person who is potentially in a position to change what he finds wrong, whether it is a law or the cut of a dinner jacket. Samuel Clemens could, had he wished, have run for political office; Marietta Holley could not. Because women—like members of racial and ethnic minorities—have largely been external to this circle of power, their humorous writing evidences a different relationship with the culture, one in which the status quo, however ludicrous, exerts a force to be coped with, rather than representing one of a number of interchangeable realities.

It is for this reason that women's humor so often seems to turn on and perpetuate traditional stereotypes of women: the gossipy spinster, the nagging wife, the inept housekeeper, the lovelorn woman, the dumb blonde. These are some of the roles in which women have been cast by men and male institutions, and as such they have, until quite recently, seemed fixed. What female humorists have done with these stereotypes, however, is to subvert them. The housewives who cannot reach perfection, such as those of Jean Kerr and Erma Bombeck, are in this situation because the standards for their performance are impossibly high; the lovelorn women of Dorothy Parker, Margaret Fishback, and others are victims of male indifference and the double standard; the dumb blonde, such as Lorelei Lee in Anita Loos's *Gentlemen Prefer Blondes* (1925), is not so dumb after all, but uses the assets she has to turn matters to her own advantage, all the while laughing at the men who perceive her as stupid.

III

One of America's earliest popular humorists, Frances M. Whitcher (1814-1852), exemplifies the central problem of the female humorist in America: the fact that humor is at odds with the conventional definition of ideal womanhood. Humor is aggressive; women are passive. The humorist occupies a position of superiority; women are inferior. Having been chided since childhood for her tendency to "make fun," Whitcher was to some extent aware of these paradoxes, and she developed a humorous strategy that has subsequently been used by many of America's female writers of humor: a text that functions on two levels, one that appears to endorse popular stereotypes of women, and another that points to the origins of these stereotypes in a culture that defines women in terms of their relationships with men.

The tradition of women's humor in America thus developed along different lines than did the standard canon of (primarily) male humor. Its subject matter, themes, and even its forms have been influenced by women's quite different relationship to authority, decision-making, and social change. The established tradition in American humor is replete with tall tales, political satire, and absurdity; women's humor presents not boasters but victims of cultural expectations, their political humor is usually directed to gender-specific issues such as female suffrage, and the absurdity they present is the fundamental absurdity of oppression. While influenced by many of the same trends and fashions in humor as men have been, such as the shift from dialect humor to a more urbane word play at the turn of the twentieth century, women writers have developed forms suited to their own lives and needs: the domestic saga, the skit, and humorous fantasy.

Reasons for such differences in women's humor are explained in large part by the complex attitudes toward women's relationship to humorous expression. Although the *appreciation* of male humor (as long as it is not bawdy or obscene) has long been considered an admirable female trait, the *creation* of humor by women, whether verbal or written, has provoked much controversy. Whether viewed from the perspective of psychology, anthropology, sociology, or linguistics, humor is tied to power, autonomy, and aggression in ways that directly affect gender relationships.

Because women have been regarded as a minority group in legal, economic, and attitudinal ways, it would be logical to suppose that their humor has elements in common with that of more clearly identified racial and ethnic minorities such as blacks, Jews, and Chicanos, and this is indeed the case. Like the humor of these other groups, women's humor embodies a "we-they" dialectic in which men are, in many ways, external to women's experience. Although women are intimately and consistently involved with men in ways that blacks, for example, are not with whites, their humor nonetheless reveals a collective consciousness: women give each other advice about dealing with men, they speak to common female experiences such as motherhood, and although they do not create specific negative stereotypes of men, they make clear that a group other than themselves has made the rules by which they must live.

The collective consciousness of women as an identifiable group with common problems and interests leads ultimately to a feminist humor. By no means is *women's* humor synonymous with *feminist* humor, but the latter is a more significant part of American women's humorous expression than has commonly been perceived. Humor that may be regarded as feminist takes two forms within this tradition. The most frequently occurring is that which makes use of a double text to pose a subtle challenge to the stereotype or the circumstance that the writer appears superficially merely to describe. When Erma Bombeck's speaker describes her dirty house or matches the ring around her husband's collar to the one around his neck, she is expressing the fundamental inequity of the expectation that cleanliness is woman's exclusive responsibility. The second type of feminist humor more overtly confronts the sources of discrimination, and has tended to emerge during periods of organized agitation for women's rights. This type of feminist humor may parody anti-suffrage arguments, or may, by the use of fantasy, posit a society in which women are powerful.

While much of contemporary women's humor is feminist humor of the second kind, much of it, too, is androgynous in the sense that it thematically resembles contemporary male humor. Whereas before the 1970s women tended to write about being plagued by boxes of cereal as part of their domestic routine, they now write about the plague of junk mail that affects both women and men. The women's movement has not effected the radical changes that it seeks in political, economic, and social freedoms for women, but the entrance of large numbers of women into the labor force, the declining birth rate, and changes in family structures have brought both men and women into each others' worlds sufficiently that it is possible for women to write humor that lacks a specific gender-consciousness.

In addition to establishing the tradition of American women's humor and the specific cultural context out of which it has come, this study has two purposes. The first, which is most directly addressed, is to show that women's humor must be read as having a complexity that many readers, especially editors and critics, have not taken into account. It must be read with a consciousness that women's lives have been radically different from those of men, and with a perception that the mere expression of humor is for women a complicated issue. The second purpose is to suggest that what has been thought to be an American humorous tradition is actually only half of one, the male half, and that re-thinking this tradition can alter our perceptions of basic American values.

1

The Female Humorist in America

"It is a very serious thing to be a funny woman."
—*Frances Miriam Berry Whitcher*
(1814-1852)

I

In her introduction to *The Widow Bedott Papers* by Frances Whitcher (1856), Alice B. Neal had words of high praise for the quality and popularity of the work of this early nineteenth-century humorist. Whitcher's satiric sketches of small-town life, she says, are "full of humor [and] remarkable for minute observation of human nature."[1] Neal quotes Whitcher's sister as saying, "Her humor was chaste and original, so true to nature that the most ignorant reader could not fail to feel its force, and the most refined could discover nothing that would shock the keenest sensibility" (xii). By endorsing this description of Whitcher's humor, Alice Neal unwittingly announced the central dilemma of the female humorist in America. She must be at the same time "chaste" and "original": the former term suggesting the innocence and moral purity long felt to be peculiarly female virtues, and the latter implying precisely the freedom from constraint that has just as surely been denied to women in American culture. The humor resulting from this paradoxical circumstance must itself be a paradox. Both "forceful" and "refined," it must be clear enough in its intent that its message is not lost on the most "ignorant" of readers, yet it must not offend the "sensibility" of more "refined" readers and consequently cast doubt upon the refinement—the "chastity"—of its author.

The popular "Widow Bedott" sketches that Whitcher published in the 1840's are narrated by the garrulous widow, whose gossipy, rambling monologues comment on small-town life and simultaneously

15

reveal her own silliness (the widow's nickname, in fact, *is* Silly, short for Priscilla). The narrator is herself the embodiment of much that she criticizes in others. Telling a story full of digressions, for example, she notes that "some folks have a way of talkin' round and round and round for evermore, and never comin' to the pint" (23). A dedicated gossip, the widow nonetheless complains that her town is "a turrible place for talkin' . . . a regular slander mill" (99). Into these self-revelatory monologues Whitcher incorporates sharp satire on the genteel pretentions of the emerging American middle class. Reminded by the new husband the widow has managed to snare that their house is "comfortable," the widow snaps, "Comfortable! who cares for comfort when gintility's consarned!" (222-23). As one of the most popular of the early-nineteenth-century dialect humorists, Whitcher explored the conflicts of values, taste, and social status that particularly affected women in the Jacksonian era.

There is ample evidence that Frances Whitcher was keenly aware of the paradox of originality and "chastity." She wrote, for example, to Joseph C. Neal, editor of *Neal's Saturday Gazette*, where her "Widow Bedott" sketches appeared, that she had few close friends, and attributed this fact directly to her sense of humor:

> I received at my birth, the undesirable gift of a remarkably strong
> sense of the ridiculous. I can scarcely remember the time when the
> neighbors were not afraid that I would "make fun of them." For
> indulging in this propensity, I was scolded at home, and wept over
> and prayed with, by certain well-meaning old maids in the
> neighborhood; but all to no purpose.   (xiii-xiv)

The only result of these efforts to suppress Whitcher's satiric bent was to encourage it: the young Miriam, as she was called, drew charcoal sketches (presumably caricatures) of these women who, as Huck Finn would say, tried to "sivilize" her, and pinned them to their shawls, "with, perhaps, a descriptive verse below" (xiv). Later, as an adult, better able to recognize the extent to which she was at odds with cultural expectations for women's behavior, Whicher was sometimes a reluctant humorist. A letter to her from Joseph Neal dated September 10, 1846, refers to doubts she has expressed about "continuing in the comic vein"; he speaks of her enormous popularity with readers of the *Gazette*, and closes by urging her to "Think on it then before yielding up the pen of comedy" (x-xi).

That Joseph Neal was as concerned about the circulation of his magazine as he was about the feelings of one of his contributors is clear from his comment in the same letter that he has withheld her identity from the editor of *Godey's Lady's Book*, who was interested in commissioning her to contribute humorous sketches to that magazine as well. But Neal also pleads the cause of humor in a less self-interested manner:

> It is a theory of mine that *those gifted with truly humorous genius, like yourself, are more useful as moralists, philosophers, and teachers, than whole legions of the gravest preachers. They speak more effectually to the general ear and heart, even though they who hear are not aware of the fact that they are imbibing wisdom.* [Italics in original]   (x)

Neal was by no means the first to point out the function of humor—particularly satire—as a corrective to society, even though he here proposes that perception as a personal "theory." The concept that advice from a moral, philosophical, or educational perspective is more easily swallowed when coated with wit and irony reaches into antiquity, and certainly informed Jonathan Swift's "A Modest Proposal" and the far gentler satires of Joseph Addison and Richard Steele in eighteenth-century Britain; and in Jacksonian America, devoted to expansion, progress, and improvement on all fronts, humor was a common mode of expressing dissatisfaction with the status quo.

It seems certain, however, that Neal was unaware of the significance his comments on the social value of humor have for America's female humorists. To the contemporary student of women's humor, his words seem ironic in several ways. The first is the most overt. Despite his perhaps commercial motive in urging Frances Whitcher to continue writing humorous sketches for his *Gazette* ("Our readers . . . almost despise 'Neal's' if the Widow be not there" [x]), Joseph Neal claims for this female writer a power that neither she nor virtually any other American woman has been granted by the culture in which she lived: the power to alter society rather than merely to live within its strictures governing her role and behavior. Neal is on the safest ground, of course, with the category of "moralists" in this passage, because women were generally regarded as innately the vessels for and enforcers of the nation's moral and religious doctrines. Yet even as the guardian of morality, the woman was responsible for maintaining and disseminating a received tradition, not encouraged to alter it. Still less were American women in the 1840s permitted to be "philosophers," and not until much later in the century were they "teachers" in large numbers. Thus editor Neal, in his eagerness to entice Mrs. Whitcher to write more humorous sketches about the Widow Bedott for his *Saturday Gazette*, attributed to her a role in American culture that the culture itself did not recognize her as having.

A second irony is that Frances Whitcher, in her creation of the Widow Spriggins, the Widow Bedott, and Aunt Maguire—her major humorous *personae*—did indeed endeavor to alter society: specifically to rid women of their sentimentality and their awkward pretentions to gentility. But ultimately she realized that she had, necessarily, failed. Permilly Spriggins, in Whitcher's earliest sketches, is a foolish sentimentalist who models her speech and her actions on those of the character Amanda, heroine of the wildly popular 1798 sentimental novel *The Children of the Abbey*, by Regina Maria Roche.[2] The Widow Spriggins is the humorous focus of these sketches, a ridiculous figure in whom dependent sentimentality and genteel pretentions are yoked with forceful satiric effect. The Widow Bedott, for whom Neal's *Gazette* readers clamored, is the stereotypical husband-hunter, whose self-centered haughtiness only increases after she is successful in catching a second husband; in her newly regained position of wife, she demonstrates a tastelessness and even a cruelty that make the satire ultimately bitter. Aunt Maguire, in a series of sketches written for *Godey's Lady's Book* in 1847, is a far more sympathetic character than either the Widow Spriggins or the Widow Bedott, but the small-town society upon which she comments is peopled with selfish social-climbers who have acquiesced fully to the artificiality and excesses of mid-nineteenth-century middle-class gentility: the sort of people whose tastelessness and hypocrisy Mark Twain would later parody in *Huck Finn*.

As accurate and pointed as Whitcher's social satire is, however— and as popular as it was with contemporary readers[3]—she became aware by the close of the 1840's that, as a social corrective, her work had been ineffectual. As Linda Ann Finton Morris, author of an unpublished doctoral dissertation on women vernacular humorists in nineteenth-century America, puts it:

> What Whitcher discovered through her humor ... was that nothing, not even the most skillful and accurate social satire could stop gentility, so deeply ingrained had it become in mid-nineteenth-century society.... [W]hen the most mean-spirited and self-serving attitudes prevailed, her humor of necessity became more personal and more bitter.... So she ... gave up humorous writing altogether.[4]

Frances Whitcher's sense of defeat had a painful personal side as well. Her husband was a minister in Elmira, New York, and some of Whitcher's "Aunt Maguire" sketches for *Godey's Lady's Book*, especially those concerning the local church's sewing society, seem to have hit too close to the bone for members of the Rev. Whitcher's congregation. He resigned his pastorate in Elmira in 1849 and moved with his wife to Whiteboro, New York, where Frances Whitcher died in 1852. Her last work, unfinished at her death, was a conventional novel titled *Mary Elmer*.

The third and most important irony in Joseph Neal's statement about the effectiveness of humor to "speak ... to the general ear and heart" is that the majority of America's female humorists have, like Frances Whitcher, spoken from women's experience to the "general ear and heart" in order to alter social attitudes and behavior or point to injustices to women promulgated by American culture. However, Neal assumes that the message of such humorous utterances is received and absorbed by those for whom it is intended, even though "they are not aware of the fact that they are imbibing wisdom." He views humor as a means of softening the message, of making the criticism acceptable to the general public, who, presumably, would then see the error of their ways. In other words, Neal assumes that the "wisdom" is indeed "imbibed" by the reader, and he may have had in mind—he would certainly have been familiar with—Seba Smith's "Jack Downing" and Thomas Haliburton's "Sam Slick," both early nineteenth-century humorous *personae* whose untutored common sense pointed out the absurdities and hypocrisies of the new nation's politics and pretensions.

But in fact the real message, the "wisdom," of women's humor has been missed by most readers. In the case of Frances Whitcher, several factors were at work to make her misunderstood and ultimately even persecuted for her humor. One, as Linda Morris points out, is that the hold of middle-class gentility was simply too strong to be checked by the time Whitcher wrote. Yet one wonders whether her readers in the 1840s even realized her satiric purpose, so enmeshed were they in the very values she attacked. It seems far more likely that Whitcher's readers merely saw the perpetuation of certain female stereotypes that had existed for centuries. The sentimental Widow Spriggins, the husband-hunting, nagging Widow Bedott, and the gossipy Aunt Maguire may be seen, in one sense, simply as 1840s avatars of common and venerable female stereotypes who have as ancestors Chaucer's Wife of Bath, Irving's Dame Van Winkle, and many more. Many twentieth-century critics have also missed the point of Whitcher's humor—as well as that of most of America's female humorists—largely because the *use* of a stereotype is assumed to constitute an *acceptance* of that stereotype. Walter Blair and Hamlin Hill, for example, in their 1978 book *America's Humor*, state that such humorous pieces as *The Widow Bedott Papers* "pictured a stable, domestic tranquility . . . in which tradition, decorum, justice, and sanity played significant parts."[5] Implicit in this statement is the assumption that it was *normal* for women to be sentimental fools and shrewish gossips—that such behavior arose from "tranquility" and "sanity," when in fact it was the very absence of these conditions that Whitcher sought to present.

Indeed, Whitcher's intention in presenting women (and, not incidentally, men) as silly social-climbers and talkative nags was not to endorse and perpetuate these stereotypes, but rather to write a cautionary tale for women and men whom she saw debasing and trivializing themselves in the scramble for middle-class gentility.[6] In addition to the fact that she has her major humorous *personae* behave in so ridiculous a manner as to discourage imitation, Whitcher also provides other characters who speak in a countering tone of reason and sanity. In the Widow Spriggins sketches, for example, Permilly Spriggins's two sisters represent opposing views of her behavior in imitating Amanda in *The Children of the Abbey*. Having worked herself into a lovesick frenzy, Permilly utters a long, derivative lament, ending by calling herself "the most onfortinate of creturs," whereupon her sisters respond contrapuntally:

"How much she talks like a book," says Ketury.

"How much she talks like a fool," says Mertilly, and off she went to bed.[7]

In the "Aunt Maguire" sketches, the title character frequently represents the author's perspective, as Mertilly does in the above passage. Aunt Maguire is more observer than participant in the society of "Slabtown," largely because she is considered too "plain" and "homemade" for acceptance into the genteel set. She is, like Whitcher, alarmed at what passes for "gentility," as is apparent in the following description of a Slabtown woman:

> Her gintility seemed to consist in her wearin' more colors than I
> ever see on to once afore in all my born days. She had on a yaller
> bunnit, with a great pink artificial on it; a red shawl, and a green silk
> frock, and blue ribbin round her neck, and I forget what all; but
> 'twas enough to make a body's eyes ache to look at her.[8]

What Whitcher provides, then, is a text on two levels: while Permilly Spriggins and the Slabtown woman are indeed ridiculous in their efforts to behave in the manner of "proper" society, and the humorist intends us to laugh at them, Whitcher as a social critic clearly blames not these individual women, but a social system that makes women economically dependent on men and provides so few outlets for their intellect and curiosity that they engage in mindless one-upmanship regarding men, clothes, food, and social status. The Widow Bedott, for example, is, as a widow, at a distinct disadvantage: lacking the education and the skills to support herself, and lacking any social standing whatever in her small town, she understandably seeks a husband to provide her with both economic security and — equally important — an identity. If Whitcher's women are ridiculous figures inspiring our laughter, they are at the same time deserving of our sympathy because the social forces that create the narrowness and shallowness of their lives are far stronger than they are.

It is difficult to know how much of this double text Joseph C. Neal understood when he encouraged Frances Whitcher to continue writing her humorous sketches, but it seems likely that while he lauded the corrective benefits of humor, he saw no further than the surface frivolity and amusing dialectical renderings of Whitcher's work. The irony is that his statement of the subtle power of humor describes precisely the manner in which America's female humorists have worked beneath the surface of the text to both define and protest the confinement and oppression of their lives. Frances Whitcher is just one of dozens of America's female writers, in a tradition going back to Anne Bradstreet and forward to Erma Bombeck, who have used humor as a means of analyzing women's place in American society and certifying their estrangement from the dominant culture.

II

In her classic 1931 study of the relationship between American humor and what cultural historians then called the "national character," Constance Rourke remarks that by the middle of the nineteenth century, "women had played no essential part in the long sequence of the comic spirit in America." Rourke does not mention the work of Frances Whitcher in the 1840s; she describes the emergence and development of an essentially white male tradition of American humor, informed by Yankee consciousness, frontier, and backwoods, and notes that "the lady ... was lost in the culture and the prevailing masculine genius stood apart from it."[9] Within the American comic spirit as Rourke defines it, the only woman writer is Emily Dickinson, whom she describes as "in a profound sense a comic poet in the American tradition" (209-10). Rourke admires Dickinson for her ability to "stand apart": "she contrived to see a changing universe within that acceptant view which is comic in its profoundest sense, which is part reconciliation, part knowledge of eternal disparity" (211). In her ironic vision of life, Dickinson stood apart from, among other things, the very genteel tradition that Whitcher had found so threatening: she refused to be defined by its expectations for women or for poets, and was impertinent enough to say "I'm Nobody"—even to challenge the "other" by asking "Who are you?"[10] For Dickinson, conformity of any sort was a violation of one's essential humanity, and she frequently uses imagery that conveys the absurdity of socially-defined "importance," as in the second stanza of this same poem (#288):

> How dreary—to be—Somebody!
> How public—like a Frog—
> To tell one's name—the livelong June—
> To an admiring Bog!

Most humor theorists agree that the creation of humor requires the ability to "stand apart" from the reality of one's own existence and to view that existence with detachment and objectivity. The ultimate logic of that detachment is the creation of a separate reality. As Neil Schmitz puts it in *Of Huck and Alice*, "[the humorist's] alogical view of things, so obstinately held, starts from a different a priori, proves to be sufficient, and brings the adequacy of our own assumptions into doubt."[11] Dorothy Parker suggested something quite similar when she defined humor as follows:

> There must be courage; there must be no awe. There must be criticism, for humor, to my mind, is encapsulated in criticism. There must be a disciplined eye and a wild mind. There must be a magnificent disregard of your reader, for if he cannot follow you, there is nothing you can do about it.[12]

The lack of "awe"—precisely what Frances Whitcher was chastised for by her genteel culture—brings the discussion inevitably to Freud, whose concept of the "super-ego" blends the psychological and the social by representing externally learned "rules," and for whom laughter signified the temporary release of the unconscious from the control of the super-ego. In his 1927 essay "Humour," Freud claimed that "humour has something liberating about it... The ego refuses to be distressed by the provocations of reality, to let itself be compelled to suffer."[13]

Despite all such statements about the freeing effect of humor, it still requires a social context, for several reasons. The first is that, like all art, humor presupposes an audience, and despite Dorothy Parker's "magnificent disregard of [the] reader," humor is a shared activity, a means of communication. Further, the subjects, forms, and limits of humor are culturally determined. Joseph Boskin, in *Humor and Social Change in Twentieth-Century America*, makes this point clearly:

> Every society defines the boundaries of what is—and is not—laughable, as well as develops a collective sense or approach to the way in which life operates. Humor thus reflects the inner mechanisms and energies of society. It classifies and distinguishes, separates and integrates, and serves as a unifying fulcrum. Community humor, particularly folk humor, is an index of the state of affairs in any given society.[14]

Boskin's statements are given added weight by the work of anthropologists who have studied the function of humor—particularly jokes and joking rituals—in a variety of cultures. Mahadev L. Apte, whose book *Humor and Laughter: An Anthropological Approach* is the first to provide a comprehensive cross-cultural study of the relationship between humor and social structures, states as one of the axioms of his study that "humor is primarily the result of cultural perceptions, both individual and collective, of incongruity, exaggeration, distortion, and any unnamed combinations of the cultural elements in external events." Apte continues:

> Humor is culture based in the sense that individual cultural systems significantly influence the mechanism that triggers the humor experience. Familiarity with a cultural code is a prerequisite for the spontaneous mental restructuring of elements that results in amusement and laughter. . . . If the foundation of most humor is cultural, then understanding how humorous experiences are cognitively formulated, either intentionally or accidentally, should lead us to better insight into the cultural system.[15]

Thus, just as an understanding of a particular culture—its values, beliefs, and social organization—is necessary for participation in its humor, so the study of a culture's humor can contribute to a deeper understanding of precisely those values and beliefs. To arrive at this understanding was the purpose of Rourke's *American Humor: A Study of the National Character* in 1931.

However, by omitting from consideration the substantial contributions of women writers to American humorous literature, Rourke's book succeeds only partly in achieving its purpose. Although it is true that American humor as traditionally perceived by editors and scholars grows, as Rourke contends, out of the restless dreams and fantasies of a young and brawny nation—wearing, she says, the "mask" of its own creation, "the unformed American nation pictured itself as homely and comic" (22)—women's comic sense, present from the beginning, complicates and enriches that tradition. The virtual absence of women's humorous writing from the conventional canon is in itself a telling statement about American culture and the relative positions that men and women have occupied within it. That is, not only are the subjects and forms of humor culture-specific, but so too is the cultural role accorded the humorist. In most human societies, the humorist adopts a position of superiority. As anthropologist Mary Douglas states, the person who tells jokes:

> appears to be a privileged person who can say certain things in a certain way which confers immunity.... He has a firm hold on his own position in the structure and the disruptive comments he makes upon it are in a sense the comments of the social group upon itself. He merely expresses consensus.[16]

Although Douglas is here referring specifically to joking as part of an oral tradition and not to humorous literature, her observation is applicable to the role of the humorist generally, and has particular relevance to the position of woman as humorist.

When Dorothy Parker wrote that humor requires "courage," she might well have been speaking particularly of the female humorist. Because the humorist adopts at least the *stance* of superiority, claiming the freedom to point out incongruity or absurdity in a world that others are accustomed to accepting on its own terms, he or she works from a position of privileged insight. Mary Douglas suggests that the figure of the joker in many cultures occupies the position of a "minor mystic," having "apparent access to other reality than that mediated by the relevant structure.... His jokes expose the inadequacy of realist structurings of experience" (108). Further, Douglas refers to the subversive power of humor:

> Whatever the joke, however remote its subject, the telling of it is potentially subversive. Since its form consists of a victorious tilting of uncontrol against control, it is an image of the levelling of hierarchy, the triumph of intimacy over formality, of unofficial values over official ones. (98)

One need not agree with Freud and Konrad Lorenz that humor is closely related to some innate human aggressiveness to perceive that the humorist places himself or herself—however momentarily—in the superior position of truth-teller, upsetting conventional assumptions of reality. In fact, Freud, in his essay "Humour," posits that the humorous impulse resides in the super-ego, that sometimes "severe master," which in laughing at the world "tries ... to console the ego and protect it from suffering."[17]

Women in American culture, however, have only rarely been granted or felt free to claim the sort of superiority required by this concept of the humorist. That is, in both official (lack of voting rights, property ownership, access to education and the professions) and unofficial (cultural expectations of submissiveness, piety, and dependence) ways, women have been denied the confidence in their own intelligence and competence that would make it natural or comfortable for them to adopt the stance of the humorist. Indeed, this exclusionary situation is by no means unique to American culture. In *Humor and Laughter*, Apte devotes a chapter to "Sexual Inequality in Humor" in which he proposes that in virtually every human culture, women's participation in humor is severely curtailed:

> ... women's humor reflects the existing inequality between the sexes not so much in its substance as in the constraints imposed upon its occurrence, on the techniques used, on the social settings in which it occurs, and on the kind of audience that appreciates it. [In general] these constraints ... stem from the prevalent cultural values that emphasize male superiority and dominance together with female passivity and create role models for women in keeping with such values and attitudes.... [M]en's capacity for humor is not superior to women's. Rather, both the prevalent cultural values and the resultant constraints prevent women from fully using their talents. (69)

In the last part of this statement, Apte touches on the controversy about whether women indeed *possess* a sense of humor, which I will explore in a later chapter, but his major point is that women's almost universal subordinate position has prevented the full flowering of this sense. Passivity and wit are diametrically opposed: the former requires acquiescence to rules and standards imposed by the dominant society, while the latter, with its associative values of intelligence, perception, and irreverence, implies the "tilting ... of unofficial values over official ones" of which Mary Douglas speaks.

American women writers, from colonial times to the present, have repeatedly articulated their awareness of the cultural prejudice against a display of female wittiness. In her "Prologue" to the 1650 edition of *The Tenth Muse*, Anne Bradstreet sought to disarm her critics by including the following stanza:

> I am obnoxious to each carping tongue
> Who says my hand a needle better fits;
> A poet's pen all scorn I should thus wrong,
> For such despite they cast on female wits.
> If what I do prove well, it won't advance;
> They'll say it's stol'n, or else it was by chance.[18]

Bradstreet's use here of the term "wit" is tied to its original definition of "intelligence" or "understanding" (from Old English *witan*), but the passage itself displays wit in the more modern sense of the word: the image of the woman's hand holding a pen instead of the more acceptable needle is subversively humorous, mocking as it does the "official" values of Puritan society. Equally witty are the lines from Bradstreet's poem in praise of Queen Elizabeth I in which she takes to task men who refuse to recognize women's intelligence:

> Nay Masculines, you have thus taxt us long,
> But she, though dead, will vindicate our wrong.
> Let such as say our Sex is void of Reason,
> Know tis a Slander now, but once was Treason.[19]

By the mid-nineteenth century, as Barbara Welter has documented, the "cult of domesticity" was so firmly intrenched that womanly wit had difficulty maneuvering around the image of ideal womanhood—an image that denigrated woman's intellect in favor of her emotional and intuitive nature: "Anti-intellectualism was implicit in the cult which exalted women as creatures who did not use logic or reason, having a surer, purer road to the truth—the high road of the heart."[20] This identification of femininity with the emotive and intuitive rather than the rational and intellectual persists in American culture, despite dramatic changes in woman's role. Anne Beatts and Deanne Stillman, both contemporary comedy writers, have commented on their struggle to counteract the passive, humorless concept of womanhood in contemporary American society. Beatts, reflecting on her high school experience, says flatly, "Real girls weren't funny.... Real girls didn't crack jokes."[21] Stillman, in the introduction to her collection of humorous essays *Getting Back at Dad* (1981), explains that one of her motives for beginning to write satire was to "get back at" a father who did not take her seriously as an intellectual. The fact that she changed her name to the masculine form "Dean" to sign her early work reveals that she, like Beatts, perceived humor as a masculine prerogative.[22]

III

If the humorist stands somewhat apart from the culture to comment on its incongruities, and women perforce *live* apart from the central realities of that culture, in what position is the woman as humorist? In one sense she would seem to be perfectly placed to observe and critique—to adopt, for example, the stance of the "wise fool" whose external position permits him to see truths that those engaged in the mainstream cannot—or will not—see. To some extent this has been true of America's female humorists. Certainly Frances Whitcher sought to expose the absurdities of creeping gentility by using the stance of one sufficiently removed to have clear vision. Similarly, Marietta Holley has her late-nineteenth century rustic sage Samantha Allen argue for women's rights in the guise of an unsophisticated woman merely using common sense, as when she counters her husband's pronouncement that women should marry, not vote, with the following statement:

> Josiah Allen, . . . Anybody would think to hear you talk that a woman couldn't do but just one of the two things any way—marry or vote, and had got to take her choice of the two at the pint of the bayonet.[23]

Two factors, however, complicate the role of the woman as humorist. One is the cultural identification of womanhood with subordination rather than superiority, with passivity rather than prescience. Holley's Samantha is rare among women's humorous *personae*, as is Dorothy Parker's fabled wit. The woman in Parker's sketch "A Telephone Call," abjectly awaiting her lover's call, is more typical in women's literature than is Parker's "Indian Summer," which ends with the line "To hell, my love, with you!"[24]

A second factor affecting the woman as humorist is her very "apartness" from the culture in which she lives. From the nineteenth-century sewing society to the post-World War II suburbs, which Phyllis McGinley dubbed the "village of women,"[25] women have in many ways inhabited a separate reality from that of men: a largely domestic reality involving housework and children instead of business and politics. The almost total separation, beginning in the the early nineteenth century, of men's and women's "spheres" is mirrored in the subjects, themes, and mechanisms of women's humor. Recognition of this difference led Martha Bruère and Mary Ritter Beard, in their 1934 anthology of American women's humor, *Laugh-*

ing Their Way, to attempt to define it. Noting that the humorous writing of women "always bears their proprietary brand," the editors continue:

> The sexes have their own directions for toleration. Naturally men's derision has centered about biological and occupational peculiarities. And among women, the flowers of their humor are as varied as their lives. Would that austere saint, Elizabeth Fry, break into ripples of joy over Beatrice Lillie? Would Harriet Beecher Stowe lose herself delightedly in *The New Yorker*? Yet the angle of vision from which women see a lack of balance, wrong proportions, disharmonies, and incongruities in life is a thing of their world as it must be—a world always a little apart.[26]

As a definition of the distinction between men's and women's humor, this is unsatisfactory: Bruère and Beard see some common thematic threads in the humor of American men, but suggest only the *variety* of themes and voices in women's humor, identifying no central concerns, stances, or techniques. Yet these comments do confront the issue of women's separation from the mainstream of American culture—lives lived "always a little apart."

One effect of the separateness of women's lives on their humor is that its subject matter has, quite naturally, been derived from the experiences of those lives. Instead of writing frontier tall tales and political satires, American women have tended to focus on more domestic issues: housework, children, community affairs, and—most important—relationships between women and men. As is the case in women's literature generally, the culture the writer describes is the one that she inhabits, which has significant differences from the majority culture. In some ways, in fact, as I will argue in a later chapter, women's humor resembles closely the humor of a racial or ethnic minority. As corollary to this point, the audience for women's humor, as has also been true of women's literature generally, is primarily other women. Erma Bombeck has remarked that one evidence that men were playing a greater role in housework and child-rearing in the late 1970s and early 1980s was that they began attending her readings and talks in greater numbers and more frequently commented that they enjoyed her newspaper column, "At Wit's End."[27] Put simply, men have increasingly found her work amusing and relevant because they understand what she is writing about.

The fact that for so long most men did *not* understand in any truly personal way what female humorists were writing about may go a long way toward explaining why women's humor has been consistently under-represented in anthologies and in studies of American humor. It should be no surprise that the only anthologies of women's humor published in this country have been edited by women—and all with the clear intention of retrieving a neglected tradition.[28] The American humorous tradition, as presented by most—male—editors and critics, has emerged as primarily a male literary tradition.

Another effect of the fact that American women's humor has typically dealt with the realities of women's lives rather than with the issues of the dominant culture has been to dictate the strategies by which this humor normally works. Speaking primarily to female readers about the conditions of lives they share, female humorists have on the surface seemed to accept and even condone the trivializing routines of women's lives and the unflattering stereotypes of women commonly used in humor. From the early nineteenth century to the present, the sketches, stories, and light verse that constitute this tradition are filled with female figures who are concerned with their appearance, afraid of technology, competitive with each other, and dependent upon men. The familiar stereotypes of the nag, the scold, the "clinging vine" and the gold-digger are present in women's humor just as they are in the humor of men.

But beneath the surface runs a text that directly counters these images and seeks to deny them. By presenting the *results* of women's cultural conditioning and subordination, America's female humorists implicitly address the *sources* of women's self-doubt, dependence, and isolation from the mainstream of American life. Whereas Holley's Samantha Allen overtly attacks discrimination against women in both the political and personal realm, most of the *personae* in women's humor are less aware than their creators of the reasons for the inherent craziness of their lives. Hazel Morse, in Dorothy Parker's story "Big Blonde," is a poignant example of this unawareness. Parker's summation of Hazel's perspective is bitterly ironic:

> Men liked her, and she took for granted that the liking of many men was a desirable thing. Popularity seemed to her to be worth all the

work that had to be put into its achievement. Men liked you because you were fun, and when they liked you they took you out, and there you were.[29]

Hazel Morse does not understand that she is captive to male expectations, but Parker and her readers are quite aware of the tragic irony of her situation. The stereotypical "dumb blonde" here quickly evokes our sympathy. More amusing and more self-aware is the narrator in Betty MacDonald's 1945 best-seller *The Egg and I*, who attempts to become the "perfect wife": "somewhere between a Grant Wood painting, an Old Dutch Cleanser advertisement, and Mrs. Lincoln's cookbook."[30] But even though she realizes that she is aspiring to popular images of model wifehood, MacDonald's narrator continues her comical—and doomed—attempts at perfection in that role. In both cases, the author locates the error not in the individual woman, but in a culture that sets the standards for her behavior and performance.

A closer examination of several different texts will demonstrate more clearly how the double text of women's humor challenges cultural assumptions. In spite of great variations in form and style, Josephine Daskam's *Fables for the Fair* (1901), Dorothy Parker's "The Waltz" (1939), and Shirley Jackson's *Life Among the Savages* (1953) all reveal both the "official" and the "unofficial" attitudes of women toward their circumstances. Daskam's "cautionary tales," written in the fable form that enjoyed a period of popularity at the turn of the century, mock the official culture's sharp distinction between male and female values and behavior at the same time that they give women tongue-in-cheek advice about how to cope with inequality. Most of Daskam's fables are stories of women trying to be "modern"—capable, intellectual, independent—and finding that men are not ready to accept the "New Woman," as is the case in "The Woman Who Took Things Literally":

> There was once a Woman who Invited a Celebrated Scientist to Take Tea with her. After Tea a Beggar came to the Door and Asked for a Meal. She remembered the Last Page of the Celebrated Scientist's last Essay, and addressed the Beggar thus:
> "While I Regret to see you Suffering from Hunger, I Realize that I Injure Society more in Catering to Your Idleness than I Hurt my Feelings in Refusing your intrinsically Vicious Request." And she Sent him Away.

31

"Great Heavens!" cried the Celebrated Scientist. "It is Hard Enough
for Me to act Thus, and I am Forced to in Order to be Consistent.
But a Woman, whose Every Instinct should be Charity and Sympathy
Incarnate — it is Disgusting!"
This teaches us that What is Sauce for the Gander may be Saucy for
the Goose.[31]

This fable turns on the traditional images of man as rational, scientific, and "consistent," and woman as charitable and sympathetic. The
woman in the fable attempts to adopt the "masculine" characteristics
of intellectuality and logic, and is found "disgusting" by the man. The
most telling part of the fable is the man's admission that he finds it
difficult to be "consistent" in his professional and personal views —
he, too, is a victim of cultural conditioning. Although the structure of
Daskam's moral tag suggests an acceptance of different standards for
male and female behavior, implicit in the fable is a protest against the
denial of women's intellectuality by men who are, themselves,
expected to be cold-heartedly rational.

Dorothy Parker employs a more obvious method of presenting
"official" and "unofficial" responses in her monologue "The Waltz."
Here the speaker uses two voices, one to speak aloud to the man
who asks her to dance and the other to provide the reader with her
actual responses to the experience. The contrast between her polite
"public" voice and her witty and angry "private" voice is both the
source of the humor and a clear statement of woman's outward conformity and inward rebellion. The speaker's public voice begins the
sketch by accepting the dance: "Why, thank you so much. I'd adore
to." This socially correct exterior is immediately undercut by her private voice:

I don't want to dance with him. I don't want to dance with anybody.
And even if I did, it wouldn't be him. He'd be well down among the
last ten. I've seen the way he dances; it looks like something you do
on Saint Walpurgis Night.

As the dance progresses, the speaker identifies her social dilemma,
as her private voice says:

What can you say, when a man asks you to dance with him? I most
certainly will *not* dance with you, I'll see you in hell first. Why, thank
you, I'd like to awfully, but I'm having labor pains. . . . No. There was
nothing for me to do, but say I'd adore to.

As the sketch continues, the speaker's public voice continues cheerfully while her partner proceeds to step on her feet and kick her shins, and the distinction between public and private voice becomes tellingly sharper. To herself she says, "Oh, my shin. My poor, poor shin, that I've had ever since I was a little girl," but aloud she accepts the blame for her own injury: "It didn't hurt the least little bit. And anyway, it was my fault, Really it was. Truly."

"The Waltz" ultimately becomes metaphoric of man's brutality and woman's powerlessness. The speaker's private voice talks of the "creature I'm chained to" as having a "leering, bestial face"; his embrace is "noxious," and the dance itself is an "obscene travesty." Yet to her partner's face, as the orchestra begins another tune, she says, "I'd like to go on like this forever."[32] The sketch ends with the speaker encouraging the man she has privately identified as a "creature" to pay the band to keep playing. The hyperbolic language that Parker uses in both the public and private utterances of her *persona* is at once an example of comic incongruity and a clear indication that the "waltz" of the title is emblematic of a continuing cycle of male domination and female submissiveness. The speaker in Parker's sketch is able to articulate her dilemma, but is doomed to go on repeating it.

A somewhat more subtle example of the double message of women's humor is found in Shirley Jackson's *Life Among the Savages*. Jackson, best-known as the author of "The Lottery," demonstrates her mastery of humorous writing in this contribution to women's post-World War II domestic humor. Her primary technique is raising the daily details of motherhood and housekeeping to the absurdity of slapstick comedy, but throughout the book are strong suggestions that the life of the average housewife is repetitive and demeaning. The clearest demonstration of social attitudes that discriminate against women is in the narrator's account of the birth of her third child. After being driven to the hospital by a taxi driver who is clearly terrified that the child will be born in his cab, she confronts the hospital receptionist for the usual interrogation. The conversation grows increasingly inane as the narrator struggles to retain her composure:

> "Name?" the desk clerk said to me politely, her pencil poised.
> "Name," I said vaguely. I remembered, and told her.
> "Age?" she asked. "Sex? Occupation?"

"Writer," I said.

"Housewife," she said.

"Writer," I said.

"I'll just put down housewife," she said. "Doctor? How many children?"

"Two," I said. "Up to now."

"Normal pregnancy?" she said. "Blood test? X-ray?"

"Look—" I said.

"Husband's name?" she said. "Address? Occupation?"

"Just put down housewife," I said. "I don't remember *his* name, really."

"Legitimate?"

"What?" I said.

"Is your husband the father of this child? Do you *have* a husband?"

"Please," I said plaintively, "can I go on upstairs?"

"Well, *really*," she said, and sniffed. "You're *only* having a baby."

Having succeeded in denigrating both the narrator's professional status and her womanhood, the clerk turns her over to the nurses and the doctor, who persists in asking her how "we" are feeling. Finally, when her husband says while she is in labor, "I know *just* how you feel," her anger erupts:

> My only answer was a word which certainly I knew that I *knew*, although I had never honestly expected to hear it spoken in my own ladylike voice.

Her husband's response is to ask her to stop using the word, whereupon she says coolly, "Who is doing this? . . . You or me?"[33]

Jackson thus manages a humor that, as Frances Whitcher's sister described her work, is "chaste and original." The anger is cloaked in inanity; the narrator remains a "lady." But the message is clear: the culture Jackson describes does not value women's professional lives, and it both fears and trivializes childbirth. The narrator in *Life Among the Savages* is part of both the humorous text of the book and its underlying critique of society.

IV

America's female humorists have not all used the subversive tactic of the double text. During several periods in this nation's history, most notably when agitation for women's rights has been most vigorous, writers have employed a straightforward feminist stance. Before the 1870s, when Marietta Holley's Samantha Allen argued with everyone who would listen (and some who would not) about the necessity of female suffrage, "Fanny Fern" (pseudonym for Sara Willis Parton), author of the popular 1855 novel *Ruth Hall*, wrote satiric essays explaining why *men* were unfit to vote, turning upon them the conventional arguments against female suffrage. In 1915, in *Are Women People?*, Alice Duer Miller expressed the same sentiments in verse, and shortly after women were granted the vote, Florence Guy Seabury satirized the helplessness of men to take care of their own basic needs in *The Delicatessen Husband* (1926). The women's movement of the 1970s and 1980s has produced a large body of feminist humor that directly confronts the sources and issues of inequality, from cultural expectations for women's physical appearance, as in Nora Ephron's "A Few Words About Breasts" in *Crazy Salad* (1975), to Ellen Goodman's annual awards to the most sexist men in politics in her syndicated newspaper column.

More commonly, however, women's humor has expressed its critique of American culture subtly, with authors and *personae* adopting a less confrontational and frequently an apparently self-deprecatory stance more in keeping with women's traditional status. Even the titles of women's humorous works suggest their separation from the dominant culture and their discomfort with their lives and relationships—Edna St. Vincent Millay's *Distressing Dialogues*; Erma Bombeck's newspaper column and her first book *At Wit's End*; Shirley Jackson's *Life Among the Savages*. Dorothy Parker suggests the double text of her collected sketches and stories with the punning title *Here Lies* (1939). More recently, Teresa Bloomingdale signals the homemaker's continued apartness from mainstream society in the title *Sense and Momsense* (1986), which implies that women must develop a different mode of thought, and one that is labeled uncomfortably close to "nonsense." The publication of Bloomingdale's *Sense and Momsense*, touted on the dust jacket as embodying "the ability to laugh at marriage and family foibles—*after* learning how to survive it all," as late as 1986 suggests that the genre of domestic humor that began in the early nineteenth century still performs an important function for its readers. The fact that gender roles have actually changed very little is evidenced in Bloomingdale's axiom, "If you want to please your mother, talk to her. If you want to make points with your father, listen to him."[34] Mothers are to be "pleased," and enjoy listening; one "makes points" with fathers, who enjoy talking.

To the extent that women's humor derives from experiences that must be *survived*—such as motherhood, waltzes with boors, and the double standard—it functions much as the humor of a racial or ethnic group does. The writer assumes the reader's familiarity with her topics and themes, and assumes further a shared discomfort or anger at the oppression they mutually endure. The humorous text, which appears to surrender to the status quo, carries within it the codes that members of the group recognize as part of their common heritage. While superficially accepting the assessment of the dominant culture—e.g., women are frivolous, gossipy, inept—on a deeper level women's humor calls into question the values that have led to these assessments.

When we compare the conventionally conceived tradition of American humor to the quite different tradition that emerges in the humor of American women, it becomes clear that what Louis D. Rubin, Jr., calls the "Great American Joke" has more than one major formulation. The classic American humorous situation, according to Rubin, has its origins in "the gap between the cultural ideal and the everyday fact."[35] America's male humorists have been quick to perceive that a nation founded on the promise of equality and freedom has largely failed to reach those goals, and have pointed out the distance between the ideal and the real. Women's humor also deals with incongruity—with the contrast between the official mythology and the daily reality—but it starts from different assumptions. Traditional male American humor rests on the premise that human events—including human failures—are somehow within our control; there is in it a consciousness that the promises that get broken were made by the same sort of people who now seek, through humor, to do the mending. In contrast, women's humor develops from a different premise: the world they inhabit is not of their making, and often not much to their liking, so their tactics must be those of survivors rather than those of saviors.

One example will suffice to illustrate this distinction before I treat it in greater depth in the next chapter. Both male and female writers satirized the figure of the sentimental female poet in nineteenth-century America. The most famous instance is the portrait of Emmeline

Grangerford in Twain's *Huck Finn*. For Twain, Emmeline is one of the results of the genteel culture that had so bothered Frances Whitcher earlier in the century, and he uses the irony of Huck's naïve admiration of Emmeline's accomplishments to convey his own view of her as ludicrous. Twain is thus doubly distanced from Emmeline: he presents her through Huck's innocent vision as an unfortunate artifact of nineteenth-century middle-class values, her sentimentality and egregious poetry merely a by-product of pretensions to lady-like behavior. Marietta Holley also satirized the sentimental female, especially in *My Opinions and Betsey Bobbet's*, written about ten years before *Huck Finn*. But although, like Twain, Holley presents a scathingly negative picture of this female stereotype, she is not distanced from it: Betsey Bobbet, the unattractive spinster whose clinging-vine characteristics provide a counterpoint to Samantha Allen's sturdy common sense, is a presence to be reckoned with. Her existence is a threat to women like Samantha because she represents culturally sanctioned norms for women's behavior—norms that undermine the feminist consciousness that Samantha represents. Even though Betsey is an exaggerated figure, she embodies the majority culture's definition of woman's role, which Samantha must resist, as in the following exchange:

> I have always felt [says Betsey] that it was woman's highest speah [sic], her only mission to soothe, to cling, to smile, to coo. . . . I feel that you do not feel as I do in this matter, you do not feel that it is woman's greatest privilege, her crowning blessing, to soothe lacerations, to be a sort of poultice to the noble, manly breast when it is torn with the cares of life. [Samantha, deeply involved in doing laundry and making preserves and sugar, counters:] Am I a poultice, Betsey Bobbet, do I look like one?—am I in the condition to be one? . . . What has my sect [sex] done . . . that they have got to be lacerator soothers, when they have got everything else under the sun to do?[36]

So the woman meets the "lady," and it becomes the task of the woman, working through the lady, to confront the culture, using humor as her weapon.

2

The Male Tradition
and the Female Tradition

The Truth I do not dare to know
I muffle with a jest.
                    —*Emily Dickinson, #1715*

I

Despite the supposed damper of Puritanism,[1] America as a nation has long been proud of its sense of humor, seeing it as evidence of a resilience and a capacity for self-criticism that accorded with the country's revolutionary origins and its rapid emergence as a world power. That which scholars have over the years identified as traditional or typical American humor, written almost entirely by men, has the swagger of the small boy who, on the one hand, is proud of his youth and strength and, on the other, is calculatedly self-deprecating in the presence of cultures with longer traditions and greater sophistication. The figure of "Jonathan," the quintessential Yankee, common in the American humorous tradition from the colonial period to the early twentieth century, is disarmingly ambivalent: he makes ignorance a virtue both to prove his innocent superiority to corrupt European values and traditions and also to arm himself against the unknowns that surround him: wilderness, "savages," new political philosophies, and the wonders of a corporate and technological society. He is insightful without being pompous; he can strut without violating his innocence. The Jonathan figure, one of whose earliest and best-known avatars appears in Royall Tyler's 1787 play *The Contrast*, is the forerunner of Huck Finn, Walter Mitty, Will Rogers, and even of Woody Allen's many incarnations of the urban Jewish male, whose bewilderment is a source of strength (in the sense that it brings him center stage in our sympathies) and a protection against accusations of snobbery.

Yet at least on an official level, Americans have also persistently denigrated humor. E. B. and Katharine S. White put the matter most directly in their preface to *A Subtreasury of American Humor*, published in 1948:

> The world likes humor, but treats it patronizingly. It decorates its
> serious artists with laurels, and its wags with Brussels sprouts. It feels
> that if a thing is funny it can be presumed to be something less than
> great, because if it were truly great it would be wholly serious.[2]

Because the Whites' is an anthology of *American* humor, we can interpret the "world" to be America, even though White may have had a larger world in mind. In any case, it is true that Americans have characteristically pretended to an official high seriousness, in part because they have wanted to be taken seriously in the potentially embarrassing face of their European ancestors.

Views of what constitutes the American humorous tradition have changed as that tradition has been enlarged and altered over the years. In 1881 a British scholar, H. R. Haweis, delivered a series of lectures on American humorists at the Royal Institution in London; the figures he selected for discussion were Washington Irving, Oliver Wendell Holmes, James Russell Lowell, and Artemus Ward. When the lectures were collected in book form the following year, he added Mark Twain—who had yet to publish his best work—and Bret Harte. Haweis summarized the essence of American humor as he perceived it:

> First, there is the shock between Business and Piety.
> Secondly, the shock of contrast between the Aboriginal and the
> Yankee.
> Lastly, the shock of contrast between the bigness of American
> nature and the smallness of European nature, or, as for the matter of
> that, Human Nature itself outside America.[3]

Haweis bases his theory of American humor on incongruity, particularly the incongruity between an essentially European sensibility and the new experience of the American continent, with its vastness, its native inhabitants, and the tension between commercial success and religious devotion. The theme that runs throughout his commentaries on all six of these writers, however, is the delicacy and gentility of their humor; in the book's Epilogue he stresses that wit is "Moral, Recreative, and Stimulating to a very high degree," and calls it "a most effective Disciplinarian, and one of the greatest sweetners and purifiers of Life."[4] In these phrases, which echo those in John Neal's 1846 letter to Frances Whitcher, Haweis essentially apologizes for dealing with humor at all by emphasizing its effectiveness as a moral force.

By 1937, in the first edition of *Native American Humor*, Walter Blair proposed that a truly "native" American humor did not even come into existence until about 1830, by which time Americans had achieved a detachment from both their awe at the vastness of the New World and the sense of high purpose inherent in colonizing and establishing a new nation. Blair does not agree with Haweis that true humor is necessarily moral; in addition to detachment, he says, another requisite for American humor is "a certain amount of frivolity." Further, he says that American writers had to develop a perception of the essential comedy of American life and devise techniques that were not merely borrowed from English and European models, as were those of Irving.[5] Blair therefore begins his study with the "Down East" humor of Seba Smith's Jack Downing and Thomas Haliburton's Sam Slick, both "Jonathan" figures who, in their innocence, poked fun at politics and commerce. Also included in *Native American Humor* is the humor of the Old Southwest, consisting primarily of tall tales; the work of the "literary comedians" such as David Ross Locke and Finley Peter Dunne; and the local color stories of the late nineteenth century.

Into this predominantly male pantheon Blair admits Frances Whitcher, as an exponent of Down East humor, and Harriet Beecher Stowe, with two of her "Sam Lawson" stories. But the tenor of both Blair's commentary and the selections he includes is decidedly masculine, from the tall-tale raucousness of Thomas Bangs Thorpe's "The Big Bear of Arkansas" to Harte's "The Luck of Roaring Camp" and Twain's "Baker's Blue-Jay Yarn." In a brief discussion of twentieth-century humor, added for the 1960 edition, Blair does acknowledge the increasing urbanity of American humor and the creation by Thurber and others of the bewildered "little man" in the early twentieth century. But in Blair's classic study *The New Yorker* seems to have gotten along without Dorothy Parker, and Marietta Holley, whose works rivaled those of Twain in popularity, is a footnote.

As recently as 1973, Louis D. Rubin's *The Comic Imagination in American Literature* included only one essay (of thirty-two) about a female writer: Eudora Welty. In his concluding essay, " 'The Barber Kept on Shaving': The Two Perspectives of American Humor," Rubin identifies the "most distinctive characteristic" of American humor as "the incompatibility of the vulgar and the genteel viewpoints within a single society." The long tradition of balloon-pricking vernacular humor, Rubin says, is evidence that the more "vulgar" or "democratic" humor has been the ascendant mode:

> There can be little doubt that this perspective—the vernacular
> perspective, set forth in opposition to the cultural, the literary—is the
> approved American mode of humor. The characteristic comic
> situation in American humorous writing is that in which cultural and
> social pretension are made to appear ridiculous and artificial. The
> bias is all on the side of the practical, the factual.[6]

Such a view is certainly consistent with the tendency toward anti-intellectualism in American culture, in which H. L. Mencken, decrying America's lack of intellectual sophistication, is almost a lone voice. Yet Rubin, like other scholars, also ignores the special contributions of women writers to the American humorous tradition.

In fact, the clash of the genteel and the vulgar that so many critics have identified as basic to American humor has another dimension that helps to explain both the conception of that humor as male and some of the prominent figures within it. Put simply, the strict, official gender-role definitions that prevailed in the nineteenth century identified the woman as genteel and the man as inherently vulgar. With responsibility for culture delegated to women, men were left free to play, to joke, knowing that the women would pull them into line soon enough. A striking example of this peculiar balancing act can be found in the life and work of Mark Twain. Not only is Huck Finn the classic "bad boy," called back to "civilization" by a series of women who clearly have the responsibility for reforming wayward men,[7] but Twain himself appears to have enjoyed a similar role, relying on his wife, Olivia, to censor both his books and his behavior. Mary Ellen Goad suggests that in Twain's view, one of woman's essential roles was that of reformer:

> Twain viewed the role of the female in a particular, and, to the
> modern mind, strange way. He operated on the theory that the male
> of the species was rough and crude, and needed the softening and

refining influence of a woman, or, if necessary, many women. The primary function of the women was thus the reformation of man.[8]

Twain's perception of the innate characteristics of man and woman is concomitant with the male fondness for the tall tale and the questioning outsider, Jonathan, and also with the nagging, scolding, unbearably sensible women who populate male humor until Thurber gets his revenge in "The Unicorn in the Garden" by having the wife who refuses to admit to the existence of unicorns hauled off to the "booby-hatch."

In *Gender, Fantasy, and Realism in American Literature*, Alfred Habegger argues a similar proposition when he adds the contrast between gender roles to the conventional analysis of the origins of an American humorous tradition. Habegger notes that "the voluminous critical literature on American humor has yet to come to terms with the American habit of regarding humor as in some way masculine," and proceeds to explain that pervasive masculinity in the following analysis:

> At a time when being a lady sometimes meant being a corseted artificial sentimentalist, the relaxed, ill-dressed loafing man supplied the literary comedians with the mask that formed the basis of their humor. The prevailing view of American humor is that it developed out of a kind of border warfare between two cultures, vernacular and refined. I am proposing an additional dialectic—between male and female. The social basis of American humor may have been the staggering difference in our ideal gender roles. What the humorist did was to play the ideal male type—the lazy unregenerate man who defied cultural norms perceived as feminine, not by saying "Don't tread on me" or "No" in thunder, but by relaxing, taking it easy.[9]

What Habegger suggests in this analysis is that the male perception of the female as guardian and embodiment of the genteel tradition allowed men to claim the freedom to be the opposite: the joking "bad boy" who rebelled against official social norms. It seems likely, in fact, that the consistently unflattering stereotype of the woman as nag and scold in male humor reflects an ambivalence about the male-female dialectic. On the one hand, the wives of Rip Van Winkle and Walter Mitty are unimaginative upholders of the status quo who serve as foils to the boyish imaginations of men; their stern common sense makes them dull and unattractive, directing the reader's sympathies to the unfulfilled yearnings of the men. To this extent they are merely humorous devices. Yet at the same time, Irving's Dame Van Winkle and Thurber's Mrs. Mitty are drawn so negatively that one perceives true antagonism in the portraits, a sense that is reinforced by the fact that in both cases the woman "wins," and the reader's sympathy is supposed to remain with the dreaming, downtrodden husband.[10]

The dominant tradition of American humor, then, turns upon the freedom of the male to enjoy, to joke, to criticize, to question. The stance of the humorous *persona* is one of superiority, whether he is the naïve but wise "Jonathan" or the carefully articulate Easterner introducing a Western tall tale. Common targets of this male tradition have been corrupt or inept politicians, the vagaries of institutions and bureaucracies, and women. What Alfred Habegger calls "the staggering difference in our ideal gender roles" provides a point of intersection between the male and female traditions in American humor; the pervasive distinctions between men's and women's roles, tasks, and talents have caused each gender to view the other as "other," and hence essentially ludicrous. However, the stereotypes born of this tension are primarily those of women, created by male writers and appropriated for different purposes by female writers.

As the "outsiders" in American culture, women have created a humorous tradition that both mirrors and challenges that separateness. Just as Anne Bradstreet recognizes in her "Prologue" the enormous dichotomy between the needle and the pen, and fends off the "carping tongue" that would hustle her back to her "proper sphere," so women's humor in general reveals a consciousness of an assigned, subordinate role within which one must operate subversively rather than with assumed superiority. At least three important distinctions between men's and women's humorous writing help to define these different traditions. The most obvious is subject matter. Until very recently, most American women's humor could be called "domestic" in a broad sense, turning as it does on the details of life *inside*—the home, the church or social group, the neighborhood—whereas men's humor typically takes place *outside* of this domestic world: on riverboats, in the legislature, in offices. The second major difference is the use of certain humorous forms, which is in turn related to subject matter and place. Both men and women have written comic plays, satiric sketches, humorous stories, and light verse, but women have not written the traditional tall tale, and when they have written political satires, these have almost uniformly dealt with the subject of women's role and rights, from "Fanny Fern" in the 1850s to Ellen Goodman in the 1980s. Finally, and most important, is the difference in the way the theme or message is presented—the manner in which the language of the text in women's humor reveals awareness of discrimination and oppression at the same time that it wears a gloss of amusement.

II

When Walter Blair suggested that a distinctive American humorous tradition began about 1830, he based his argument on socio-political realities: the emergence of a sense of national identity, the veneration of rural, rustic values made possible by Jacksonian ideals, and freedom from slavish imitation of European literary models. For quite different reasons, the female tradition in American humor may be said to begin about the same time. As the production of goods increasingly took place outside the home in the early nineteenth century, the roles of men and women became more sharply differentiated. The rapid industrialization of American society, which relegated many poor and single women to factory jobs, had the effect of reinforcing in the middle classes the separation between "man's work" and "woman's work," so that as early as the 1840s, Catharine Beecher and others were urging that women receive an education fitting them for lives in the domestic sphere.[11] Whether in a settled town or on the frontier, women increasingly spent their time at home, in the company of children, household chores, and other women.

Other factors combined with this enforced domesticity to make the early nineteenth century a propitious starting point for a women's humorous tradition. The cult of gentility, which Frances Whitcher and Mark Twain so deplored because of its excesses and crude interpretations, sanctioned women's involvement in the arts—including literature—and in a variety of women's social and benevolent groups, such as the sewing societies that Whitcher and others describe. At the same time, outlets for women's writing began to exist in greater numbers than before. Local and regional newspapers frequently published poetry and brief essays or sketches,[12] and more prestigious national publications, such as *Godey's Lady's Book*, founded in 1830, published both male and female writers, among them Harriet Beecher Stowe and Frances Whitcher. By the 1850s, when Hawthorne referred to the "mob of scribbling women," a large body of women's literature existed in America, and it is not surprising that, even amid the flood of sentimentality that prevailed, the authors of some of that literature employed the critical eye of the humorist, as women surveyed the world they inhabited.

The domestic setting in which women have located their humor has undergone many changes since the early nineteenth century. For Frances Whitcher, as for other writers of the early national period, household chores required a great deal of time and physical drudgery, but included in the definition of women's domestic realm were church-related social functions, such as the sewing society and "donation parties" for the minister's family. At the same time, women on the frontier, such as Caroline Kirkland in Michigan, attempted to create a domestic environment with scant resources. In *A New Home — Who'll Follow*, Kirkland writes amusingly of her neighbors' habit of borrowing all those items they have not succeeded in providing for themselves — including sheets, churns, and shoes. By mid-century, in the work of Fanny Fern (Sara Willis Parton) and others, women's humor arose from their understanding that the domestic sphere was inseparable from issues of women's rights, including property ownership, education, and suffrage, all of which had a direct bearing on the quality of their lives as wives and mothers. The work of Marietta Holley, beginning in the 1870s, combines the domestic world in its strictest sense with these larger social concerns as her character Samantha Allen argues for women's rights while washing her husband's shirts and making preserves and pies.

In the early twentieth century, as a more urban and urbane humor became the vogue, domesticity as defined by household tasks and childrearing retreated briefly to the background, to be replaced by another aspect of women's lives — relationships with men — as in Josephine Daskam's *Fables for the Fair* and Dorothy Parker's light verse and sketches. By the 1920s, however, a different sort of domestic dilemma became the subject of women's humor as more middle-class women entered the work force and found that, as Florence Guy Seabury points out in *The Delicatessen Husband*, men were ill-prepared to take part in the domestic routine while their wives worked outside the home. After World War II, middle-class women's lives were located increasingly in suburban America, and as the "back-to-the-kitchen" movement gained force, a generation of female humorists that includes Jean Kerr, Phyllis McGinley, and Peg Bracken wrote about the domestic life of the woman in terms that were strikingly similar to those of their nineteenth-century counterparts. The bridge club and the PTA replaced the sewing circle, and the beauty parlor replaced the dressmaker, but the separation of men's and women's lives was as distinct as it had been a hundred years before.

Despite changes in the definition of the domestic setting over time, the world in which female humor is located exhibits two constants: first, it is a world peopled primarily by women; and second, women's experience in this world is repetitive, trivializing, and demeaning. Traditional male American humor may take place in a predominantly male environment, such as a mining camp or a corporation office, but the occasion for the humor is normally a moment of high drama, instead of a depiction of sameness and routine. Frequently, women are present—as wives, mothers, teachers, or girlfriends—whereas in women's humor the sense of men as "other" often leads to their absence from the scene.

The dominant forms and devices of humorous literature, like those of all popular literature, change in response to alterations in the public taste, which are in turn influenced by an array of demographic and ideological shifts. The great popularity of dialect humor in the nineteenth century, for example, can be explained in part by the striking differences between the elegant rhetoric of official speech and the less formal dialects in which most people spoke, and the divergence of dialects in various parts of the country, all of which were amusing to the nineteenth-century reader.[13] The tall tale as a form also belongs to the nineteenth century and has its origins in the frontiersman's need to be somewhat larger than life in order to deal with a threatening wilderness. By the end of the century, as America became more urban and Americans more literate, such vernacular devices and forms gave way to a more subtle and sophisticated humor featuring word-play, wit, and irony. The image of the humorous *persona* changed from the unlettered bumpkin to the figure of Eustace Tilley surveying a butterfly through his monocle: the emblem of *The New Yorker*, which its founding editor, Harold Ross, intended to be "gay, humorous, satirical but to be more than a jester."[14] Because it produced many of the dominant figures in American humor of the twentieth century, such as James Thurber, Robert Benchley, S. J. Perelman, Dorothy Parker, and Phyllis McGinley, *The New Yorker* has had great influence on the humor of twentieth-century America.[15]

Women writers, like men, have followed and helped to create these and other changes in American humorous taste, but to understand the full range of the American humorous tradition and the place of women within it, it is important to note the ways in which women writers have diverged from these patterns. Most obvious is the absence of women writers from the American tall-tale tradition. There are at least two reasons why women did not write tall tales like those of Mark Twain and Thomas Bangs Thorpe. The first is the fact that women did not normally inhabit the environments where such stories take place: mining camps, riverboats, hunting trips. Women's experience of the frontier environment had much more to do with cooking, laundry, and caring for the ill than with storytelling around a campfire, and in more settled communities, female competition found expression in accomplishments of dress or cooking rather than in boastful accounts of physical prowess. Second, the requirements of genteel society dictated that women's writing be characterized by a delicacy of language and subject matter to which the tall tale did not conform. The classic American tall tale contains obscene and even scatological elements that also found their way into other forms of masculine humor of the period. In fact, Samuel Cox, an early student of American humor, noted in 1876 that it lacked "refinement," insisting that "three-fourths of our humor will not bear rehearsal in the presence of women."[16]

The women's humorous tradition, however, includes several forms that are not characteristic of male humor, all of them expressing women's sense of isolation from the dominant culture and frustration with their assigned role. The most pervasive of these forms is the domestic saga—an account of a female *persona* in a domestic setting struggling to cope with the many demands of her role as homemaker. The domestic saga has its origins in the early nineteenth century, in the work of Caroline Kirkland and Fanny Fern, and reached its full flowering in the mid-twentieth century in such works as *The Egg and I* by Betty MacDonald (Anne Elizabeth Campbell Bard), Jean Kerr's *Please Don't Eat the Daisies*, and Shirley Jackson's *Life Among the Savages.* The narrator in these works frequently uses the hyperbole and slapstick comedy of the tall tale, but the setting is the home or neighborhood, and the issues raised in these works are those of concern specifically to women.

Caroline Kirkland, using the pseudonym "Mrs. Mary Clavers," wrote *A New Home — Who'll Follow? Glimpses of Western Life* (1839) about her brief sojourn as a frontier wife earlier in the decade in what is now Michigan. Always, like most women, a reluctant pioneer, Kirkland describes various aspects of the domestic experience in a new western settlement from the safe distance of New York City, to which she returned after six years of frontier living. Kirkland's are the observations of a well-educated outsider who can afford to be amused by what is not, for her, a constant way of life, but the realities of women's lives in a frontier community are clearly presented. Kirkland is struck, for example, by the neighbors' propensity to borrow whatever they need from each other:

> Whoever comes into Michigan with nothing, will be sure to better his condition; but wo [sic] to him that brings with him any thing like an appearance of abundance, whether of money or mere household conveniences. To have them, and not be willing to share them in some sort with the whole community, is an unpardonable crime.... I have actually known a stray martingale to be traced to four dwellings, two miles apart, having been lent from one to another, without a word to the original proprieter, who sat waiting, not very patiently, to commence a journey.[17]

The climax of Kirkland's passage about the evils of borrowing comes when a local woman has a baby, and a neighbor sends word that she wishes to borrow the child because her own infant's mouth is too sore for him to nurse:

> "LEND MY BABY!!!" — and her utterance failed. The new mother's feelings were fortunately too big for speech and Ianthe wisely disappeared before Mrs. Doubleday found her tongue.[18]

The domestic saga is also one of the forms used by Sara Willis Parton, writing as "Fanny Fern" for several publications in the 1850s and 1860s. One reason for Fanny Fern's enormous popularity with readers, in both her brief newspaper sketches and her novel *Ruth Hall*, was her ability to write both tearfully sentimental accounts of dying children and the virtues of motherhood, and witty, pointed sat-

ires about issues of concern to nineteenth-century women. She addressed many topics—such as prostitution, birth control, and the
need for women's economic independence—that were considered
"unladylike," using wit and sharp sarcasm. Among her most amusing
sketches are those about women's domestic role, such as "Aunt Hetty
on Matrimony," a soliloquy in which an older woman lectures a
group of girls on the evils—for them—of marriage. Her attitude is
summarized in the following passage:

> Oh girls! set your affections on cats, poodles, parrots or lap dogs; but
> let matrimony alone. It's the hardest way on earth of getting a
> living—you never know when your work is done.[19]

In "Mrs. Adolphus Smith Sporting the 'Blue Stocking,'" Fanny Fern
describes a woman's attempts to finish writing an article amid constant interruptions from her children, husband, and servant. When
one of the children swallows a button, the husband follows his wife's
advice to turn him upside down—*"Reverse him*, dear"—and nearly
kills him in the process. The sketch ends with the woman giving up
her writing, and with her comment, "There! it's no use for a married
woman to cultivate her intellect" (265-66).

By the 1920s, when a certain amount of role-reversal began to
occur as more married women pursued careers, the domestic saga
was likely to focus on the inability of the husband to take care of his
own basic needs without his wife constantly present to cook and
clean. Such is the message in the title piece of Florence Guy Seabury's *The Delicatessen Husband*. The point of view in this sketch is
that of Perry Winship, who has great difficulty making the transition
between the life of his childhood, with a stay-at-home mother to provide for him, and life in an urban apartment with a professional wife
whose long hours force him to depend on the local delicatessen for
sustenance:

> He hated going to the delicatessen. Despite his needs those
> indispensable institutions ... were not, to him, convenient places at
> which to purchase ready-to-eat foods. They were emblems of a
> declining civilization, the source of all our ills, the promoter of equal
> suffrage, the permitter of the business and professional woman, the
> destroyer of the home. They were generations removed from his
> ideals.[20]

Although Seabury satirizes Perry Winship's anguish—especially in light of the fact that it never seems to occur to him to learn to cook—she sees him also as a transitional figure caught between his mother's apparent fulfillment in motherhood and the professional life of the "New Woman."

The full-length domestic saga became popular in 1945 with Betty MacDonald's *The Egg and I*, in which the anguish of a woman attempting to be a model housewife is close beneath the surface of the comedy. The actual isolation of the narrator on a chicken ranch in the Northwest is a metaphor for the essential isolation of the woman whose life revolves around cooking, cleaning, and laundry, and the book chronicles her futile attempts to live up to the ideal promulgated by advertising, her mother, and her neighbors—as well as by her husband's expectations. In *The Egg and I*, as is commonly the case in women's domestic humor, it is clear that the female *persona* is almost entirely without self-determination: in virtually every aspect of her life, she is expected to abide by standards set by others, and, further, to derive her fulfillment as a person from any success she may experience in trying to attain ideal domestic womanhood.

The initial influence on Betty's life is her mother, who has taught her daughters that "it is a wife's bounden duty to see that her husband is happy in his work."[21] When her husband decides to start a chicken ranch, she therefore does not protest, but takes with her into this new adventure the knowledge of "how to make mayonnaise and mitre sheet corners and light candles for dinner" (39). When these skills prove insufficient for life on a remote farm, Betty has the examples of two neighbor women, Mrs. Kettle and Mrs. Hicks, for instruction. The former is a sloppy, earthy mother of fifteen who bakes wonderful bread, and the latter is a meticulous housekeeper and notorious gossip. Neither of these women approves of Betty's rather tentative devotion to life as a farmer's wife, but Betty's most consistent critic is her husband, Bob, who is quick to make clear his requirements for her work. He insists, for example, that she scrub the floors every day:

> . . . it was a badge of fine housekeeping, a labor of love, and a
> woman's duty to her husband. The more I was shown of that side of
> the life of a farmer's good wife, the more I saw in the life of an
> old-fashioned mistress. (75)

By the end of *The Egg and I*, the relationship between Betty and Bob has deteriorated to the point that, as they sit waiting for a babysitter she thinks to herself, "Heavens, we act like neighbors who suddenly find themselves in a hotel bedroom together" (285). Although contemporary reviewers described the book as "hilarious" and "one long chuckle," the book in fact chronicles the mounting frustration and resentment a woman feels when forced into society's mold.

Most of the domestic sagas of the post-World War II period are lighter in tone than *The Egg and I* and depend for their humor less on hyperbole and more on wit and slapstick comedy. But the basic elements of all domestic sagas are the same: a female *persona* or first-person narrator recounts, with some degree of self-deprecation, her chaotic attempts to achieve a level of ideality as a homemaker that is dictated by the culture in the form of older women, men (usually husbands), advertising, and women's magazines. Such sagas presuppose that the reader will identify with the central character's struggles; while offering no solutions to the problems of the homemaker, they have served as a relatively safe means of protest about those problems.

Another form that female humorists have made peculiarly their own is a brief sketch that Martha Bruère and Mary Ritter Beard, editors of the 1934 anthology *Laughing Their Way*, call the "skit." Bruère and Beard define the skit as "a caper, a prance, a puff of whimsy with such truth as it may contain treated incidentally." Relating the skit to the monologue or newspaper column, the editors continue their definition:

> The Skit is usually written in the first person and always has the air of being spoken. And if there is one time more than another when a woman's tongue is in her cheek, when she nudges herself in the ribs, and points a derisive finger at her own personality, it is when she writes a Skit. Sometimes she does this to disarm criticism. In a kind of bravado, she stands up and faces the music she has provoked.

Bruère and Beard's definition of the skit touches upon both method and purpose in ways that are suggestive of the essence of women's humor generally. The fact that the skit has "the air of being spoken" is related to the need of the female humorous *persona* to "talk to" someone; the skit may also be a dialogue, either between the speaker and herself, as in Dorothy Parker's "The Waltz" and Tess Slesinger's "Upon Being Told That Her Second Husband Has Taken His First Lover," or between two people, as in many of the pieces in *Distressing Dialogues* (1924) by Nancy Boyd. The tendency to self-deprecation in women's humor is indicated here also, as Bruère and Beard note that the writer of the skit "points a derisive finger at her own personality." Although the speaker in the skit is no more self-deprecatory than the domestic saga, there is a tendency in this form for the speaker to lecture herself on her own shortcomings or to speak to the reader about a social problem that affects not only her, but other women as well.

The editors of *Laughing Their Way* further define the skit by locating it in a particular era:

> ... it will appear only in such an atmosphere of well-being and urbanity as had begun recently to envelop a large part of literate America. It is a type of buoyant conversation which cannot flourish without a flippantly sagacious audience.[22]

The period of time to which Bruère and Beard refer is the early years of *The New Yorker*, founded in 1925; most of the examples of this form in *Laughing Their Way* are reprinted from that magazine and are written by both well-known humorists such as Dorothy Parker and Cornelia Otis Skinner and now-obscure writers such as Katharine Best and Frances Warfield. What Bruère and Beard call the "skit" is a form of what Harold Ross, *New Yorker* founding editor, referred to as the "casual," a brief, usually unsigned commentary on some aspect of contemporary life. In fact, however, the skit as a form can be traced to the mid-nineteenth-century newspaper columns of Fanny Fern and others. Fern's "Hungry Husbands" fits the definition of this subgenre, as do many others of her "Fern Leaves."[23]

The skit, or "casual," was also written by men, including *New Yorker* writers James Thurber, E. B. White, and S. J. Perelman, but there are significant differences in tone and subject matter between the sketches by these male writers and the female writer's skit. The male writer, freer to "play," frequently spins the skit out into pure fantasy or nonsense, and the humor depends to a great extent on word-play. E. B. White's classic sketch "The Door," for example, a satire on modern synthetic materials, expresses frustration with things not being what they seem:

The names were tex and frequently koid. Or they were flex and oid
or they were duroid (sani) or flexan (duro), but everything was glass
(but not quite glass) and the thing that you touched (the surface,
washable, crease-resistant) was rubber, only it wasn't quite rubber
and you didn't quite touch it but almost.[24]

The speaker here has entered a reality different from the one to
which he is accustomed, and the reader only gradually realizes that
the origins of his confusion and discomfort are the products of
modern technology. S. J. Perelman's skits usually deal with more
ephemeral topics and have a lighter, more frivolous tone. But they
share with those of White the elements of fantasy and playfulness.
Perelman's *New Yorker* casuals are frequently comments on manners, fads, and affectations in urban culture, and, like those of White,
Perelman's *personae* seem drawn into some vortex of absurdity. A
piece on *Harper's Bazaar*, for example, begins:

Just in case anybody here missed me at the Mermaid Tavern this
afternoon when the bowl of sack was being passed, I spent most of it
reclining on my chaise longue in a negligee trimmed with marabou,
reading trashy toffees and eating French yellow-backed novels.[25]

More recently, Woody Allen has raised the skit to the apotheosis of
absurdity, as when in an imagined speech to a graduating class he
defines "modern man" as "any person born after Nietzsche's edict
that 'God is dead,' but before the hit recording 'I Wanna Hold Your
Hand.'"[26]

The woman's skit is far more likely to be grounded in the reality of
her everyday life, and to express in more straightforward fashion an
immediate discomfort with that life, usually arising from the speaker's experience *as a woman*. Instead of fantasy or absurdity, these
sketches commonly turn on a humorous rendering of reality that
evokes in the reader more thought than laughter. Some of Fanny
Fern's mid-nineteenth-century "Fern Leaves" are brief, witty lectures
on social issues. In her 1867 *New York Ledger* piece, "Fashionable
Invalidism," for example, Fern attacks the habits of fashion and diet
that caused so many nineteenth-century women to feel unwell much
of the time. She takes to task the woman "who laces so tightly that she
breathes only by a rare accident; who vibrates constantly between the
confectioner's shop and the dentist's office," and urges sensible
clothes and a sensible diet.[27] Fern's "Hungry Husbands" is a mono-

logue turning upon the adage that "the way to a man's heart is through his stomach," which the speaker both agrees with and deplores. "There's nothing on earth so savage—except a bear robbed of her cubs—as a hungry husband," says the speaker, and she urges the reader to "feed him well," so he will "stay contentedly in his cage, like a gorged anaconda." The humorous twist, proving that her advice has been tongue-in-cheek, comes at the end:

> If he was my husband, wouldn't I make him heaps of *pison* things! Bless me! I've made a mistake in the spelling; it should have been *pies-and-things!*[28]

Edna St. Vincent Millay's *Distressing Dialogues* more nearly conform to the definition of "skit" as the term is normally used. Many of the pieces in this collection are dialogues between speakers identified only as "He" and "She," and the pervasive theme is the difficulty of male-female relationships. The conflicts range from the trivial, such as a man leaving the cap off the toothpaste tube in "No Bigger Than a Man's Hand," to the more serious failure of a man to appreciate a woman's career, as in "The Implacable Aphrodite." The *personae* in these sketches are urbane, privileged, and often world-weary socialites, whose brittle sophistication Millay satirizes. Although both genders are caricatured, the women are presented as even sillier and more vain than the men; these unflattering stereotypes are reminiscent of those in the work of Frances Whitcher and Marietta Holley, here transferred to an urban setting. In "Tea for the Muse," for example, the male poet who is invited as the guest of honor is first patronized and then ignored as the women chatter idly, delivering caustic insults, as in the following exchange about Mrs. Blackburn's taste in tea and men:

> Mrs. Blackburn: It's all right darling. I filled up at Dolly's before I came.
> Mrs. Lang-Jennings: Teresa! And you dare say that in my presence! What's the matter with *my* tea?
> Mrs. Blackburn: Nothing, dear,—
> Miss Lenox (*interjecting*): It's the best tea this side of Tokio!
> Mrs. Blackburn: But I'm not one of those who can wait for the best. I always take the first, for fear it should be the last.
> Miss Dunning (*to Miss Hutton, in a whisper*): As in the case of her husband, my dear.[29]

Most of the skits that Bruère and Beard include in *Laughing Their Way* have similar urban settings and deal primarily with social situations, and although their form is commonly the monologue or sketch form of the *New Yorker* "casual" rather than the dialogues that Millay uses, there is a similar focus on the particular dilemmas that women encounter, from Dorothy Parker's monologue about breaking a garter at a party to Thyra Samter Winslow's "Semi-Professional Astrology," in which an inept astrologer reads the author's horoscope. Several of the skits address directly the issue of women's competence, including the ability to play tennis, in Alice Frankforter's "Tennis Game," and the ability to read, in Cornelia Otis Skinner's "Municipal Efficiency." In this latter piece, the speaker must take a literacy test in order to register to vote, and her confrontation with the bureaucracy, whose "uncleaned cuspidors bear honest testimony to the simplicity of our Tammany Fathers," causes her to feel childlike and inept. Even the elevator is a source of disquietude, and Skinner's speaker holds her breath as it goes into "delicate swoons" between floors. The clerk she encounters at the voter-registration office looks at her with a "savage glare" that makes her feel apologetic:

> I tried to win him with a smile, but he seemed only to hate me more, and asked in a growl where I lived. . . . He then asked me if I had ever voted, and I had to admit I never had.
> "Ya never voted?" he asked with such utter scorn I felt like replying "No. But I can sew."[30]

The clerk's challenge to her involvement in the political process tempts her to announce her skill in a typically "feminine" pursuit, but she refrains from saying this, knowing that it will only remove her further from this "masculine" world.

Because it deals primarily with manners and mores, the skit features allusions to people, events, and fashions that tie it to an era; its topicality frequently makes it almost inaccessible to later generations of readers. Published chiefly in newspapers and popular magazines, the skit presents the woman's immediate response to circumstances that she finds annoying, and therefore provides a measure of the changes in women's concerns over time. In 1860 Fanny Fern wrote a sprightly, satiric piece titled "Shall Women Vote?"; more than sixty years later, during the first decade in which women were allowed to vote, Skinner's *persona* is chastized for not having done so sooner, as though she has neglected a long-standing civic duty.

If the skit is located in time, the third form that women have appropriated for humorous purposes projects a time or place in which contemporary realities are left behind in the creation of a new order. Speculative literature—utopian fantasy and science fiction—has allowed women writers to satirize the patriarchal culture they inhabit by contrasting it with imagined worlds in which the values and welfare of women are ascendant if not exclusive. The utopian impulse is implicit in the work of a number of female humorists. By arguing, for example, for sexual equality in all areas of life, Holley's Samantha Allen proposes a better—if not perfect—world for women; and in viewing Perry Winship, in "The Delicatessen Husband," as a casualty of the transition to a culture in which women are free to follow their own talents and preferences, Seabury expresses optimism about fundamental changes in the social order. But it is in full-blown fantasies such as Charlotte Perkins Gilman's *Herland* (1915) and Joanna Russ's *The Female Man* (1975) that the merger of humor and futurist vision demonstrates the author's ability to detach herself imaginatively from cultural restrictions.

Gilman's *Herland*, serialized in her magazine *The Forerunner* in 1915, is one of three utopian novels by the writer best known in her own day as the author of *Women and Economics*, and today as the author of "The Yellow Wallpaper," a study of a woman's descent into insanity. *Moving the Mountain*, published in 1911, posits a world in which men and women have learned to live together in a humanist-socialist society, whereas *Herland*, and its sequel *With Her in Our-land* (1916), supposes a culture composed only of women, who reproduce by a sort of mystic self-fertilization and who have developed a society based on principles of love, harmony, and nurturance. Into this society, located somewhere on the planet Earth, come three young men, the first to be seen in Herland in 2000 years, and the most pervasive source of humor in the book is the contrast between the serene, competent inhabitants of this utopia and the bewildered male adventurers who are the "outsiders." The novel is narrated by one of the three men, Vandyke Jennings, who is a sociologist by profession. With, as Ann J. Lane puts it, "a characteristic mischievousness," Gilman makes her narrator a "man of reason" who "uses his scientific knowledge to argue 'learnedly' about the well-known physiological limitations of women,"[31] and who is made to appear ridiculous in the process.

As is frequently the case in utopian fiction, the flaws of the "real" society, inhabited by the reader, emerge by contrast with the utopia. In *Herland*, the women function as the *eiron*, or "wise innocent" figures, asking detailed questions about the world outside Herland; in their answers, the three men reveal not only the hypocrisy and violence of the world from which they have come, but also their own acculturated chauvinism. One issue about which the men are most curious is how a society composed only of women perpetuates itself, and Jeff struggles to find a parallel to their process in the world he knows:

> "Well—there are some rather high forms of insect life in which it occurs. Parthenogenesis, we call it—that means virgin birth."
>
> She could not follow him.
>
> "*Birth*, we know, of course; but what is *virgin?*"
>
> Terry looked uncomfortable, but Jeff met the question quite calmly. "Among mating animals, the term *virgin* is applied to the female who has not mated," he answered.
>
> "Oh, I see. And does it apply to the male also? Or is there a different term for him?"
>
> He passed this over rather hurriedly, saying that the same term would apply, but was seldom used.
>
> "No?" she said. "But one cannot mate without the other surely. Is not each then—virgin—before mating?"[32]

Before the calm, common-sensical questioning of the residents of Herland, the flaws of a patriarchal society are one by one exposed.

Gilman's premise in *Herland* is that these evils are a result of habit and cultural tradition, not of an inherent superiority of one gender. Further, as Van, the narrator, comes to realize, many of the characteristics thought to belong "naturally" to women have developed in response to male demands. When Terry, who is ultimately expelled from Herland for rape, laments the fact that the Herland women are not "feminine," Van comes to this realization:

> ... those "feminine charms" we are so fond of are not feminine at all, but mere reflected masculinity—developed to please us because they had to please us, and in no way essential to the real fulfillment of their great process. (54)

The most pervasive instance of the unquestioning acceptance of a received tradition is organized religion, and the women of Herland, who strive continually to change and improve their own religious beliefs, find such blind adherence to ancient doctrines astonishing. In a culture that glorifies motherhood and devotes much of its energy to raising children, the concept of infant damnation is particularly repugnant; when Van tells Ellador, his Herland fiancée, of this concept, she cannot accept it:

> "They believed that God was Love—and Wisdom—and Power?"
> "Yes—all of that."
> Her eyes grew large, her face ghastly pale.
> "And yet that such a God could put little new babies to burn—for eternity?"
> She fell into a sudden shuddering and left me, running swiftly to the nearest temple.

Ellador is comforted by the temple-keeper's reminder that "people who are utterly ignorant will believe anything" (110), a statement that deftly places the Herland women in a position of superiority. In a subsequent conversation, Ellador as *eiron* challenges biblical authority and leaves Van with no logical rejoinder:

> "We consider it inspired—'the word of God.'"
> "How do you know it is?"
> "Because it says so."
> "Does it say so in as many words? Who wrote that in?"
> I began to try to recall some text that did say so, and could not bring it to mind. (114)

Gilman's ironic method calls into question the basis of many of the beliefs that have for centuries subordinated women to men, and *Herland* describes a culture free of patriarchal condescension.

Shortly before publishing *Herland*, Charlotte Perkins Gilman wrote a short story that similarly uses irony to point out ways in which woman's fate is determined by man. In "If I Were a Man" (1914), Mollie Mathewson, a "true woman" in the sense that she conforms to society's expectations for her behavior and demeanor, finds herself inhabiting her husband Gerald's body, her consciousness of herself as "Mollie" coexisting with his male consciousness. She is pleased by the ease of movement afforded by a man's clothing, but is shocked by her increasing awareness of "what men really think of women"[33] as she overhears the conversations on the train her husband is taking to work. An Episcopalian minister fears that women will "overstep the limits of their God-appointed sphere," and notes that "she [woman] brought evil into the world" (37), whereupon the female consciousness contributed by Mollie's presence causes Gerald to defend women: "Women are pretty much *people*, seems to me" (38).

This fantasy of dual consciousness is one of the forerunners of Joanna Russ's 1975 *The Female Man*, a science-fiction novel that explores the nature of gender-identity while satirizing cultural expectations for female behavior. The title of *The Female Man* comes from the decision by one of the novel's protagonists to deal with sexism by regarding herself as a man rather than a woman:

> For years I have been saying *Let me in, Love me, Approve me, Define me, Regulate me, Validate me, Support me.* Now I say *Move over.* If we are all Mankind, it follows to my interested and righteous and rightnow very bright and beady little eyes, that I too am a Man and not at all a Woman.[34]

Rather than presenting a single utopian vision of the ideal society, Russ presents four female characters from parallel universes, one of which, Whileaway, is inhabited solely by women. The four women who alternately narrate the story are in some ways different aspects of the same woman, and all of them are aware that women are regarded as a joke. Russ's method in this strongly feminist novel is to turn the joke back on its perpetrators, primarily by parodying submissive behavior and the male need for it. The following catalog of women at a party is one of many examples of the novel's attack on conventional female behavior:

> Sposissa, three times divorced; Eglantissa, who thinks only of clothes; Aphrodissa, who cannot keep her eyes open because of her false eyelashes; Clarissa, who will commit suicide; Lucrissa, whose strained forehead shows that she's making more money than her husband; Wailissa, engaged in a game of ain't-it-awful with Lamentissa; Travailissa, who usually only works, but who is now sitting very still on the couch so that her smile will not spoil. (34)

In "A Female Man? The 'Medusan' Humor of Joanna Russ," Natalie M. Rosinsky argues that Russ uses humor as a subversive device to lay bare and thus disarm the forces of patriarchy. After reading passages such as the one quoted above, Rosinsky says, "having recognized this folly for what it is, as something we have participated in but need do no longer, we move on. We remove ourselves as participants in patriarchal scenarios, as the butts of patriarchal humor."[35] In Whileaway, from which Janet comes as an emissary, there is no patriarchy because there are no men, and there is a great deal of laughter. Whileaway is not a utopia: there are disagreements, hurt feelings, and even duels. But, Russ says:

> ... there is too, under it all, the incredible explosive energy, the
> gaiety of high intelligence, the obliquities of wit, the cast of mind that
> makes industrial areas into gardens and ha-has, ... comic nude
> statuary ... and the best graffiti in this or any other world. (54)

In short, humor is a principle of life in Whileaway, but it is not composed of jokes at the expense of others; instead, it is a free expression of joy in human equality.

Although Whileaway is not so completely utopian as Herland, the two imagined worlds have similarities. Both began as "bisexual" (to use Gilman's term) societies, but a catastrophe has long since eradicated the male population, leaving the women to develop both a social order and a means of reproduction. In both societies, the traditional parent-child nuclear family is nonexistent; children are largely raised and educated by those other than their mothers, and are thus given the sense that they belong to the entire society. Further, in both Whileaway and Herland, the dominant values are those traditionally associated with women: nurturance, patience, and love. The differences between these two fantasy societies are related to the periods of time in which their authors composed them. The women of Herland are not themselves humorous; the humor in Gilman's novel derives from the ironic contrast between Herland and what Gilman called in her sequel "Ourland." Gilman imagined that the perfect society could be attained only by the total removal of values associated with a patriarchal culture; Russ depends upon parody to free women from male domination: writing during the early years of the current women's movement, she uses hard-biting satire as a means of expressing anger at male dominance and awakening women to their own submissiveness.[36]

III

Natalie Rosinsky notes that Joanna Russ in *The Female Man* uses stereotypical images of women in order to free women from such stereotypes. Indeed, the use of common female stereotypes as either a
means for writing a cautionary tale, as in Russ's novel, or an expression of frustration with an assigned subordinate role is a dominant
technique in women's humorous writing. Most of these stereotypes—the nags, the gossips, the clinging vines—are centuries old,
originating as unflattering portraits created by male writers in both
serious and humorous literature. The fact that women have used
these same stereotypical portraits may, on the surface, seem to represent an imitative borrowing of humorous stock or, worse, an acquiescence to the accuracy of such portraits. A recent article in *Ms.* magazine on female stand-up comics, for example, is subtitled, "Can You
Be a Funny Woman Without Making Fun of Women?"[37] A close examination of these stereotypes as they are used in women's humor,
however, makes clear that they are intended as parts of a critique of
cultural realities.

In Russ's *The Female Man*, the devices of hyperbole and irony
make the method clear. In her thumbnail sketch of "Superwoman,"
for example, Russ describes the woman who "does it all"—raises
eight children, bakes bread, and succeeds in a demanding job—but
is adored by her husband primarily because:

> she comes home at night, slips into a filmy negligee and a wig, and
> turns instanter into a *Playboy* dimwit, thus laughingly dispelling the
> canard that you cannot be eight people simultaneously with two
> different sets of values. *She has not lost her femininity.*

Russ underscores her distrust of this image in the line that follows:
"And I'm Marie of Rumania" (119). The Superwoman stereotype is
used here to attack not only the mentality that would cause a woman
to fall into this trap, but also men who demand submission ("femininity") from women.

Such uses of female stereotypes in women's humor are not new,
but are part of the tradition of women's humor in America. Two clus-
ters of stereotypical images are most common in this tradition, suggesting that these two culturally determined modes of behavior have
been most problematic for these authors. One group of images

emphasizes woman's tendency to submissiveness, and includes the "clinging vine," the sentimentalist, the "dumb blonde," and the weak, incompetent woman. The other is in many ways the obverse, including the nag, the gossip, the obsessive housekeeper, and the domineering bitch—images that derive from either feelings of use-lessness or misguided efforts to perform well in women's "proper sphere." Florence Guy Seabury, commenting on Perry Winship's professional wife in "The Delicatessen Husband," describes the origins of this latter behavior:

> If she had lived a hundred years ago, with no outlet for the forces of her nature, nothing to exist for except a domestic routine, she would probably have been one of those irritable, inefficient wives and tart mothers who make an entire family miserable, seeing their duty and doing it.[38]

These stereotypes of women are not always discrete: elements of several may be found in a single character. Frances Whitcher's Widow Bedott, for example, is a gossipy, domineering woman who yearns to be dependent upon a man in marriage so that she may have an identity in her community. Marietta Holley's Betsey Bobbet, on the other hand, is a more "pure" example of the sentimental cling-ing-vine type, and Holley obviously intends her to be a warning to women who might behave similarly. Not only is Betsey presented as unattractive and foolish; it is also true that men are not attracted by her flutterings and her sentimental poetry. As Samantha Allen comments:

> ... the men that are the most opposed to wimmin's havin' a right, and talk the most about its bein' her duty to cling to a man like a vine to a tree, they don't want Betsey to cling to them, they *won't let* her cling to 'em. ... says I to 'em "which had you ruther do, let Betsey Bobbet cling to you or let her vote?" and they would every one of 'em quail before that question.[39]

Yet Betsey does eventually marry, and it is here that Holley makes clear the extent to which Betsey's values and behavior are the result of submission to cultural norms. Betsey marries Simon Slimpsey, a poor widower with numerous children who needs someone to mend his clothes and take care of the children. After her marriage Betsey becomes an ill-tempered drudge. When Samantha asks her whether she is happy, her responses—"I feel real dignified" and "I have got something to lean on" — reveal that although she has achieved her goal in life, success brings with it no joy or love.[40]

In twentieth-century women's humor, the stereotype of the submissive, dependent woman is commonly found in the speaker or narrator herself, who comments ironically on the circumstances of her life even as she outwardly submits to them. Such an approach is most obvious in the work of Dorothy Parker, in which the speaker in both poems and sketches realizes that she puts herself at the mercy of a man's changeable affections and yet seems doomed to repeat this behavior again and again. In "For a Favorite Granddaughter," for example, the speaker gives her granddaughter sage advice about avoiding certain types of men, but closes the poem with the lines, "Should you heed my words, my dear, /You're no blood of mine,"[41] acknowledging her inability to follow her own advice. Over and over in Parker's prose pieces, the situation involves a faithless man and a woman who, though aware of his inconstancy, wishes to ignore it. The following passage from "Just a Little One" is typical of this stereotypical female attitude:

> Oh, is this where you were Thursday night? I see. Why no, it didn't
> make a bit of difference, only you told me to call you up, and like a
> fool I broke a date I had, just because I thought I was going to see
> you. I just sort of naturally thought so, when you said to call you up.
> Oh, good Lord, don't make all that fuss about it. It really didn't make
> the slightest difference.[42]

Knowing she has been a "fool," the woman nonetheless continues her submissive behavior by denigrating her own feelings of rejection.

The anger underlying the submissive woman's awareness of her own dependence frequently causes her to adopt the characteristics of the opposite stereotype, the bitch. In the same Parker sketch, for example, the speaker launches into a sarcastic diatribe against the woman her companion has been with on the Thursday in question:

> Now to me, Edith looks like something that would eat her young.
> Dresses well? *Edith* dresses well? Are you trying to kid me, Fred, at
> my age? You mean you mean it? Oh, my God. You mean those
> clothes of hers are *intentional*? My heavens, I always thought she was
> on her way out of a burning building. (243)

Such bursts of nastiness, however, are soon revealed as bravado;

before the end of "Just a Little One," Parker's speaker has dissolved into boozy, apologetic self-pity.

The stereotype of the domineering, self-assured, or impossibly competent woman most commonly occurs as a friend or acquaintance of the narrator or *persona*. Joanna Russ's satiric description of "Superwoman" is one in a long line of hyperbolic portraits of female characters who are satirized for their ability to more than measure up to society's requirements. Caroline Kirkland's Mrs. Davenport, in *A New Home*, who is "possessed with a neat devil" is an early avatar of the woman who seems superior in housekeeping, appearance, or some other accomplishment expected of women. In a 1920s *New Yorker* series titled "Metropolitan Monotypes," Baird Leonard described the "Class-A Wife," whose virtues include the following:

> She does not quote poetry, diet, or read anything aloud except by request. . . .
> Her wardrobe is extensive and shipshape, so that she can start for a world cruise on an hour's notice.
> She knows a good joke when she hears it, even for the fifteenth or sixteenth time. . . .
> And her chequebook is as neat and accurate as that of a certified accountant.[43]

Mrs. Hicks, the immaculate housekeeper and gossip in MacDonald's *The Egg and I*, is another of these stereotypes of impossible perfection, as is the mother of one of the narrator's friends in Shirley Jackson's *Life Among the Savages*:

> She is one of those impressive women who usually head committees on supervising movies, taking the entire sixth grade on a tour of one of our local factories, or outlawing slingshots, and I daresay she would be the first person everyone would think of if there should arise an occasion for the mothers to lift the school building and carry it bodily to another location.[44]

The persistence of images of submissive or impossibly capable women in women's humor suggests that rather than endorsing or even accepting these extremes of women's behavior, the authors are rejecting the cultural forces that have created them. Such negative satiric portraits create a distance between reader and subject that allows the reader to disclaim elements of similar behavior in herself. However, the humorist's attitude toward these two different sets of images is not the same. The submissive woman, such as Betsey Bobbet and the speaker in Parker's "Just a Little One," is an object of pity as well as of scorn; so completely has she accepted traditional notions of her subordinate role that she has negated any possibility of personal power or achievement, and the author evinces some sympathy for her limited experience. No such sympathy, though, is shown for the woman who is outstandingly capable or beautiful, because her very accomplishments are a mirror that reflect the average woman's own shortcomings. More important, because she succeeds according to the culture's rules for her success—by having a shiny kitchen floor or perfectly behaved children—she reinforces those rules and thus works against the efforts of other women to challenge them. The use of such stereotypes is one of the methods by which female humorists have protested the condition of women in American culture.[45]

Another method by which America's female humorists have contrived a subversive subtext for their work is the careful use of language. Puns, malapropisms, and ironic statements are common in all written humor, but these and similar devices in the humorous writing of American women are frequently directed toward the single intention of revealing women's subjugation. That language may define us and our relative importance in a culture is an axiom familiar to anyone who has ever been called "nigger," "kike," or "slut," and one of the tactics of language in women's humor is to reveal its ability to classify women. A striking example is the narrator's exchange with the hospital admittance clerk in Jackson's *Life Among the Savages*:

> "Age?" she asked. "Sex? Occupation?"
> "Writer," I said.
> "Housewife," she said.
> "Writer," I said.
> "I'll just put down housewife," she said.[46]

It is this confining, excluding use of language that Joanna Russ parodies in *The Female Man* when one of her protagonists decides that if the term "mankind" is *indeed* intended to include women, she will simply refer to herself as "man" rather than "woman." Perhaps the ultimate questioning of the validity of language to name, define, and confine occurs in the work of Gertrude Stein. In *Q.E.D.*, the heroine says ironically, "I always did thank God I wasn't born a woman."[47] The irony masks a truth, and reveals a different truth.

In nineteenth-century dialect humor, misspellings, mispronunciations, and malapropisms are common methods of denoting the speaker's social class and educational level. The contrast between the dialect speech of some characters—often the *eiron* figures—and a more sophisticated speaker is frequently the source of the humor. Such language is a major element in establishing the ironic (*eiron*-ic) stance of Huck Finn. Neil Schmitz describes what he calls "Huck-speech" as the language of the outsider:

> ... the speech of the illiterate, the speech of the preliterate, of the poor, and of children, which, in its proper place, is charming, but which is also, in other places, in the schoolroom, in courts of law, inadequate, wrong, the excluded language of the vulnerable, the ignorant, the innocent.[48]

This "excluded language," when used in women's humor, points directly to the circumstance of being "other" and therefore deficient—"housewife" rather than self-proclaimed "writer." Linda Morris has shown how Samantha Allen's malapropisms in Marietta Holley's work contribute to this sense of "otherness." Samantha continually refers to the female "sect" rather than the female "sex" as, Morris says, "an integral part of her social criticism":

> ... its primary function is to call attention to a society that has tried to turn a whole sex into a quasi-religious cult. Likewise, when Samantha Allen refers to woman's "spear" rather than her "sphere," her author alerts us that in her writings she is going to insist that women's relegation to the private sphere be transformed into a weapon for social change.[49]

In nondialect humor, such malapropisms are rare, but language is used in much the same way to call attention to woman's separateness from the majority culture. The narrator in MacDonald's *The Egg and I*, for example, instructed by her husband to move a chest of drawers into the bedroom, responds, "Why, me?" Whereupon he snaps, "Who else? ... and my lower lip began to tremble because I knew now that I was just a wife." Later in the book, the narrator emphasizes the different "spheres" of male and female:

> Bob went native the minute he saw another rancher and became a

big, spitting bossy *man* and I was jerked from my pleasant position
of wife and equal and tossed down into that dull group known as
womenfolk.[50]

If MacDonald's narrator is ambivalent about the wife's status as
"equal," Phyllis McGinley's language consistently conveys the consciousness of a subordinate position. In McGinley's light verse about
suburban living, men are absent commuters, eagerly awaited by
women who cook, clean, care for children, and polish their nails. It is
a way of life approved by the surface lightness of the verse and by its
overt message, but this message is undercut persistently by McGinley's use of language. In "Confessions of a Reluctant Optimist," for
example, McGinley's speaker professes contentment with her life as
a suburban housewife, yet speaks of herself as "trapped, tricked,
enslaved," and notes that she "wear[s] [her] chains like ornaments,
/Convinced they make a charming jingle."[51] Just as revealing are
McGinley's remarks about women's suburban lives in her introduction to *A Short Walk From the Station* (1951). Referring to the high
point of the day—meeting the husbands' evening train from the
city—she speaks of the "delightfully ritualistic" moment when the
women "*move over* from the driver's seat, *surrender* the keys, and
receive an *absent-minded* kiss" [emphasis mine].[52] Whether con-
sciously or not, McGinley presents a culture in which women will-
ingly surrender control to men.

Recent feminist humorists are far more direct in their approach to
language. As the women's movement has increased our awareness of
sexism in many forms, America's female humorists have confronted
the sources of gender inequality, and use language ironically to
attack these sources. One form of sexism is the exploitation of
women's insecurities about their attractiveness. Nora Ephron, in
"Dealing with the, uh, Problem," exposes the motives of the manufacturers of feminine hygiene deodorant products, who, in the opinion of many feminists, have created both a "problem" and a product
to solve it. Referring to the euphemisms used by those who make
and promote such products, Ephron says:

They speak of "the problem." They speak of "the area where the
problem exists." They speak of "the need to solve the problem."
Every so often, a hard-core word slides into the conversation. Vagina,
perhaps.[53]

The message conveyed by such euphemisms is that women are inherently too dirty to talk about openly, and that, as Ephron continues, "sex—in the natural state, at least—is dirty and smelly" (82). The fact that such products are exploitative is made explicit in the response by Bill Blass that Ephron quotes without comment: "Honey, . . . if there's a part of the human body to exploit you might as well get onto it" (96). Ephron's satiric method, which is similar to Gilman's method in *Herland*, is to let the language of the male culture speak for itself.

A similar method is employed by Pat Mainardi in her 1970 essay "The Politics of Housework." Mainardi describes the unequal distribution of household chores in the two-career marriage by quoting and then translating some common male responses to sharing the burden, as in the following example:

> "I don't mind sharing the work, but you'll have to show me how to do it."
> *Meaning*: I ask a lot of questions and you'll have to show me everything every time I do it because I don't remember so good. Also, don't try to sit down and read while I'm doing my jobs because I'm going to annoy the hell out of you until it's easier to do them yourself.[54]

Such "translations" have become common in feminist humor. Joanna Russ, in "Dear Colleague: I Am Not An Honorary Male," provides a long list of statements titled "What You Say to Her" and "What You Mean," sometimes providing more than one translation of a statement. For example, the line "It was only a joke" could mean, according to Russ:

> I love the sex war because I always win.

> or

> I find jokes about you funny. Why don't *you* find jokes about you funny?

Feminist humor deals with the *creation* as well as the *translation* of language. Part of the agenda of the women's movement has been to examine the English language for evidences of its male bias, and terms such as "chairperson" and "herstory," although they have not been widely accepted, are one result. The fact that the creation of new language can be carried to absurd extremes is the subject of

Deanne Stillman's "The Feminish Dictionary: A Guide to Defining Ourselves." Stillman points out that "person" is not an adequately nonsexist replacement for "man" because of the masculine ending "son." She thus comes up with the tongue-in-cheek suggestion of "woperone" for "woman," and goes further:

> ... even the word female must be altered to the more fair and meaningful term *feperone*, which rhymes with *pepperone*, the sausage that goes on pizza. The transformation of the plural, *females*, would naturally be *fepeople*.

The list of changes goes on to include "apeople" for "amen" and "hything" for "hymen."[55] Stillman's satire is not a rejection of feminism, nor does it ridicule the idea that a sexist language is confining and degrading. Like women's humor generally, it mocks excesses that are more likely to jeopardize than to further women's efforts for equality.

IV

The tradition of women's humor in America owes its characteristics of theme, form, and language quite simply to the experience of the women who have created it. Just as the dominant humorous tradition springs from incongruities in America's political and business arenas, so the distinctive characteristics of women's humor are derived from the disparity between the "official" conduct of women's lives and their "unofficial" response to that conduct. Implicit in this humor is protest of a very specific sort, whether presented as direct satire or masked in irony; through apparent self-mockery and confrontation of the "other," women's humor seeks to correct a cultural imbalance. Writing about the comic novels of Virginia Woolf and Muriel Spark, Judy Little identifies the source of this humorous impulse:

> We can expect, ... especially in a time of social change, that the work of writers who perceive themselves as "outsiders," as persons assigned to the threshold of a world that is not theirs, will manifest the distinctive features of inversion, mocked hierarchies, communal festivity, and redefinition of sex identity. If the work of such writers

is comic, it will be comedy that mocks the norm radically, and perhaps generates hints and symbols of new myths.[56]

An essential purpose of humor is to call the norm into question. What Little suggests here is that the humor of those on the "threshold" is apt to reveal a perception of incongruity that not only questions the rules of the culture, but also suggests a different order. Behind Frances Whitcher's gossips and Dorothy Parker's uncertain ladies are the shadows of women granted the freedom to move through the world with reason and dignity, and the utopian dream of Herland and Whileaway breaks through the trivializing ritual of housework.

Recognition that there has been a distinct tradition of women's humor, with its own subjects, forms, and devices, motivated Kate Sanborn to publish *The Wit of Women* in 1885, and Bruère and Beard to publish *Laughing Their Way* in 1934. None of these editors, however, offered particularly cogent analyses of the humor they anthologized, and the very act of marking off women's humor as a discrete body of literature may in fact have ghettoized it and made it invisible to scholars. In addition, by the time American humor became the subject of serious academic study in the 1930s, when Rourke and Blair published their influential works, a great deal of women's humorous writing was being published in periodicals intended for female readers—magazines such as *Ladies' Home Journal* and *Good Housekeeping*. While the humor in these magazines served the important purpose of assuring readers that they were not alone in their private domestic chaos, such publications could easily be regarded as ephemeral by male critics and scholars, for whom American humor remained the province of male writers.

Perhaps the most penetrating—and itself satiric—analysis of the omission of women's literature from the canon is Joanna Russ's *How to Suppress Women's Writing* (1983). Russ lists the reasons critics have stated or implied for such omission:

She didn't write it.
She wrote it, but she shouldn't have.
She wrote it, but look what she wrote about.
She wrote it, but "she" isn't really an artist and "it" isn't really serious, of the right genre—i.e., really art.

She wrote it, but she wrote only one of it.
She wrote it, but it's only interesting/included in the canon for one,
 limited reason.
She wrote it, but there are very few of her.[57]

Two of these reasons apply most directly to the exclusion of women's humor from the literary canon. The fact that " 'it' isn't really serious" plagues both men's *and* women's humor, as one humor anthologist after another has lamented. More significant for women's humor is "look what she wrote about." The fact that humor, to be successful, requires that the reader be familiar with the social context it describes has worked against the appreciation of much of women's humor by the dominant culture: the very separation of male and female "spheres" and values that it describes means that men have been hard pressed to understand and find amusing what women have created. Related to this is the common — if often subtle — protest against a male-dominated culture that is embedded in women's humor. To find such humor amusing requires that the reader assents to the political proposition it contains, and just as women find uncomfortable the negative images of themselves found in male literature, so men find it difficult to appreciate accusations that they occupy the role of oppressor.[58]

Recent efforts to recover the woman's humorous tradition have been spurred on by the more comprehensive revision of the American literary canon that feminist scholars have undertaken since the early 1970s. Doctoral dissertations by Jane Curry, Linda Morris, and Zita Dresner have provided important groundwork for a re-evaluation of American humor.[59] Excerpts from Marietta Holley's work are now back in print, as are Fanny Fern's *Ruth Hall* and a number of her newspaper columns.[60] A study of this emerging tradition reveals how closely tied the issue of woman's sense of humor is to controversy regarding her intelligence, her independence, and her "proper sphere" in American culture.

3
Humor, Intellect, and Femininity

"She knew too much, you see, for her own good."
> *Fay Weldon,* Letters to Alice on First
> Reading Jane Austen

I

The publication of Kate Sanborn's anthology *The Wit of Women* in 1885 was a direct response to a debate in America's literary community about whether women possessed a sense of humor. Richard Grant White, a New York art and literature critic, commented in an 1884 issue of the weekly magazine *The Critic* that a sense of humor was "that rarest of qualities in woman," prompting Alice Wellington Rollins to respond in two subsequent issues of the same magazine that although "we have had no feminine Artemus Ward," women indeed displayed wit in both conversation and writing.[1] To demonstrate the truth of Rollins's assertions, Sanborn set out to collect examples of women's humorous writing in a volume that proved to be so popular that it was reprinted twice. Sanborn's search of literature anthologies then in print was initially discouraging. In humor anthologies she found no women writers represented, and when she turned to collections of women's literature, she encountered the prevailing sentimentality of nineteenth-century women's prose and poetry. In Griswold's *Female Poets of America* (1849), for example, she found the atmosphere discouraging:

> The general air of gloom—hopeless gloom—was depressing. Such mawkish sentimentality and despair; such inane and mortifying confessions; such longings for a lover to come; such sighings after a lover departed; such cravings for "only"—"only" a *grave* in some dark, dank solitude.[2]

Despite the lugubrious tone of so much popular women's literature of the period, Sanborn was able to present in *The Wit of Women* an impressive collection of humorous writing, including the dialect stories of Harriet Beecher Stowe and "Grace Greenwood," local-color stories by Rose Terry Cooke and Sarah Orne Jewett, literary parodies, and humorous poetry for children. Sanborn assumed her readers' familiarity with the work of Frances Whitcher and Marietta Holley, commenting on the latter's creation of a "tidal wave of laughter" (31).

The debate about woman's sense of humor originated long before Sanborn sought to settle it and lingered long afterward. The prologue to Anna Cora Mowatt's satiric play *Fashion*, first produced in 1845, is strongly reminiscent of Anne Bradstreet's prologue to *The Tenth Muse* in its plea that a woman's writing be regarded as significant, and one of the issues it raises is woman's comic ability:

> What! from a woman's pen? It takes a man
> To write a comedy — no woman can.

The prologue, written by Epes Sargent, ironically proposes that *Fashion*, a comedy, might be suspect on two grounds: that it was written by a woman and that it was written by an American — and the prologue ends with an appeal to the audience:

> Friends, from these scoffers we appeal to you!
> Condemn the *false*, but O! applaud the true.
> Grant that *some* wit may grow on native soil,
> And Art's fair fabric rise from woman's toil.[3]

Shortly before Mowatt's *Fashion* was first presented, a writer in *Graham's Magazine* issued a categorical statement denying woman's sense of humor:

Women have sprightliness, cleverness, smartness, though but little wit. There is a body and substance in true wit, with a reflectiveness rarely found apart from a masculine intellect. . . . We know of no one writer of the other sex, that has a high character for humor. . . . The female character does not admit of it.[4]

So pervasive was the idea that women were incapable of humor that works written by women were sometimes assumed to have instead been written by men. Such assumptions about the work of Marietta Holley, who used the pseudonyms "Josiah Allen's Wife" and

"Samantha Allen," finally prompted her, in 1883, to have her picture used as the frontespiece in one of her books. Kate Winter, Holley's biographer, reports that this was probably a necessary step:

> The rumor that the writer of the Allen stories was really a man had some credence, particularly in the rural areas. After all, with the notable exception of Whitcher, most humorists were men. For some it was as difficult to believe that a woman had written the books as it was that a woman they *knew* had done it. One old gentleman complimented the Samantha work saying he "had a high opinion of the man who wrote that book." When informed that it was indeed written by a woman, he stubbornly declared, "That book was written by a man." Replied Marietta, "I have always supposed it was a compliment."[5]

Earlier in the century, Fanny Fern, whose satiric portraits of men in her novel *Ruth Hall* had caused critics to call her "unwomanly," wrote, "Isn't it the funniest thing in life that a woman can't be vital and energetic without being thought masculine?"[6]

Kate Sanborn's 1885 anthology did not prevent further assertions of female humorlessness, and the debate about woman's sense of humor has continued into the twentieth century. Arthur B. Maurice, then editor of *The Bookman*, wrote in *Good Housekeeping* in 1910 that "the new school of American humor" was "at least three-fifths feminine,"[7] but in 1922, extolling the talents of Dorothy Parker, Thomas L. Masson reflected an ongoing resistance to the woman as humorist. Calling Parker "the best humorous writer in America among the women," Masson continues in terms that acknowledge the long-standing controversy:

> I fancy I hear some of her admirers exclaim, "Why drag in the women?" Well, I drag them in because I probably don't know any better. The fact is that you cannot make any comparisons in humor between men and women. There are fewer humorists among the women than among the men. Many people declare that women have no sense of humor, but I have no doubt that there are people who will even deny them the talent for having children.[8]

In his zeal to be even-handed, Masson dismisses the great differences between men's and women's humor, but his remarks make clear that the debate about women's *sense* of humor was still alive.

Given the number of magazine articles devoted to the subject, the discussion of women's sense of humor seems to have been particularly heated during the 1920s and 1930s, no doubt fueled by women's newly acquired freedom to vote and the dramatic image of the "Flapper" that seemed to presage a host of other freedoms. Female commentators who entered into this debate tended to agree that women's sense of humor had merely been stifled by social convention and suggested that greater social freedom and increased self-esteem would allow their humor to flourish. In a 1931 issue of the *Outlook and Independent*, for example, Margaretta Newell notes that "feminists, determined to be the equals of men, writhe under a sense of inferiority well-nigh intolerable when confronted by the assertion that our sex lacks humor." Newell identifies woman's role as the nourisher of the male ego as the source of such assertions:

> Is it not woman's role to be man's helpmeet, to inspire him in every enterprise, to urge him on to each endeavor? With this in view, must she not persuade herself that he is amusing when his aim is such? . . . And this role of woman, to make of man what he would be, explains why even literal-minded men view themselves as more humorous than women as a whole. What man chooses to say, woman in her urge to be successful with man chooses to applaud.[9]

Newell does not find it surprising that wives laugh at their husbands' jokes instead of telling their own — it is a matter of economic survival: "If she is so ill-advised as to indulge in mirth at man's expense, she risks the loss of his material support — a consideration of which the woman in the home is very much aware" (207).

Because the "woman in the home" faces great risks by displaying a sense of humor, Newell looks to the new class of professional women, those "who lead their lives in the broader environment," to counter the gender's reputation for humorlessness. That they have not yet done so she attributes to the fact that they are "pioneers," too busy struggling to survive in an alien world to have the energy for humor (207). For these women, she advises "courage":

> Obviously, if courage brings out humor, women must get more courage, and if courage depends on danger, then women, in order to become a humorous sex, must welcome danger. . . . If woman is to cultivate wit and grow in humor, let her seize the world by the tail, her tail. (224)

Elizabeth Stanley Trotter, writing for *The Atlantic Monthly* in 1922, also finds the source of woman's supposed humorlessness in her role as man's supporter:

> Neither education nor humor had been an essential part of a woman's equipment; undoubtedly, it had been conducive to matrimonial harmony that she should echo her husband's ideas—so why not his jokes as well?[10]

And Mary Austin, in a 1924 *New Republic* article, reinforces this link between humor and unwelcome competition when she proposes that it is man's requirements of woman that have denied her the sense of humor:

> The element of corrective criticism informing humorous observation upon life is, no doubt, responsible for the chief inhibition against exhibitions of it in women. The inhibition has grown with the growing competition of civil life, and man's mounting need to find in the mother-wife, the relief of uncritical response.[11]

Despite these severe limitations on women's expression of humor, both Trotter and Austin believed that the women of their day had begun to free themselves from a humorless response to life; Austin refers to "the swift rise of comedy among women writers [in the 1920s]" (11).

By 1934, when Martha Bruère and Mary Beard edited *Laughing Their Way: Women's Humor in America*, these two women adopted an even more sanguine attitude toward the acceptance of woman's sense of humor. They acknowledge that in the nineteenth century "men appear to have assumed that they alone enjoyed a sense of humor," but they refer to Sanborn's *The Wit of Women* as an adequate refutation of this assumption, and presume that the situation has changed:

> It now seems a long, long way from 1885, when such a corrective for ill-conceived assumptions was necessary!
>
> No one today can pick up a newspaper, read a magazine, or work in a library without meeting face to face laughing women who peer through the printed pages.

Bruère and Beard express relief that they no longer have to "emphasize the mere fact that American women have been merry as well as gloomy and righteous," and can move on to an analysis of the humorous works they have collected in their anthology.[12] And yet, fifty years later, Deanne Stillman admits to submitting humorous work under the name "Dean" because she perceived that "writing funny was something girls didn't do,"[13] and a recent article about Nicole Hollander's comic strip "Sylvia" notes that the strip has "brought women's humor out of the closet."[14]

Resistance to women's humor is not unique to America. In a 1961 article titled "We Witless Women," Siriol Hugh-Jones, a writer for the British publications *Punch* and the *Tatler*, reports on the British assumption that women are "rarely witty." Hugh-Jones cites an advertisement for the London *Observer* in which the author says of its female film critic, "She is also that unusual thing, a woman who is a wit"—a remark that recalls, 77 years later, Richard Grant White's 1884 comment that humor is "that rarest of qualities in woman." Hugh-Jones proceeds to analyze the import of the *Observer* statement in her own witty style:

> A witty woman is automatically suspect, and when feeding her little goodies between official meals you don't want to poke your fingers through the bars; but the "unusual" label reassures and lends confidence. No need to alarm yourself by imagining they're *all* going to be like this.[15]

What is the source of this persistent denial of woman's sense of humor and its products? That it is related in part to woman's subordinate role in the male-female relationship was suggested by Kate Sanborn in *The Wit of Women*:

> There is a reason for our apparent lack of humor.... Women do not find it politic to cultivate or express their wit. No man likes to have his story capped by a better and fresher from a lady's lips. What woman does not risk being called sarcastic and hateful if she throws back the merry dart, or indulges in a little sharp-shooting. No, no, it's dangerous, if not fatal.
>
> > "Though you're bright, and though you're pretty,
> > They'll not love you if you're witty." (205-6)

Sanborn's comments, like similar ones by Newell, Trotter, and Austin, raise two issues. One is male-female competition: the woman bows out of the humorous exchange to allow the man his sense of dominance. The second, closely related, issue is male expectations of "feminine" behavior. Humor's inherent posture of superiority— even aggression—is in conflict with traditional notions of female submissiveness and passivity. By the middle of the twentieth century, little seemed to have changed since Sanborn's time. Ann Beatts, a comedy writer, recalls the socialization of her high-school years:

Real girls weren't funny. Real girls were pretty and fluffy and could do the splits in cheerleader tryouts. Real girls didn't crack jokes. Did you ever hear Sandra Dee crack a joke? Annette Funicello didn't even laugh; she just put her hands on her hips and got mad at Ricky or Tommy or Eddie or whoever was carrying her surfboard, so that they could tell her how cute she was when she was mad.[16]

As this example demonstrates, film and television have replaced the nineteenth-century advice manual as influences on woman's proper behavior, but the message is much the same: the aggression and dominance of the humorist's stance is not "appropriate" to women.

This stance, and woman's vulnerability when she occupies it, is nowhere more obvious than in the world of the stand-up comic, in nightclubs and on television. Whereas in written humor the method can be subtle and subversive, in a live, personal confrontation a comedienne runs the risk of alienating rather than amusing her audience if she steps too far from conventionally conceived "female" behavior. As more and more women have entered the field of live comedy, they have introduced perspectives and subject matter relevant to women, but have discovered the restrictions on their performances. Julia Klein interviewed a number of female comics for a 1984 *Ms.* magazine article, and found considerable agreement about these perceived restrictions:

The women agree that stand-up comedy is, in itself, an aggressive act; making someone laugh means exerting control, even power. But a woman cannot come off as overaggressive or she will lose the audience.

Klein quotes Carol Siskind, then an emcee at the Improv in New York, on the subject of these limitations:

In a way, we have to be more careful. Men can be gross and get away with it. We have to be very careful not to step on the male ego. There are things you learn early on to phrase very carefully.[17]

Siskind's remarks reflect a continued expectation of female gentility that began in the nineteenth century to influence the themes and methods of women's humor.

II

The debate about woman's sense of humor is closely related to the debate about her general intellectual capacity that occupied educators, clergymen, and scientists in the nineteenth century. As Barbara Welter and others have shown, the increasing separation of male and female "spheres" as the century progressed was accompanied by an emphasis on the difference between male and female abilities to think and reason. Logic, reason, and analytical thought became the provinces of man, whereas to woman were ascribed the qualities of intuition, feeling, and morality. The two prevalent idealizations of the nineteenth-century woman—the intuitively spiritual being and the Earth-mother—are equally nonintellectual; as Welter puts it, "whether she drew man to a higher spiritual plane or bound him to earth by her life-force, female nature and functions were untouched by human intellect."[18] Leading medical authorities pronounced that woman's brain was smaller than man's; phrenologists felt on her skull larger bumps of Benevolence and Ideality than of Self-Esteem and Firmness,[19] and religious leaders decreed that woman was "naturally" religious: "A natural religion avoided speculation, doubt and controversy and was exempt from the musings of a restless intellect" (260).

Such qualities had direct implications for the manner in which women were to be educated. Not only were women assumed to be deficient in the intellectual attributes that would enable them to master disciplines requiring logic and reason, but they were presumed to be too weak physically to withstand the rigors of the traditional male education. Susan P. Conrad, in *Perish the Thought*, quotes the predictions of the Rev. John Todd, whose hyperbole makes his statements unintentionally amusing to the contemporary reader:

> As for training young ladies through a long intellectual course, as we do young men, it can never be done. They will die in the process. . . . She must be on the strain all the school hours, study in the evening till her eyes ache, her brain whirls, her spine yields and gives way, and she comes through the process of education, enervated, feeble, without courage or vigor, elasticity or strength. Alas! must we crowd education upon our daughters, and, for the sake of having them "intellectual," make them puny, nervous, and their whole earthly existence a struggle between life and death?[20]

The speciousness of such claims of female frailty is obvious when one thinks of the hard physical labor involved in ordinary household tasks before the invention of vacuum cleaners, washing machines, and prepared foods, and it is the illogic of such an appeal to woman's physical frailty that Holley's Samantha Allen exposes when her husband, Josiah, maintains that "poles and 'lection boxes" are "too wearin for the fair sect":

> Josiah Allen, . . . you think that for a woman to stand up straight on her feet, under a blazin' sun, and lift both her arms above her head, and pick seven bushels of hops, mingled with worms and spiders, into a gigantic box, day in, and day out, is awful healthy, so strengthenin' and stimulatin' to wimmin, but when it comes to droppin' a little slip of clean paper into a small seven by nine box, once a year in a shady room, you are afraid it is goin' to break down a woman's constitution to once.[21]

The always reasonable Samantha, though an uneducated farm wife, counters arguments regarding women's weaknesses with persistent logic; it is Samantha, not Josiah, who remarks, "Now I love to see folks use reason if they have got any" (86). Others besides humorists used wit to expose the unreasonable fervor of those who insisted on woman's inferior intellectual capacity. Susan Conrad cites the writings of Caleb Atwater, the founder of the Ohio public school system, who took to its logical conclusions the sharp division between women's intellectual and domestic lives. To those who opposed education for women because it rendered them unfit for domestic life, Atwater responded:

> For the consolation . . . of men, who fear that our system of female education will soon become so perfect that they cannot find ignorant women enough for wives and companions . . . , we can assure them that we do all we can to educate them, yet there will always be ignorant women enough for all such men. We hope this idea will console them. (37)

The most sobering effect of an attitude toward women that denies their intellectual capacity is the stunting of natural curiosity and ambition—the waste of potential talent and the narrowing of lives that might otherwise be expansive and fulfilled. Margaret Fuller's famous exhortation, "Let them be sea captains if they will," was a stirring appeal for recognition of women's ability to succeed in virtually any career, but despite the voices of Fuller and many others, a cultural perception of women as nonintellectual has persisted, creating the frequently undefined frustrations that Betty Friedan documented in *The Feminine Mystique* in 1963. The narrator in Charlotte Perkins Gilman's story "The Yellow Wallpaper" suffers acutely from the medical prescription that reading and writing will exacerbate her depression, and must keep in secret the diary that documents her progress toward insanity. Similarly, Alice James, caught in the shadow of her older brothers William and Henry, found emotional survival only in suppressing her active intellect. As she expresses it in her diary, she early learned the lesson that "the better part is to clothe oneself in neutral tints, walk by still waters, and possess one's soul in silence"; yet to her diary she also impishly confides, "My Mind is *Great!*"[22]

Intellectual freedom, independence, and the free play of a sense of humor are closely interdependent. The creation and perception of humor are above all the activities of an intellect that can perceive irony and incongruity, and a consciousness that is sufficiently detached from self-effacement to be able to play. The humorous vision requires the ability to hold two contradictory realities in suspension simultaneously—to perform a mental balancing act that superimposes a comic version of life on the observable "facts." The intuition of illogic requires a prior perception of accepted logic, and those who deny woman the sense of humor thus have begun by denying her the capacity for logical thought.

A different rationale for the claim that women's sense of humor is inferior to that of men may be found in Freudian psychoanalytic theory. Those who accept Freud's formulation of the difference between male and female ego development suggest that men have a greater need for—and therefore are naturally more adept at—humorous release. Freud maintained that the humorist, because of his momentary stance of superiority, gains control of his super-ego, that voice of external authority that ordinarily places a check on his natural impulses. Freudian theorists argue that the need to control the super-ego is greater in men than in women because of the severe threat of castration posed by the male super-ego, whereas the female super-ego cannot make this threat and therefore does not maintain such rigid control. This interpretation was put succinctly by Alfred Winterstein in a 1934 article in *The Psychoanalytic Quarterly*. Beginning from Freud's assumption that humor is a device to protect the ego from the "instinctual demands" of the id, which are either sadistic or masochistic, Winterstein proposes that "in both cases, narcissistic masculinity is threatened by the same external danger (and it now becomes clear why humor is a masculine trait)."[23] More recently, David Zippin, in "Sex Differences and the Sense of Humor," seems to contradict both Winterstein and himself in his own analysis of the relationship between humor and the super-ego:

> Women, . . . being more consistently narcissistic than men, should have less of a need for humor since vanity, flirtatiousness, and whimsicality are considered essential feminine traits. Structurally as well, there is far less superego to prevent the manifestation of humor.[24]

Zippin, following Freudian theory, suggests here that the "essential feminine traits" that make women more self-absorbed reduce their need to take control of a threatening super-ego through humor. At the same time, however, he proposes that the woman is freer to use humor, precisely *because* she is less constrained by a super-ego that attempts to dictate her behavior.

Such a logical tangle is perhaps the inevitable result of a psychoanalytic theory that posits and reinforces woman's subordinate position. Zippin is on much safer ground when he locates the source of women's unequal participation in humor in cultural conditioning rather than in an inherently different psychological makeup, even though he reaches this ground unwittingly. Writing about the aggressive, "male" nature of the comedian, Zippin says, "Comediennes are numerically rare compared with male comics. This suggests that humor is somehow alien to femininity" (50). Although he continues by associating the role of the comedian with the possession of a phallus, Zippin has hinted—unintentionally, it seems—at a more logical basis for the denial of female humor: the fact that it is at odds with common cultural definitions of "femininity."

These and most other psychological studies of gender differences in relation to humor are based on comparisons between male and female responses to jokes, cartoons, and, more recently, stand-up comics. In general, such studies show that males, from early childhood through late adolescence,[25] have a greater tolerance for and appreciation of aggressive and obscene humor than do females, and that both males and females respond more favorably to male rather than female comedians. Commenting on this latter phenomenon, psychologist Alice Sheppard Klak points to its origin in cultural conditioning rather than inherent emotional or intellectual differences:

> I would suggest that this male bias may be related to cultural expectations. That is, because men are supposed to be competent, strong, and unemotional, their admission of weakness is perceived as funnier than the same admission by a woman. Similarly, aggression as a form of wit—and most humor is to some degree aggressive—is accepted and serves to release repressed emotion from the audience when the comedian is male, whereas a display of hostility from a female comedian is suspect and renders her less effective as a comedian.[26]

Klak thus echoes Zippin's view that "humor is somehow alien to femininity," but she bases her argument on differences in culturally determined gender roles rather than on the relative strength of the super-ego.

This cultural rather than intrinsic approach to the development of woman's sense of humor is supported by other psychologists and by anthropological studies, many of which equate the expression of the sense of humor to the relative degrees of freedom enjoyed by women and men. In a 1977 article in *Signs*, Greer Litton Fox proposes that of the three basic methods used in most cultures to control and determine the behavior of women—confinement, protection, and normative restriction—the last is the most complex because while it appears to allow women a great deal of freedom, it places the burden of compliance with social restrictions on the individual woman and therefore requires her to censor her own behavior. Fox uses the term "normative restriction" to refer to the set of cultural expectations, or "value constructs," embodied in the concepts of "good girl," "nice girl," and "lady"—what Ann Beatts calls the "real girl." "As a value construct," Fox says, these terms connote "chaste, gentle, gracious, ingenuous, good, clean, kind, virtuous, non-controversial, and above suspicion and reproach."[27] (One is reminded of the careful praise accorded the nineteenth-century humorist Frances Whitcher by her sister, who said that Whitcher's humor was "chaste and original," containing nothing that would "shock the keenest sensibility."[28]) In contrast to confinement (keeping the woman physically restrained in the home) and protection (requiring supervisors, such as chaperones, when she goes out into the world), normative restriction depends upon a set of inter-nalized rules for proper behavior, and being a "nice girl" or a "lady" is the work of a lifetime. As Fox puts it, "one's identity as 'lady' or as 'nice girl' is never finally confirmed. Rather, it is continually in jeop-ardy, and one is under pressure to demonstrate one's niceness anew by one's behavior in each instance of social interaction" (809).

In his cross-cultural study of humor, anthropologist Mahadev L. Apte finds that such forms of social control have a direct relationship to the free expression of the sense of humor. In both pre-industrial and industrial cultures, women participate rarely if at all in such rit-uals as clowning and joking relationships, and Apte locates their absence in the social constraints on women's behavior:

> Women seem not to engage in the development of certain categories of humor because they do not have the same degree of freedom that men do. Sociocultural reality in many societies means in part that men's activities usually take place in public arenas, while women's activities occur in more private ones. Women's relative lack of freedom to engage in certain types of activities in the public domain seems closely related to their socially inferior status in that domain and to the emphasis that many societies place on such cultural values as modesty, politeness, and passivity in the context of the female role.[29]

The circumstances under which women's humor is permissible tend to be those in which women are in groups composed only of women—and thus are invisible to men—and when they have achieved the status conferred by advanced age, at which point "the sex-specific norms of behavior are relaxed for them" (79).

Research in joke-telling behavior by folklorist Carol Mitchell, com-pleted in the mid-1970s, leads to similar conclusions. Mitchell stud-ied not only the types of jokes told by males and females, but also the settings in which each gender typically "performs." Whereas men enjoy public, competitive joke-telling situations, women seldom par-ticipate in these competitions, preferring to tell jokes to "very small groups of close friends."[30] One consequence of this preference is the relative invisibility of women's joking behavior and the resultant misunderstanding of its nature. As Mitchell points out, such misun-derstanding inevitably leads to a perception of women as humorless:

> It has been assumed by Legman and Freud and many of the

experimental psychologists that obscene jokes are primarily male humor. This is true to the extent that 5 percent more of men's jokes than women's jokes are obscene. However, women do participate in the telling of obscene jokes, even if to a lesser extent than men. Male scholars simply have not realized the extent of the joke-telling tradition among women, since women do most of their joke-telling privately to other women and not to men. (173)

Further, Robin Lakoff, a linguist who studied differences between men's and women's spoken utterances in the mid-1970s, identifies women's reluctance to be openly humorous as both source and evidence of discrimination. Lakoff's thesis in *Language and Woman's Place* (1975) is that "women experience linguistic discrimination in two ways: in the way that they are taught to use language, and in the way general language use treats them."[31] One of the distinguishing characteristics of "women's language," according to Lakoff, is the absence of joke-telling:

> Women don't tell jokes.... [I]t is axiomatic in middle-class American society that, first, women can't tell jokes—they are bound to ruin the punchline, they mix up the order of things, and so on. Moreover, they don't "get" jokes. In short, women have no sense of humor. (56)

What such studies suggest is that instead of lacking a sense of humor, women have lacked opportunities for free expression of that sense because of cultural expectations regarding their status and behavior. As a result, women have typically masked their humorous utterance with a pose of anxious adherence to cultural norms. Believed to be sinful yet admired for their purity, women have steered their way through such ludicrous incongruity by means of a subversive laughter. French scholar Hélène Cixous, in an essay encouraging women to break the bonds of cultural conditioning and write in their own voices, perceives this incongruity: "You only have to look at the Medusa straight on to see her. And she's not deadly. She's beautiful and she's laughing." This triumphant laugh, Cixous believes, emerges whenever woman uses her true voice, for "writing is *the very possibility of change*, the space that can serve as a springboard for subversive thought, the precursory movement of a transformation of social and cultural structures."[32]

III

America's women humorists have responded in two general ways to the charge that women are nonintellectual creatures incapable of independent thought and witty utterance. One response is to satirize that assumption, as does Marietta Holley when her character Samantha compares the rigors of picking hops to those of casting a ballot "once a year in a shady room." Throughout American literary history, women writers have used irony and satire as ways of asking to be taken seriously as women and as writers. A second response is to convert the image of the nonintellectual woman into a form of self-mockery that displays the absurdity or the destructive nature of such assumptions about women's intellectual capacity. The latter is a more subtle, subversive approach than the overtly satirical one, but both embody women's attempts to counter cultural stereotypes of them as fragile and emotional rather than intelligent and capable.

Like Marietta Holley, who promotes a common-sense feminism throughout her more than twenty books, Alice Duer Miller urges logic and reason as arguments for female suffrage in the verses in *Are Women People?* (1915). In "Many Men to Any Woman," she adopts the voice of the condescending male who proposes that women *might* be allowed to vote if they promise to retain "the best standards of their womanhood," and also if they can instantly right all the world's wrongs:

> If you can show a clearly thought-out scheme
> For bringing the millennium in a day:
>   Why, then, dear lady, at some time remote,
>   I might consider giving you the vote.[33]

Those who adopt such stances, Miller suggests, are secure in the notion that women are incapable of devising such a "clearly thought-out scheme," and thus the promise of suffrage is a safe and empty one. In another poem in the same volume, Miller makes clear that it is cultural expectations rather than lack of innate ability that deter women from intellectual pursuits. The speaker in "The Protected Sex" counsels a young girl against intellectual competition with men:

> There, little girl, don't read,
> You're fond of your books, I know,

But Brother might mope
If he had no hope
Of getting ahead of you.
It's dull for a boy who cannot lead.
There, little girl, don't read. (34-35)

Miller's ironic modification of "There, little girl, don't *cry*" implicitly juxtaposes the intellectual and the emotional.

Earlier, in Josephine Daskam's *Fables for the Fair* (1901), women repeatedly attempt to determine the balance between intellectual attainment sufficient to attract a man and yet minimal enough to avoid scaring him away. In "The Woman Who Used Her Theory," for example, Daskam presents "a Woman who had a Theory that Men did Not Care for Too Much Intellectuality in her Sex." Accordingly, she professes not to understand Ibsen and to find Maeterlinck "silly," but when she pretends to believe that there is little "sense" in Shakespeare, she crosses an invisible line that causes her suitor to leave in disgust. In his final speech, the suitor reveals the rules he has set up for her intellectual responses:

> Not to Understand Ibsen shows that you are a Good Woman; to think Maeterlinck Silly augurs Well for your Intelligence; but not to see Much Sense in Shakespeare implies that you are Uneducated.[34]

The woman in Daskam's fable is in a double bind: she knows that men do not want intellectual competition from women, but she is unaware of the subtleties within this rule that set a trap for her. Similarly, in Daskam's "The Woman Who Caught The Idea," the man breaks his engagement to a woman who has learned to be a "clinging vine" and finds one who will "March Abreast" of him. But he, too, has established unspoken limits on a woman's competence, and he rejects the second woman when "Not Only did she March Abreast, but it Seemed Probable that she would Get Ahead. Also she had a Work of Her Own, which sometimes Interfered with His" (84).

If, on the one hand, women are constrained by a male culture that feels threatened by female intellectuality, they are themselves threatened by women who acquiesce to the passive, "clinging vine" role. In the nineteenth century in particular, female humorists time after time satirized the woman who represented capitulation to the emotive, nonintellectual ideal of womanhood; such women belied the authors' own intellectual attainments by representing virtues at odds with them—virtues such as piety and submissiveness that were more widely sanctioned. It is no accident that such women, as they appear in women's humorous writing, are usually themselves writers of sentimental verse or prose, because the conflict between humor and sentimentality was a literary representation of the battle between female assertiveness and female passivity. Sometimes, like Holley's Betsey Bobbet, these women have their sights fixed on marriage and practice to be "clinging vines" in search of a "sturdy oak"; sometimes their piety causes them to seem too pure for this world and to yearn for one more nearly ideal, whether on Earth or in Heaven. In Louisa May Alcott's satire on the experimental community of Fruitlands, for example, there is Miss Jane Gage, "a stout lady of mature years, sentimental, amiable, and lazy":

> She wrote verses copiously, and had vague yearnings and graspings after the unknown, which led her to believe herself fitted for a higher sphere than any she had yet adorned.[35]

In a community in which all must work for the common good, the laziness and general uselessness of such a person are sufficient cause for satiric treatment, but Miss Gage also represents the type of woman who is guided by emotion rather than by intellect, which so many in the nineteenth century believed to be suitable for "true womanhood." Similarly, earlier in the century Caroline Kirkland described a visit to frontier Michigan by a Miss Fidler, whose dreamy immersion in sentimental poetic clichés is matched by the unsuitable daintiness of her clothes:

> It was unfortunate that she could not walk out much on account of her shoes. She was obliged to make out with diluted inspiration. The nearest approach she usually made to the study of Nature, was to sit on the woodpile, under a girdled tree, and there, with her gold pencil in her hand, and her "eyne, grey as glas," rolled upward, poefy by the hour.

It is Miss Fidler's earnest desire to marry, and she is eventually betrothed to a young store clerk who, not surprisingly, believes that changes in social position and education would assist women's equality "in all but strength of mind, in which very useful quality it was his opinion that men would still have the advantages."[36] One assumes that Miss Fidler will not quarrel with this premise of masculine intellectual superiority.

Juxtaposed to these passive women are more admirable women possessing common sense and, frequently, a sense of humor. In Alcott's sketch about Fruitlands, for example, there is Mrs. Hope, who is forced to feed her family without access to foods the community rejects on vegetarian principle—milk, butter, cheese, meat, and tea among them. But Mrs. Hope copes with stoicism: "A ten years' experience of vegetarian vagaries had been good training for this new freak, and her sense of the ludicrous supported her through many trying scenes" (72). Significantly, Mrs. Hope has the last word in the sketch, and it is one that reveals her sense of humor. Fruitlands, with its constant diet of apples, bread, and water, has failed as an experiment in communal living, and as her husband bemoans its demise, Mrs. Hope says, "Don't you think Apple Slump would be a better name for it, dear?" (83).

As if in accord with Samantha Allen's comment "I love to see folks use reason if they have got any," the narrators and *personae* in nineteenth-century women's humor provide frequent examples of the woman of reason who functions as the *eiron* or "wise innocent" figure, whose sense of irony reveals her intelligence and capacity for logic. One of the most significant and well-known instances of this voice in women's humor is Fanny Fern (Sara Willis Parton), whose enormously popular newspaper columns, collected in two volumes of *Fern Leaves* (1853, 1854), address such topics as woman's health, her lamentable economic dependence, and the tyranny of husbands. Parton, like other humorists of her day, provided unflattering portraits of weak, self-indulgent women, such as the "Model Lady," who:

> Puts her children out to nurse and tends lap-dogs;—lies in bed until noon;—wears paper-soled shoes, and pinches her waist; ... goes to church when she has a new bonnet ... runs mad after the last new fashion [and] adores any man who grins behind a moustache.[37]

In several of her "Fern Leaves" sketches, Parton urges the importance of the sense of humor for both women and men. In "Important for Married Men" she counters the negative stereotype of the talkative woman by proposing that men are often amused by the witty conversation of women. The sketch involves a woman whose friend drops by for a chat. All her efforts to get her husband to leave them alone fail, so the women decide to have their conversation anyway:

Kitty tells you a most excruciating story, and you tell her another; and you laugh till the tears start. Well, now you just creep slily round Moses' chair, and take a peep at him. St. Cecelia! if that book is not upside down, and his mouth stretched from ear to ear! He has swallowed every word with the avidity of a cat over her first mouse banquet; and yet, if you did not face him up with that upside down book, he would persist he had been reading the funniest book alive! And so he has, but it was not bound in "calf" or "sheep-skin!" (350)

Not only, Parton proposes, do women have a sense of humor, but men, however grudgingly, enjoy it. Further, in "Owls Kill Humming-birds," she advises women to marry men who have a sense of humor: "if you have the bump of mirthfulness developed, don't marry a tombstone" (391). A man who is "about as genial as the north side of a meeting house," she continues, will have a woman "plodding through life with him to the dead-march of his own leaden thoughts" (392). Parton assumes that the sense of humor is not the sole province of men, and her own sprightly satires in *Fern Leaves* effectively combine logic and irony.

Thus, amid the controversy about whether women possessed a sense of humor, women writers continued to both demonstrate it and argue for its value. A second response to the cultural denigration of women's intelligence and wit has been to present female *personae* who overtly conform to and demonstrate an image of womanhood in keeping with the stereotype of the nonintellectual, silly, dependent woman. Although this response originated in such nineteenth-century works as Frances Whitcher's *Widow Bedott Papers*, with its gossips and husband-hunters, it became more common in the twentieth century in the works of Anita Loos, Dorothy Parker, Jean Kerr, Shirley Jackson, and others. One reason for this shift in emphasis from the rational, ironic narrator who comments on the foibles of others to the narrator who embodies these same weaknesses may be traced to a change in both locale and tone of American humor generally. As the progressive optimism and pervasive sense of reform and self-improvement of the nineteenth century gave way to the self-doubt and bewilderment of an increasingly urban and bureaucratic culture, American humorists turned from broad social satire to introspective studies of individuals and relationships. The timid "little man" created by James Thurber and Robert Benchley replaced the easygoing raconteur of the tall tale, and a corresponding "little woman," in the works of Parker and others, expressed insecurity about her appearance and her abilities. With the advent of *Vanity Fair* and *The New Yorker*, Americans' taste in humor favored the urban sophisticate over the rural sage who spoke in dialect, and the humorous *persona* who revealed his or her insecurities about coping with modern life mirrored the insecurities of the middle-class American who aspired to greater sophistication, yet who felt intimidated by new ways of life and thought.

Perhaps the best-known of the twentieth-century figures who represent an apparent capitulation to the nonintellectual, dependent role for women is Lorelei Lee, the narrator and main character in Anita Loos's *Gentlemen Prefer Blondes* (1925). Loos's book did more to establish the stereotype of the "dumb blonde"—a twentieth-century version of the "clinging vine"—than did any other single work. Lorelei lacks the assumed purity of the nineteenth-century stereotype; she is, in fact, a "kept" woman who prefers diamonds to affection, whose attractiveness to men is purely physical. In fact, the dichotomy between woman as sex object and woman as intellectual is one of the sources of humor in Loos's book. Throughout the novel, the reader is able to see through Lorelei's naïve statements to the reality of her life, and thus can feel intellectually superior to her; further, one of the subterfuges that men use to justify spending time with her—and that she at least superficially accepts—is that they are trying to "educate" her. In the first chapter, for example, Lorelei tells us about Gus Eisman:

> I mean Mr. Eisman is in the wholesale button profession in Chicago and he is the gentleman who is known practically all over Chicago as Gus Eisman the Button King. And he is the gentleman who is interested in educating me, so of course he is always coming down to New York to see how my brains have improved since the last time.

Lorelei adopts the same subterfuge to gloss over her sexual activities. She reports that normally, after an evening on the town, "Mr. Eisman shows me to my apartment. So of course when a gentleman is interested in educating a girl, he likes to stay and talk about the topics of the day until quite late."[38] There is no question that both Lorelei and Gus Eisman see their relationship as a form of business arrangement from which both of them benefit: he buys her food and gifts in exchange for the pleasure of her company and the privilege of being seen with an attractive woman. Nor is Lorelei above negotiating to get her way. When Gus shows up on her birthday with a diamond smaller than she has expected—"a little thing you could hardly see"—she tells him she has a headache and sends him away; and when he, understanding the terms of the negotiation, comes back later with "really a very very beautiful bracelet of square cut diamonds," she is "quite cheered up" and agrees to go out with him (19).

Despite such evidences of Lorelei's materialism, however, Loos's intentions in *Gentlemen Prefer Blondes* are more complex than merely presenting the "dumb blonde" stereotype. As Zita Dresner has pointed out, Lorelei is a victim of cultural attitudes toward women:

> The temptation to blame Lorelei is balanced by the objective
> recognition that the relationship between Eisman and Lorelei is
> mutually exploitive and that the social moralism that traditionally
> condemned such relationships is also responsible for creating the
> conditions for such relationships by making woman's sex appeal her
> most marketable asset. When Lorelei's maid reminds her of "the old
> addage [sic]: Leave them while you're looking good," she is reflecting
> a cultural reality.[39]

Moreover, Lorelei is in some ways an *eiron* figure whose very naïveté is a mask for her perceptions. Not only, as Dresner points out, has she "learned . . . what it takes for a woman to get ahead in American society" (66); she is also the vehicle for incidental bits of Loos's social satire. For example, in Lorelei's description of Gus Eisman lurks a commentary on the intellectual level of American politicians:

> [Mr. Eisman] ought to know brains when he sees them, because he is
> in the senate and he spends quite a great deal of time in Washington,
> d. c., and when he comes into contract [sic] with brains he always
> notices it. (11-12)

Thus the stereotype of the "dumb blonde" as Loos uses it does not represent acquiescence to society's view of women as nonintellectual; instead, Lorelei Lee is an example of the *effects* of such a view: valued only for her appearance, she uses her wits to turn the situation to her own—material if not emotional—advantage.

Hazel Morse, in Dorothy Parker's "Big Blonde," is in many ways the same "dumb blonde" stereotype. Like Lorelei, Hazel has no assets except her physical appearance, and she depends for her livelihood on the approbation of men. But in Parker's story, the woman is even more clearly a victim of cultural assumptions about women's value, with results that are nearly tragic. Part of the difference in tone and emphasis is caused by the difference in the authors' perspective on their main characters. Whereas Loos uses a first-person narration, allowing Lorelei Lee to tell her own story, Parker adopts the third-person narrative approach; instead of the brisk, slangy speech that characterizes *Gentlemen Prefer Blondes*, Parker uses a restrained, ironic perspective that makes the reader see Hazel Morse as a case study in social conditioning. The ironic distance of the author's voice in "Big Blonde" allows Parker to provide a double view of Hazel: that of the objective narrator who understands how Hazel is viewed by those around her, and that of Hazel herself, whose understanding is severely limited. At the beginning of the story, for example, the author's voice identifies the stereotype Hazel represents and the male response to it:

> Hazel Morse was a large, fair woman of the type that incites some men when they use the word "blonde" to click their tongues and wag their heads roguishly.[40]

Shortly thereafter, Parker presents the same situation from Hazel's perspective, in language that testifies to the limitations of her perception:

> Men liked you because you were fun, and when they liked you they took you out, and there you were. So, and successfully, she was fun. She was a good sport. Men like a good sport. (214)

This uncritical, reflexive relationship to life is underscored by many of Parker's comments about Hazel: "She was not a woman given to recollections" (213); "She never pondered if she might not be better occupied doing something else" (214).

As the story progresses through Hazel's brief marriage to Herbie Morse, to his leaving her, to her slide into virtual prostitution, Parker consistently emphasizes the extent to which Hazel is the product of others'—primarily men's—requirements. The most important requirement is that she be "fun"; when she gives serious consideration to the plight of the world or herself and ceases to laugh, the man leaves and she must await another to replace him. Because Hazel is expected to react rather than to think, she does precisely that, and the only action she plans entirely for herself is her abortive attempt at suicide.

Although Lorelei Lee and Hazel Morse differ sharply in their ability to manipulate life to their own advantage, both are victims of cultural assumptions about women's intelligence and self-determination. Instead of being educated for independence, both women are rigorously schooled in the notion that woman's function is to please man; and beneath the surface of Lorelei's comic misspellings and Hazel's ironic bewilderment is the same message: the denial of women's intellect leads directly to their exploitation.

By the middle of the twentieth century, when the location of women's humor had moved from the urban apartment and the speakeasy to the suburban home, the terms of women's conformity to a nonintellectual ideal shifted from pleasing men with sexual attractiveness to demonstrating their competence as homemakers. In the domestic humor that flourished after World War II, women are seldom portrayed as sex objects in the overt manner of Loos and Parker. Attractiveness is still a virtue, as the frequent mention of beauty parlors and diets attests, but far more pervasive are struggles to perform acceptably the myriad monotonous tasks involved in housekeeping and child-raising. Women are still not supposed to *think*, but they are supposed to *do* rather than simply *be*. The self-deprecation of the humorous *persona* centers on her self-perceived inability to meet a set of culturally determined standards for her role as homemaker.

The titles of many of the works of domestic humor testify to the conflict between ideal fulfillment of this role and woman's sense of her actual performance. Erma Bombeck's *Aunt Erma's Cope Book* is subtitled *How to Get from Monday to Friday . . . in 12 Days*; Shirley Jackson's *Life Among the Savages* chronicles the perils of motherhood; Jean Kerr's *How I Got to be Perfect* is an ironically titled account of just the oppsite; and the most overt statement of all is made by Peg Bracken's *The I Hate to Cook Book*. What these works and others record—albeit amusingly—is failure. In "Tales Out of School: The Sandwich Crisis," Jean Kerr describes standing in front of the refrigerator at one in the morning trying to find something to fix for her children's lunches the next day, and locating little except a "sinister-looking turkey carcass that must have been there since Christmas." She muses about her inefficiency:

> Another woman could make a tasty sandwich spread by mixing evaporated milk and mayonnaise with some curry powder. But I lack the dash for this kind of experimentation. For that matter I lack the curry powder, and—what is more to the point—I lack qualities of leadership. Yes, I do. I'm an unfit mother and a rotten housekeeper, as shiftless and improvident as a character out of *God's Little Acre*.[41]

The "other woman" also provides a point of comparison for Peg Bracken, who notes that some women are able to do creative things with leftovers. "But," she adds, "when you hate to cook, you don't do this. You just go around thinking you ought to."[42] Erma Bombeck's speaker often points to the example of other women as well, but in *Aunt Erma's Cope Book* she speaks of the pressure of advertising, especially television commercials:

> If commercials were supposed to make me feel good about myself, they were failing miserably. My paper towels turned to lace in my hands. My cough medicine ran out at 2 a.m., and my garbage bags broke on impact with the garbage.

The message of advertising, as Bombeck makes clear, is that the woman is responsible for everything that happens to her family:

> I was responsible for my husband's underarms being protected for twelve hours. I was responsible for making sure my children had a well-balanced breakfast. I alone was carrying the burden for my dog's shiny coat. . . . When my daughter's love life fell through it was up to me to remind her that whiter teeth would bring him back.[43]

If the speaker in these humorous works falls short of the ideal of performace in her assigned role, she does not even attempt to do what is considered "man's work," involving reason, numbers, and technology. Phyllis McGinley provides a litany of male skills in her poem "Apology for Husbands," which includes the following:

> He layeth rugs, he fixeth sockets,
> He payeth bills from both his pockets, . . .
> He jousts with taxi-men in tourney,
> He guards your luggage when you journey,

> And brings you news and quotes you facts
> And figures out the income tax.[44]

These "male" responsibilities require skills that women presumably
do not have; the man deals with electricity, money, "facts," and arith-
metic—fields alien to the woman as nonintellectual. In another
poem, McGinley deals directly with the differences between male
and female mental capacities in terms that reacall the sharp distinctions of the nineteenth centruy:

> A lady is smarter that a gentleman, maybe.
> She can sew a fine seam, she can have a baby.
> She can use her intuition instead of her brain.
> But she can't fold a paper on a crowded train.[45]

To be "smart," for a woman, is thus defined as using those abilities
that are both biological and culturally determined *for* her; even the
manual dexterity required for folding a newspaper is beyond the
scope of "intuition" and requires the reasoning power of the male
brain. Shirley Jackson's speaker in *Life Among the Savages*, confronted with a furnace that has quit working, describes her fear of
technology:

> I am wholeheartedly afraid of fuses and motorcycles and floor plugs
> and lightning rods and electric drills and large animals and most
> particularly of furnaces. Laboriously, over the span of years of
> married life, my husband has taught me to use such hazardous
> appliances as a toaster and an electric coffee pot, but no one is ever
> going to get me to go down cellar and fool around with a furnace.

So completely has Jackson's *persona* absorbed the notion that
women are incapable of dealing with such mechanisms as furnaces
that, despite her husband's announcement that "*no* furnace ... has
ever exploded because some woman pressed the third little button
from the left," she calls a repairman instead of attempting it.[46]

The female humorist's creation of the inept, nonintellectual *persona* is a subtle form of protest against cultural conditioning: by presenting the results of such rigid expectations of women's behavior,
the writer shows the enforced shallowness and emptiness of women's lives. Further, to reinforce this cultural critique, these humorous *personae* often make remarks that reveal their awareness of dis-

criminatory treatment. Phyllis McGinley, for example, speaks of the repetitive triviality of the housewife's existence:

> Some lives are filled with sorrow and woe
> And some with joy ethereal.
> But the days may come and the weeks may go,
> My life is filled with cereal.[47]

Similarly, in "The Children's Hour After Hour After Hour," Jean Kerr's narrator speaks of the wearying repetition involved in child-rearing: "Every night for almost twenty years I have felt obliged to make the banal but stunningly prophetic remark, 'Don't leave that glass there, you're going to knock it over with your elbow.'" The narrator proceeds to yearn wistfully for a more intellectually stimulating life:

> I'm sick of talking about milk. When do we get to the great topics,
> like art, music, McLuhan? And what about people like the Kennedys,
> who, they say, had such brilliant converations at the dinner table,
> even when the children were young? How? Didn't those kids get any
> milk?[48]

More recently, Judith Viorst continues this questioning of the woman's assigned role when she addresses the difference between male and female activities:

> Where is it written
> That husbands get twenty-five-dollar lunches and
>   invitations to South America for think
>   conferences while
> Wives get Campbell's black bean soup and a trip to
>   the firehouse with the first grade . . .[49]

The issue of women's sense of humor is not, then, an isolated or trivial concern. Instead, it is part of a complex web of cultural assumptions about woman's intelligence, competence, and "proper role." As long as woman is viewed as helpmate, sex object, and domestic servant, she cannot at the same time be allowed the capacity for humor, with its implication of superiority and its fundamental critique of social reality. The "lady" and the "real girl" are not funny; at best, they appreciate the humor of the male. Yet one of the dominant themes in women's humor in America has been the rejection of these passive, nonintellectual stereotypes that deny women's independence and selfhoods. Whether in the form of overt satire or in more subversive ways, women have laughed at the accusation that they are "witless," and through that laughter have spoken to each other about the absurdity of their common dilemma.

4
The Humor of the "Minority"

"I do not feel like no weekend house guest."
—*Alice Childress,* Like One of the Family (1956)

I

In his prefatory note to *The Book of Negro Humor* (1966), Langston Hughes provides his own definition of humor:

> Humor is laughing at what you haven't got when you ought to have it. Of course, you laugh by proxy. You're really laughing at the other guy's lacks, not your own. That's what makes it funny—the fact that you don't know you are laughing at yourself. Humor is when the joke is on you but hits the other fellow first—before it boomerangs. Humor is what you wish in your secret heart were not funny, but it is, and you must laugh. Humor is your own unconscious therapy.[1]

Hughes's definition is applicable more widely than to the humor of American blacks collected in his anthology; in fact, it echoes definitions put forth by many other humor theorists. The concept of humor as "therapy" parallels Freud's theory that humor protects the ego from the super-ego; and the notion that humor "hits the other fellow" accords with the widely held belief that humor is inherently aggressive. Yet several of Hughes's comments here suggest that he has reference in particular to the humor of the underdog, the have-nots of society who learn to cope with deprivation and discrimination in part by using humor. To laugh at "what you haven't got when you ought to have it" implies a consciousness of both one's rights and the denial of those rights; to laugh when "you wish in your secret heart [that the situation] were not funny" suggests an awareness of the disparity and incongruity that members of minority groups constantly endure: the distance between the official promise of equality and the actual experience of subordination to the dominant culture. Such an awareness of disparity—and of humor as a way of dealing with it—is inherent also in the remarks of Martha Bruère and Mary Beard concerning the humor of American women. In their introduction to *Laughing Their Way*, Bruère and Beard note that "the angle of vision from which women see a lack of balance, wrong proportions, disharmonies, and incongruities in life is a thing of their world as it must be—a world always a little apart."[2]

To a large extent, women have lived apart from the mainstream of American culture, as have members of ethnic and racial minorities. Their angle of vision has been that of the outsider—the one who lives by someone else's rules in a culture that has denied them independence and power. In both personal relationships and public life, white American women[3] have shared with members of minority groups the experience of discrimination, subordination, and oppression. Yet, because in some senses they are also members of the ruling class, white women cannot be perceived in precisely the same ways as can blacks, Puerto Ricans, or members of any other identifiable minority group. William Chafe, in *Women and Equality*, points to this paradox by noting that "women are connected, directly or indirectly, to the operation of society at every level, and at the same time occupy the aggregate position of outsiders."[4] In terms of family and social interaction, and the enjoyment of economic and social privilege, most white American women have escaped the exclusion and prejudice that have been the lot of America's racial and ethnic minorities. The overt social discrimination exemplified by signs reading "No Irish Need Apply" and the Jim Crow laws has been, in the case of American women, transmuted into the more subtle forms of role definitions and behavioral expectations.

Yet, as Chafe points out, there are some significant similarities between the experiences of women and those of groups of people more clearly understood to be minorities. He adopts Louis Wirth's definition of a minority as "a group of people who, because of their physical or cultural characteristics, are singled out from the others in the society in which they live for differential and unequal treatment," a group that may be numerically a majority, but whose members are treated as "members of a category, irrespective of their individual merits."[5] The sense of cultural identity shared by members of most minority groups does not, in the case of women, derive from a common place of origin or from a set of foreign ideas; yet, Chafe argues, women in America have developed the institutional structures (groups, clubs, societies), the consciousness of separation, and even the distinct linguistic patterns common to minority groups. Thus the sewing society may promote group solidarity in a way similar to the Jewish synagogue; suburban isolation may be analogous to the ghetto experience; and culturally determined habits of speech may stand for the foreign language of an immigrant group (Chafe, 4-6).

These parallels between the experience of American women and the experience of members of minority groups are, of course, approximations rather than evidence of identical status. They suggest, however, that even middle-class American women have enough in common to be considered a group with shared interests and concerns. Chafe's distinction between aggregate and collective group behavior is useful in distinguishing between the response to discrimination by the majority of American women and the response of groups more obviously tied by a common racial or national origin. "Aggregate" behavior includes those activities which are "distinctive in nature and appear to be based on gender, but which do not reflect conscious group planning," whereas "collective" behavior consists of activities that "grow out of a conscious sense of group purpose and reflect group self-awareness and intent" (7). Collective behavior thus requires a strong sense of group solidarity, such as would exist among slaves living in close proximity or among Irish laborers, whereas aggregate behavior reflects a spontaneous, individual response whose consonance with the responses of others seems on the surface to be accidental.

This is not to suggest that American women have never acted collectively, out of a sense of group purpose. A variety of political and social issues — temperance, suffrage, the Equal Rights Amendment — have unified groups of women for specific action on their behalf *as women*. Yet the majority of American women have at the same time been engaged in social, intimate, and, increasingly, professional relationships with men, and so have not experienced the almost-total separation of the ghetto, the ethnic neighborhood, or the barrier of skin color. This fact, as Carolyn Heilbrun has explained in *Reinvent-*

ing Womanhood, has prevented both men and women from being conscious of women as "outsiders":

> Men, who perceive women as by their sides, . . . have rarely if ever described women as outsiders. Generally speaking, outsiders are conceived of in a context of alternate or excluded cultures. The outsider is expected to have a culture of his or her own (Jewish in America, Irish in England) that women, as women, patently lack. One might, in this context, persuade oneself that women are not even outsiders, because they do not all "come" from any particular place or culture. If a woman is an outsider, it is supposed that she is so only by virtue of being Black, or Jewish, or foreign born, but not by virtue of being a woman.[6]

Furthermore, as Nina Auerbach has pointed out, communities composed solely of women have been regarded with great suspicion in Western culture, and the recurrence of the female community as a literary image, from the Muses of Greek mythology to the schoolgirls in *The Prime of Miss Jean Brodie*, testifies to a cultural fascination with a phenomenon both abnormal and threatening:

> As a recurrent literary image, a community of women is a rebuke to the conventional ideal of a solitary woman living for and through men, attaining citizenship in the community of adulthood through masculine approval alone. The communities of women which have haunted our literary imagination from the beginning are emblems of female self-sufficiency which create their own corporate reality, evoking both wishes and fears.[7]

Because women have been traditionally defined by their relationships with men, rather than by their intrinsic capabilities or individual accomplishments, the separate subcultures that have been mandated for most conventionally-defined minority groups have been effectively prohibited for women, at least on an official level. The aggregate rather than collective behavior of women that Chafe describes is explained by Auerbach in terms of "codes":

> All true communities are knit together by their codes, but a code can range from dogma to a flexible, private, and often semi-conscious set of beliefs. In literature at least, male communities tend to live by a code in its most explicit, formulated, and inspirational sense; while in female communities, the code seems a whispered and a fleeting thing, more a buried language than a rallying cry, whose evocations, like Cranford's reiterated "elegant economy" or the ostensible

etiquette of Jean Brodie's "la crème de la crème," have more than a
touch of the impalpable and the devious. (8-9)

The rules or "codes" by which the dominant culture operates are
announced, articulated—whereas those of the community of women
are whispered and subversive, like those of the racial or ethnic
minority group, who maintain a more or less invisible subculture
within or alongside the larger society.

In a very real sense, of course, virtually *all* Americans are immigrants—at least ancestrally—a fact that led William Dean Howells to
champion the literature of ethnic writers such as Abraham Cahan and
Charles Chesnutt in the late nineteenth century, and more recently
has caused Werner Sollors to equate ethnic literature with American
literature.[8] In *Pocahontas's Daughters: Gender and Ethnicity in
American Culture*, Mary V. Dearborn proposes that it is the double
position of "otherness"—gender and ethnicity—that gives the
woman writer a special perspective on American values. Defining
"ethnic" as "other," Dearborn relates the concept to power—especially to woman's comparative powerlessness:

> Only in relation to other groups can a group be defined as ethnic.
> Ethnicity has always been defined as otherness; the other is always
> ethnic. The Indians of North America became ethnic only when
> European settlers appeared, who, first by gunpowder and goods and
> later by sheer numbers emerged as dominant, i.e., nonethnic. . . .
> [E]thnicity *is* related to power, however broadly defined. When
> gender is introduced, the relationship becomes more clear.
> Pocahontas, a sexually and culturally colonized woman, reminds us
> that, in effect, white males exist as a dominant group only insofar as
> there are other entities whom they can perceive as ethnic and
> female, or colonizable. When John Smith—an immigrant, after all—
> arrived in Jamestown, Pocahontas began to be ethnic.[9]

In terms of technique, the woman writer as ethnic writer must
employ subversive methods, or codes, that parallel the method of the
humorous writer; in Dearborn's terms, "the authorial strategy of the
trickster, purporting to tell one story and project one persona and
actually implying another message, setting out to mediate but only
pretending to do so" (29).

Humor is one of the expressions of the codes by which a group
operates. The topics and forms of humorous expression are an index
to the values and the taboos of the group, and the humor can be so

intimately tied to group identity as to be almost unintelligible to anyone outside the group. These principles apply to the humor of distinctive ethnic and racial minorities as well as to the aggregate humor of American women, and they point up ways in which women's humor both does and does not function as the humor of a true minority. Women's humor, like minority humor, displays a consciousness of a group identity, often posing a "we-they" dialectic, and both types of humor feature common stereotypes of members of the dominant culture. Women's humor, like that of minorities, is usually expressed within the group, rather than in mixed company — orally, in groups composed only of women, and in print, in publications intended primarily for other women. Finally, the humor is frequently a means of dealing with frustration or anger, rather than simply celebratory or fun.

The differences between women's humor and that of minority groups are related directly to women's less isolated position in American culture. Minority humor, especially that of blacks, demonstrates a sharp awareness of the group's difference from the majority culture, and within that difference asserts a superiority to those in power; the speaker frequently has the "last laugh," or, alternatively, is superhumanly skilled at bowing, at least ostensibly, to the wishes of those in charge. For example, Langston Hughes recounts the story of the black woman who went to a fashionable Washington, D.C., restaurant soon after the official end of segregation and asked for black-eyed peas, cornbread, and collard greens. Told that the restaurant had none of these items on its menu, the woman rose to leave, saying, "Honey, ... I knowed you-all wasn't ready for integration" (*Book of Negro Humor*, 256). The absurdity of segregation is also pointed up by the popular joke about the black man who, in the midst of falling from a great height, sees that he is about to land on a white woman, and manages to reverse his direction.[10] Women's humor is, overtly at least, more accepting of circumstance; the speaker is more apt to be self-deprecatory as a way of acknowledging that she has difficulty living up to the standards established for her behavior. All of these similarities and differences are matters of degree rather than clear demarcations, just as women both are and are not a "minority" in the conventional sense of the term.

II

The humor of black American women points up most clearly the minority-group experience as it has affected those who have participated in this experience in a double sense: as members of a true minority group, they demonstrate a consciousness of separation from the dominant culture, and yet as women they have bonds with *all* women because of the shared experience of gender. The work of Zora Neale Hurston, Mari Evans, Alice Childress, and others provides an instructive counterpoint to the humor of white women, a contrast that illuminates similarities and differences in the minority experience. The first book by Alice Childress, playwright and author of *A Hero Ain't Nothin' but a Sandwich* (1973), is the ideal case in point. *Like One of the Family*, subtitled *Conversations from a Domestic's Life*, was first published in 1956, at the height of the suburban movement that isolated America's white, middle-class women in the "villages of women" that are described in the domestic humor of Phyllis McGinley, Jean Kerr, Margaret Halsey, and Shirley Jackson. The title of Childress's book, drawn from the common white liberal claim that black servants were regarded as family members, is ironic in several senses. Most obviously, the black woman who cleans and cooks for a white family is *not* "one of the family," either racially or in terms of equal status and privilege. On a more complex level, the black domestic servant is required to live in two communities at once: that of her white employer, in whose household she spends much of her waking life, and that of her own family and friends, with whom she shares radically different customs, tastes, and privileges.

Like One of the Family consists of a series of conversations between the narrator, Mildred, and her friend Marge, detailing Mildred's experiences with a series of white employers. The "conversations" are actually monologues, because Marge's responses to Mildred are recorded only in what Mildred says; like Anne Warner's Mrs. Lathrop, in her "Susan Clegg" stories at the turn of the century, Childress's Marge is a sounding board, an occasion for Mildred's storytelling. Yet Marge also represents the minority culture to which Mildred belongs and in which she feels comfortable, in contrast to the white families for whom she works. Mildred does not allow herself to be victimized by the families whose housework she performs;

in fact, much of the humor in *Like One of the Family* arises from her confrontations with those whose behavior would demean her. In the title sketch, for example, Mildred reports to Marge on a conversation with "Mrs. C.," who is fond of saying to her guests, "We *just* adore her! She's *like* one of the family and she *just adores* our little Carol! We don't know *what* we'd do without her!" Mildred confronts Mrs. C. with reality:

> I wish you would please stop talkin' about me like I was a *cocker spaniel* or a *poll parrot* or a *kitten*. . . . I am *not* just like one of the family at all! The family eats in the dining room and I eat in the kitchen. . . . You think it is a compliment when you say, "We don't think of her as a servant. . . ." but after I have worked myself into a sweat cleaning th bathroom and the kitchen . . . making the beds . . . cooking the lunch . . . washing the dishes and ironing Carol's pinafores . . . I do not feel like no weekend house guest.[11]

On other occasions Mildred functions as the *eiron*, pretending to her employers an innocence she does not possess in order to reveal the racist attitudes of whites. In "The Pocketbook Game," she tells Marge about "Mrs. E.," who keeps a tight grip on her purse all the time Mildred is in her apartment. Tired of having her honesty impugned, Mildred leaves the apartment on an errand but comes running back to grab her own purse, imitating Mrs. E.'s behavior and thus demonstrating to her its absurdity. In "The Health Card," an employer, having ascertained that Mildred lives in Harlem, asks to see her health card: "I don't mean any offense, but one must be careful, mustn't one?"

> Well, all she got from me was solid agreement. "Sure,["] I said, "indeed *one* must, and I am glad you are so understandin', 'cause I was just worryin' and studyin' on how I was goin' to ask you for yours, and of course you'll let me see one from your husband and one for each of the three children." (43)

In one situation after another, Mildred proves herself to be morally superior to the white families for whom she works, and she uses wit and irony as her methods.

Mildred is thus part of a long tradition of servants who outwit or see more clearly than their masters, a tradition that turns upon class differences as well as upon racial differences. In opera, there are the examples of Susanna in *The Marriage of Figaro*, Adele in *Die Fleder-*

maus, and Despina in *Cosi Fan Tutti,* and on television, the popular series *Hazel,* in which Shirley Booth played the part of a maid who, because of her intelligence and common sense, solved the problems of the family for which she worked. The response of the domestic servant to taking on this kind of responsibility may well be encapsulated in the joke that Lawrence W. Levine cites in *Black Culture and Black Consciousness,* in which a black cook announces that she is quitting her job. When her white employer asks, "Haven't we always treated you like one of the family?" the black woman replies, "Yes, you have, and I've put up with it just as long as I'm going to" (316).

Levine points out the long tradition in black American humor of "laughing at the man." By calling attention to absurd or foolish behavior on the part of whites, blacks could invert the social order, achieving "the trivialization or degradation of ideas or personages normally held to be lofty or noble, and the advancement of those normally consigned to an inferior or inconsequential position" (300-301). Black American humor was directed not only at slave-owners, but also at other minority groups with whom blacks faced economic competition from the early nineteenth century on—notably, Irish and Jews—but inevitably the system of slavery and its long aftermath of racial discrimination has been the major target of black American humor. Jokes told by blacks since the late nineteenth century point up the absurd extremes of racism, the inability of whites to survive without the black servant class on which they have come to rely, and—most important—the shared sense of community among blacks. As Levine says, "The salient function of these jokes was to rob the American racial system of any legitimacy long before the courts and the government began that still uncompleted task" (311).

Yet in addition to belonging to the black minority that could see so clearly the hypocrisy of white society, Childress's Mildred also belongs to the community of American women—both black and white. Although employed ostensibly by families, Mildred associates most closely with the women of these families, and for all her outspoken resistance to racism, Mildred feels more pity than hatred for these women who are in turn subjugated by white men. She understands their struggle to relate to her, their discomfort in the role of "superior." In "If You Want to Get Along with Me," "Mrs. M." finally confesses, "I . . . want to get along but I don't know how," and Mildred sympathizes with her:

Marge, in that minute I understood her better and it came to my
mind that she was doing her best to make me comfortable and havin'
a doggone hard go of it. After all, everything she's ever been taught
adds up to her being better than me in every way and on her own
she had to find out that this was wrong. (21)

However, no such sympathy is reserved for "Billy Alabama," the big-
oted Southern cousin of one of her employers, who loudly opposes
school integration while claiming that he has known "some really
fine Nigras over the years" (185), or for her friend Tessie's husband,
Clarence, the demanding tightwad in "Men in Your Life."

The fact that *Like One of the Family* is a series of conversations
between two women, often in a kitchen, underscores the separateness of the community of women. From the sewing society of
Frances Whitcher's *Widow Bedott Papers*, to the "just between us
girls" tone of Erma Bombeck's work, American women's humor has
typically been located in kitchens, on front porches, and in other
places where women have traditionally congregated to tell each
other their stories. One effect of this tradition has been to blur the
distinction between life and art, as Trudier Harris points out in her
introduction to *Like One of the Family*:

> In its conversational form, *Like One of the Family* is an example of
> one of the patterns of interactions so characteristic of women who
> frequently integrated art into their life-styles. . . . In the traditional
> places that characterize the differences between the gathering and
> storytelling sites of men and women, kitchens become comparable to
> barbershops and cooking takes the place of shooting pool. Instead of
> moving out of the usual realms of their environments to share
> experiences with others, women frequently tell their tales where they
> are—in the dining room or living room while they are shelling
> beans for dinner. . . . Tasks do not interfere with performance, and
> art and life are synonymous. (xv-xvi)

As Mildred moves back and forth between the cultures of black and
white, she retains both her identity as a member of a racial minority
and her consciousness of being a part of a female community that
includes both black and white women. Although she feels closer
bonds with black than with white women, it is also clear that men of
either race are effectively "outside" the community of women.

Zora Neale Hurston is another figure whose movement between the cultures of black and white, female and male, is instructive in a consideration of women's humor as minority humor. Hurston, whose fiction and nonfiction drawing upon black Southern culture and folklore have been rediscovered in recent years, grew up in the all-black town of Eatonville, Florida, where she absorbed the speech patterns that she would later transform into the rollicking, high-spirited prose of novels such as *Their Eyes Were Watching God* (1937) and *Moses, Man of the Mountain* (1939), and her autobiography, *Dust Tracks on a Road* (1942). Hurston's work is typically located in all-black communities, and her humor differs sharply from that of Alice Childress and Mari Evans in that instead of using irony and wit to confront racism, Hurston celebrates black culture with its jokes, its linguistic exaggerations, and its flamboyant storytellers.

This distinction can be seen more clearly by comparing one of Mari Evans's poems with passages from Hurston's *Dust Tracks*. Evans's "Mattie," like Childress' Mildred, works as a maid for a white family, and in "When in Rome" Evans presents a dialogue between Mattie and her employer in which Mattie's part is thought but not spoken:

> Mattie, dear
> the box is full ...
> take
> whatever you like
> to eat....
> (an egg
> or soup ...
> there ain't no meat.)
> there's endive there
> and cottage cheese ...
> (Whew! if I had some
> black-eyed peas ...)
> there's sardines
> on the shelves
> and such ...
> but
> don't
> get my anchovies ...
> they cost
> too much!

> (me get the
> anchovies indeed!
> what she think, she's got—
> a bird to feed?)
> there's plenty in there
> to fill you up . . .
> (yes'm. just the
> sight's
> enough!
> hope I lives till I get
> home
> I'm tired of eatin'
> what they eats in Rome. . . .)[12]

Mattie identifies herself with the stereotypical black community by longing for black-eyed peas; the contrast between this traditionally Southern/black food and the white employer's endive and anchovies is emblematic of much else that separates the two women.[13] Further, Mattie's subservience to white culture is demonstrated by her silence: her responses to white condescension remain as thoughts, not utterances, so that the face she presents to the white world is one of acquiescence, even while the reader perceives the humor of incongruity.

Hurston, by way of contrast, revels in the colorful language of the black community. She describes her father's family as having "no more to 'em than the stuffings out of a zero,"[14] yet she defines bitterness as "the underarm odor of wishful weakness" (280). Her youthful contacts with white people are described in terms that affirm black solidarity and assumed superiority. Some of the selections in the hymnal given to her by wealthy whites do not please her: "If white people liked trashy singing like that, there must be something funny about them that I had not noticed before" (52). And when white visitors come to her school, the black students and teachers are all conscious that they are putting on an act:

> We always sang a spiritual, led by Mr. Calhoun himself. Mrs. Calhoun always stood in the back, with a palmetto switch in her hand as a squelcher. We were all little angels for the duration, because we'd better be. She would cut her eyes and give us a glance that meant

trouble, then turn her face towards the visitors and beam as much as to say it was a great privilege and pleasure to teach lovely children like us. (46-47)

Even as a child, Hurston was aware of the differences between her life in Eatonville and the more heroic and exciting lives she read about: "Stew beef, fried fat-back and morning grits were no ambrosia from Valhalla. Raking back yards and carrying out chamber pots, were not the tasks of Thor" (56). But her tone is one of joy, and the juxtapositions create humor, not bitter irony.

Yet as an adult during the Harlem Renaissance, Zora Neale Hurston was resented—even by members of her own race such as Wallace Thurman and Langston Hughes—for her verbal humor. She was accused of playing the role of the funny "Darkie" for the amusement of whites, and of refusing to let go of her Southern folk heritage to be assimilated into Northern black society. It is likely that Hurston used humor as a shield, and just as likely that she was resented for it because she was a woman. In "Hurston, Humor, and the Harlem Renaissance," John Lowe points to Hurston's contemporaries' portrayals of her as opportunistic, willing to play the "Darkie" role for white benefactors, and notes that many of the Harlem literati were eager to eschew their rural origins and behave with a seriousness that befitted their positions as the black literary "elite." Thus Hurston's boisterousness was an embarrassment—not least because she was female. "At first charmed by her wit and appearance," Lowe says, "they began to have reservations about her 'seriousness.' ... Hurston's humor was enjoyed, but found suspect, partially because it was 'unladylike.'"[15]

For much the same reason, Dorothy Parker, that well-known wit of the Algonquin Round Table in the same period, was the object of resentment and suspicion. Though Parker has been remembered in print more kindly than has Hurston, her talent for humor kept her at arm's length from those assumed to be her closest associates. John Keats, in his biography of Parker, asserts that few people around her understood the deep current of despair that gave rise to Parker's wit:

At this time in her life [the early 1920s], Dorothy Parker had not one female confidante. She had never had one. She was quite popular among men, who enjoyed what they believed to be the sharp and masculine play of her wit, but her relationship with virtually all of the men she knew was a superficial one. Most of the women she knew were suspicious of her. The one person who served as her faithful counselor, comforter, and spiritual adviser was [Robert] Benchley. She could depend on him to gently say, "Dottie, don't be a damned fool."[16]

Cultural prejudice against the witty woman thus cuts across racial and ethnic lines, affecting the black Zora Neale Hurston and the half-Jewish Dorothy Parker—not on the specific grounds of their blackness or Jewishness, but because humor violates ladylike behavior.

To violate the standards of ladylike behavior involves crossing an invisible but real boundary, and several theorists have emphasized the concept of "boundary" as critical in defining ethnicity. Fredrik Barth has maintained that the boundary of an ethnic group is more important than the cultural content of the group,[17] and Wsevolod W. Isajiw states that "ethnicity is a matter of a double boundary, a boundary from within, maintained by the socialization process, and a boundary from without established by the process of intergroup relations."[18] That is to say, in America particularly, those cultural elements often thought to determine ethnic identity—elements such as language, religion, dress, and customs—are not fixed, but are subject to change, so that the boundaries between one group and another may continually be redrawn.

Humor is a means of both establishing and testing the boundaries between groups of people, and it is for this reason that Werner Sollors has recently argued that "in all cases the community of laughter itself is an ethnicizing phenomenon, as we develop a sense of we-ness in laughing with others."[19] The experience of shared humor creates a bond that replicates to some degree the sense of belonging that arises from identifying oneself with a distinct cultural group. When Alice Childress's Mildred, in *Like One of the Family*, laughs with Marge about the ways she has outwitted her white employers, she is doing more than asserting black solidarity against white discrimination; she is also acknowledging her participation in the group known as "servants," which includes Mari Evans's Mattie—another black woman—but which also includes anyone of any color or gender or ethnic background who has dealt with the assumed superiority of a dominant group.

America's ethnic and racial minorities have been major contributors to the nation's humorous tradition, both as creators of humor and as its targets. Indeed, the earliest American humor was predicated on differences of caste and class: colonists versus Europeans, urban versus rural colonists, the orthodox versus the heretical. As W. Howland Kenney notes in *Laughter in the Wilderness*, "the comic insists on telling the whole truth when the pretenders to majesty, power, and control are imposing their various systems and definitions of life."[20] The single group that has affected American humor more than any other is the Jews. With their long tradition of minority status, the Jewish people developed, centuries before their immigration to the United States, a highly refined humorous tradition that both acknowledges their position as a minority and makes fun of the oppressor. This tradition of Jewish humor is, as Allen Guttman puts it, "a product of the social situation of a minority group within a hostile majority, . . . the result of a proud people acutely sensitive of their lowly social status." The irony of the fact that "the Chosen People of God were also the despised people of the Polish or Russian village"[21] has led to the Jewish writer's ironic consciousness, a consciousness that has influenced American literature from Abraham Cahan to Woody Allen.

The fact that humor has long been an essential component of Jewish culture, coupled with the relatively rapid rate at which Jews have become, if not assimilated into, at least socially and materially successful within, American culture, accounts for their significant participation in American humor, especially in the twentieth century: Groucho Marx in film, S. J. Perelman on the pages of *The New Yorker*, and books by Leo Rosten and Harry Golden have taken their place in mainstream American humor. Until the Civil Rights Movement of the 1960s, on the other hand, the humor of American blacks was largely unknown to white Americans. What white Americans took to be the humor of blacks was, in fact, largely created by whites. The minstrel show, with whites in black-face, and the popular *Amos 'n' Andy* radio program, featured language and behavior based on stereotyped views of blacks that originated in the majority culture.

Yet the humor of these two groups is similar in its consciousness of group solidarity and identity, and its tendency to reverse the balance between those in dominant and subordinate positions. In *The Book of Negro Humor*, Langston Hughes records an enduring anecdote:

> During a battle the white general of a colored regiment noticed one of his soldiers seemed to be devoted to him and followed him everywhere. At length he remarked,
> "Well, my boy, you have stuck by me well during this engagement."
> "Yes sir," said the soldier. "My old mama back in Alabama told me to be sure to stick with the white generals and I'd never get hurt."[22]

Here the black soldier functions as the *eiron*, and the message concerns the cowardice of powerful whites, which the black has used to his advantage. A similar instance of one-upmanship, this time by a Jew, is the kernel of the following joke:

> An orthodox rabbi and a Catholic priest were playing golf together and were discussing religious differences when the priest turned to the rabbi and said, "Quite confidentially, Rabbi, have you ever eaten ham?"
> The rabbi in a very soft voice answered, "Confidentially, yes."
> As the two continued to play, the rabbi thoughtfully asked the priest, "Very confidentially, Father, have you ever gone to bed with a woman?"
> The priest blushed, and, in a whisper, answered slowly, "Yes, I have."
> "Better than ham, wasn't it?" The rabbi exclaimed.[23]

A similar kind of cultural reversal characterizes Mildred's dealings with her employers in *Like One of the Family*, and is also present in the unspoken thoughts of the black speaker in Mari Evans's "When in Rome," in the sense that the food of the black community is implicitly better than that of whites.

A group of women even more marginal in American culture, for whom humor—indeed, writing at all—is a recent development, is Chicana women. In "Walking the Thin Line: Humor in Chicana Literature," Tey Diana Rebolledo observes that the Chicana is "thrice oppressed" because she is "a woman in a male-dominated culture, a minority in the white/Anglo culture, and because of her own ambivalence of place and state in society."[24] The Chicana writer, Rebolledo says, is "hovering between laughing and crying" (96), and she typically uses humor as a means of expressing anger and frustration at cultural restriction and conflict. One example is the story "The Paris

Gown," by Estela Portillo Trambley, in which a young woman thwarts her father's plan to marry her to a wealthy widower by descending the staircase at her engagement ball not in the dress ordered from Paris for the occasion, but instead wearing nothing at all. Margarita Cota-Cárdenas, in "Mischievous Soliloquy," similarly deals with the concept of Chicana-as-object when she plays upon the stereotype of the woman as a flower:

> we concentrate real hard   like this
>   and wrinkle up our brow
>   so that we'll wither beforehand
>   and when we get to the market   hee hee
>   they can't sell us. (100)

Jewish women humorists, because of their far more thorough assimilation into mainstream American culture, identify more strongly with being female than with being Jewish. Their backgrounds are typically urban and middle-class, and although their humor sometimes refers to elements of Jewish culture, the issues they explore tend to be those that affect middle-class women of any ethnic background.[25] Judith Viorst, for example, in her several books of verse, alludes to her Jewish background and family members, and sometimes uses the syntax of the urban Jewish population. In "The First Full-Fledged Family Reunion," in her 1971 collection *People & Other Aggravations*, Viorst comments on several cousins:

> 1 cousin who has made such a name for himself
>   he was almost Barbara Streisand's obstetrician
> 1 cousin who has made such a name for himself
>   he was almost Jacob Javits' CPA
> 1 cousin don't ask what he does for a living[26]

The upward mobility that is part of the stereotypical image of American Jews is evident here, as are the speech rhythms associated with this group. But more commonly, Viorst's verse deals with her struggles as a woman to combat overweight and aging, and to accommodate herself to a world in which men are the privileged gender. In a poem that reflects the traditional dilemma of the female writer who is also housewife and mother, Viorst echoes—among others—Anne Bradstreet and Fanny Fern:

Did Edna St. Vincent Millay rise at dawn

> For a first-grade production called Snowflakes?
> Did Marianne Moore put her symbols aside
> To wipe Quaker Oats off the table?
> Excuse me, my husband would like a cold beer.
> I'll be back just as soon as I'm able. ("The Writers" 105)

Other Jewish writers, such as Nora Ephron and Fran Lebowitz, occasionally allude to their ethnic identification, but this is not a major focus of their humor. In one of her *Esquire* articles, Ephron muses about why she buys *Gourmet* magazine: "it occurred to me that perhaps I bought *Gourmet* because I figured it was the closest I would ever get to being a gentile."[27] Lebowitz begins a piece in *Social Studies* (1981) by referring to herself as "a practicing member of several oppressed minority groups."[28] But in both cases these are passing remarks—Ephron's point is the elitist materialism of *Gourmet*, and Lebowitz is satirizing the oppression of smokers by nonsmokers—and their tone is tongue-in-cheek. In contrast to the speakers in Childress's and Evans's work, these are in no sense pleas for tolerance or acceptance. The humorous literature produced by America's minority women embodies a dual consciousness—a consciousness of both ethnic background and gender—but its themes and its language most clearly differentiate it from the humor of men.

III

In the early 1970s, at the height of the women's movement, two female scholars—both, perhaps coincidentally, Jewish—wrote about connections between women's humor and the humor of minority groups. Naomi Weisstein, in "Why We Aren't Laughing . . . Anymore," argues that for several reasons women had not developed a tradition of humor similar to that of other oppressed groups—"a humor which recognizes a common oppression, notices its source and the rules it requires, identifies the agents of that oppression." For one thing, Weisstein proposes, women have lacked the sense of group identity that would have produced such a humor: "our base has not generally been a social grouping of women, but some particular man with whom we live." More significantly, she notes that "the humor of the oppressed is based on a knowledge of shared oppression, and this has been hidden from us in curious ways":

One of the paths of coming into consciousness, into politics, of an oppressed group is the realization that their misery is not due to some innate inferiority, to their own flawed characters, but that there is something going on outside that is keeping them down, and that it is *not fair*.

The curious thing about our own oppression is that we were taught that it *is fair*: that it was in the divine order of things.[29]

Sharon Weinstein, writing in *American Humor: An Interdisciplinary Newsletter* a year later, refers to Weisstein's argument and discusses the many obstacles to women as humorists—obstacles that I have described at length in the previous chapter. Weinstein compares men and women to the *schlemiel* and the *schlemazel*, respectively, in the Jewish tradition—the *schlemiel* being the one who has bad luck, such as spilling his soup, and the *schlemazel* the one on whom the soup gets spilled. She continues by comparing women's experience to that of minority groups generally:

Is the woman's experience not only akin to the *schlemazel's* (granted the *schlemiel* is no more than inept, he is just active, rather than passive in his ineptness) but akin also to the Black experience? Are women in the same position as Ellison's black protagonist in *Invisible Man*, who only realized after many sour adventures that he'd been the butt of the joke and not the joker, that he'd been the receiver rather than the doer, and that however inept the doer, the receiver can do little more than decide if the soup was split pea or bean?[30]

If, as Weinstein argues, women have the been the victims—the butt of the joke and not the joker—a shared sense of that victimization could have created a shared humorous response to oppression, as has been the case with other groups; yet she does not find a cohesive tradition of women's humor, partly because of the public suppression of the sense of humor in women. The absence of such a tradition could also be traced, as Naomi Weisstein suggests, to the fact that the subjugation of women has been sufficiently subtle and sufficiently sanctioned by the official values of the culture that it has frequently been hidden from women themselves.

Yet the striking fact is that such a tradition of women's humor— one that testifies to a sense of shared oppression—*does* exist, even though it has seldom been recognized as such. For at least 150 years, the question of woman's sense of humor has been debated, and women have sought, apparently in vain, the humor of their own gender. Yet all the while, women have written and published humorous work, often, as in the case of writers such as Marietta Holley, Betty MacDonald, and Erma Bombeck, becoming nationally known for their work. What exists, then, is a paradoxical situation in which a tradition has been effectively submerged or hidden—hidden not least from the members of the group that have created it and whom it most directly concerns.

There are at least two reasons for this paradox. One is that the absence of women's humor from most anthologies and critical studies of American humor has made it difficult for women to be conscious of a tradition involving the realities of their own lives. Whereas male readers or writers could look back to the tall-tale tradition, the bitter satire of Mark Twain, or James Thurber's henpecked husbands and find the expression of certain values affecting their lives as men in American culture, women have not had access to their own tradition because it has been largely omitted from the official canon. Whether because of conscious or unconscious bias on the part of male editors and critics, or because women's humor has seemed somehow irrelevant to dominant cultural patterns, it has been allowed to go out of print, to disappear from all but the dusty reaches of library shelves. A second reason why women have been largely unaware of the commonalities in their own humorous tradition is that, until recently, few readers were alert to the subtext of women's humor that carries the message of oppression. That is, even if the work had been readily available, readers not prepared to understand the subversive methodologies of women's literature might well have carried away from it an impression that directly counters the subtextual content.

A brief comparison of the work of two well-known female humorists will illustrate this latter point. Marietta Holley, writing as "Josiah Allen's Wife" around the turn of the century, presented overt challenges to the sexism of her day, arguing openly for the right to vote and complaining with vigor about the drudgery and trivialization of housework. One need not look for any subversive messages or codes in Holley's work. Her narrator, Samantha Allen, is an outspoken feminist who sees marriage as an economic necessity for most women rather than a relationship shared for mutual benefit and love. Samantha's method of logical argument is encapsulated in the comment she makes to her neighbor: "Cant you see daylight ... when the sun is mountin' up into the clear horizon?"[31] Although Holley's Samantha favors a great many different reforms for women, including equal participation in religious observance and governance, and economic independence, the issue she raises most commonly, as do other nineteenth-century feminists, is female suffrage. This is also the issue over which she butts heads most frequently with her husband, Josiah, who adopts the standard view that women are too frail to be exposed to the political process. In *Samantha at the Centennial*, Josiah asks Samantha to accompany him to Jonesville, where he will vote and she can buy material to make shirts for him. Pretending shock that he will allow her to get so close to the polling place, Samantha once again exposes the weakness of arguments against women voting:

> "Oh!" says I almost wildly, "a woman can plunge up head first ag'inst the pole, and be unharmed if she is in search of cotton flannel; she can pursue shirt buttons into the very vortex of political life, into the pool of corruption, and the mirey clay, and come out white as snow, and modest as a lilly of the valley. But let her step in them very tracks, a follerin' liberty and freedom, and justice, and right, and truth and temperance, and she comes out black as coal." And says I in a almost rapped way, liftin' up my eyes to the ceilin': "Why are these things so?"[32]

There is never any doubt about Samantha's stand on feminist issues; though she is far too "meegum" to approve of bloomers and free love, she is a clear spokeswoman for women's rights.

But such overt challenges to the status quo are rare in women's humor. More typical is Betty MacDonald's *The Egg and I*, in which a housewife views her various failures at household tasks as evidence of her inability to live up to the standards of her husband and the society in which she lives. As the wife of a chicken-rancher, MacDonald's narrator finds her time spent on endless, repetitive tasks, and her complaints about them are embedded in comments about her failure to be adequate to these demands:

> I felt as if I were living in a nightmare, fleeing down the track in front of an onrushing locomotive. I raced through each day leaving behind me a trail of things undone. . . . I relegated my ironing to something I would try and finish before small Anne entered college—my washing I tried to ignore, although it assumed the proportions of a snowball rolled from the top of Mt. Olympus.[33]

Underlying the self-deprecatory stance of the narrator, however, is the same challenge as that embodied in Holley's work: as long as women are economically enslaved to men and relegated to the ritual of housework, human equality and dignity are not served. Readers who themselves accept the subordination of women, or who are not alert to the message of feminist protest encoded in the narrator's anguish, will miss the fact that MacDonald and Holley speak as members of the same "minority," with common concerns and a sense of community with other women, at the same time that these authors speak of their own isolation—Holley as an unheeded spokeswoman for feminist principles and MacDonald as the lonely housewife who seems to accept cultural norms for her behavior.

The invisibility of the tradition of women's written humor in America, coupled with women's usual isolation from one another, would suggest that women's humor has functioned differently from that of other minority groups, in which humor both arises from and reinforces a sense of group solidarity.[34] Lawrence W. Levine points to this aspect of the role of humor in group identity:

> Humor is primarily an interactive process among those who share a sense of commonality of experience and situation. . . . Laughter . . . not only helps to strengthen a sense of group cohesion, it assumes the presence of at least the rudiments of an already existing sense of identification. The widespread existence of laughter throughout Afro-American history is in itself evidence of the retention and development of forms of communal consciousness and solidarity among a group that too often and too easily has been pictured as persistently and almost totally demoralized and atomized. (358-59)

What Levine proposes here is that the existence of an Afro-American humorous tradition is evidence of a greater sense of common identity and purpose than is thought to have been the case among blacks in this country. A shared tradition of reiterated themes, characters, and devices—especially one largely hidden from the dominant culture—testifies to common concerns and aspirations.

Precisely the same has been true of the humor of American women, with one notable exception: the invisibility of the tradition, not merely to the dominant culture, but *to women themselves*. This invisibility is all the more striking when we consider the large body of written humor by American women, as opposed to the largely oral Afro-American tradition, yet it can be explained by both the pervasive critical neglect of women's literature and the cultural prejudice against women's sense of humor. Neil Schmitz, in *Of Huck and Alice*, makes the point that blacks and women have shared a cultural stereotyping that has interfered with their creation of humor:

> [Humor] is particularly hard for women writers, for black writers, who have no desire to mystify or demystify their sense of humor, who bring, as it were, a previous skepticism to their humorous writing or performance. The mode in which they find themselves, the forms that are present, popular, belong to a tradition that produces women and blacks as figures of innocence, as figures of ignorance. So they work within the constraint of a double bind.[35]

Those who are truly innocent and ignorant are incapable of humor; the "double bind" to which Schmitz refers is the struggle to believe in one's own abilities and then to believe that they will be accepted by the culture that has already effectively denied them.

Such a double bind is the source of the self-deprecatory humor that women share with members of other groups. Although, as I will discuss later, the women's movement has created a type of feminist humor that abandons the self-denigration of most earlier women's humor, the put-down of self has long been a staple of the woman's humorous stance, even when the underlying message has been the absurdity of the cultural requirements to which the humorous *personae* fail to measure up. Self-deprecation is ingratiating rather than aggressive; it acknowledges the opinion of the dominant culture— even appears to confirm it—and allows the speaker or writer to participate in the humorous process without alienating the members of the majority. Thus the Jew or the black tells stories that play upon ethnic characteristics identified by the majority culture, not only to demonstrate an ability to "take" the joke, but also to render it harmless. As Lawrence Levine states, "Marginal groups often embraced the stereotype of themselves in a manner designed not to assimilate it but to smother it. . . . To tell jokes containing the stereotype was not invariably to accept it but frequently to laugh at it, to strip it naked, to expose it to scrutiny" (336).

Further, members of ethnic groups are often the subjects of contradictory stereotypes. Levine points out that blacks "have been pictured as senselessly violent and dangerous even while they were also depicted as docile, passive, and obedient." Such a paradox makes what may be considered stereotypical behavior difficult to avoid. In the case of blacks, "antithetical aphorisms such as 'to work like a nigger,' and 'lazy as a nigger,' had them conforming to a stereotype if they worked hard or if they did not" (336). Women, too, have been assigned contradictory stereotypes, particularly in American humor. They are innocent and pure, but also temptresses; they are incapable of intellectual endeavors, but at the same time are clever manipulators. In Twain's *Huck Finn*, for example, girls and very young women are chaste, pure, and sweet, whereas older women are righteous nags bent on "sivilizing" boys and men. And Joseph Peck, in *Life with Women and How to Survive it*, manages in one paragraph to compare women to elephants who are "liable to go berserk and wreck the whole circus for no apparent reason," and to violins "with only four strings ranging from the high, sweet tones of an angel to the deep-throated growls of the devil."[36] Caught in, and aware of, this web of stereotypes, women have used self-deprecation in a complex way: to appear to adopt the stereotype, yet to challenge it and the cultural assumptions that underlie it at the same time.

Before the "back-to-the-kitchen" suburban movement that followed World War II, and which was heralded in humor by MacDonald's 1945 *The Egg and I*, the focus of women's humorous self-deprecation was the social arena, involving the search for beauty, for social skills, and for the right man. Sketches such as Dorothy Parker's "The Waltz" show women resenting—and failing to succeed in—a world of social competition that is not of their own making. One of the most popular humorists of the pre-war period was Cornelia Otis Skinner, whose publisher referred to her as "the leading feminine humorist of the country" in 1938.[37] Like so much of women's humor, Skinner's work is a record of amusing failures: the failure to learn yoga, to wear English tweeds properly, to attain an ideal beauty. Yet Skinner implicitly attacks the standards set for her behavior by causing them to seem ridiculous. In "The Skin-Game" in her collection *Dithers and Jitters* (1938), Skinner both records her inability to follow a beauty regimen and calls into question its necessity and validity. The essay opens with a series of negative statements that establish the speaker's self-deprecatory stance: "It's not that I don't want to be a beauty, that I don't yearn to be dripping with glamor." But she then proceeds to use hyperbole to make such aspirations seem ridiculous:

It's just that I can't see how any woman can find time to do to herself all the things that must apparently be done to make herself beautiful and, having once done them, how anyone without the strength of mind of a foreign missionary can keep up such a regime.[38]

Further, Skinner locates the source of her and other women's search for beauty not in their own vanity, but in the advertising industry: "the cosmetic ads for which I am a complete sucker." Even as she acknowledges her own weakness for such advertising, she issues a subtle warning to others who might succumb: "the purchaser of the product is assured of romance, seduction, and general hell-raising. In fact, with every jar comes a free ticket down the primrose path" (122). Thus, at the same time that Skinner admits her own inability to do what is necessary to live up to her culture's standards for female beauty, she simultaneously identifies the agency of that culture which benefits from her adherence to stereotypical behavior, and issues a warning to other women about the lure of the "primrose path."

As the subject of twentieth-century women's humor increasingly became the domestic realm following World War II, the humorous *personae* in both verse and prose reported her failure to live up to the standards of ideal wife and mother. Concern with appearance and gender relations appears in this later period as well, but as the officially sanctioned role for middle-class women increasingly emphasized homemaking skills, the self-deprecatory stance primarily involved the duties of the housewife. In the work of Jean Kerr, Phyllis McGinley, Shirley Jackson, and others, the woman attempts unsuccessfully to cope with cooking, children, household repairs, and community activities. Yet the tactics of the humorist are the same as in earlier periods: the admission of failure is made finally unconvincing by the exaggerated nature of the standards the woman is expected to meet, so that what appears superficially to be capitulation to the stereotype of the inept woman becomes an indictment of the values of a culture that trivializes her life. In one of the most recent examples of the domestic-humor genre, Teresa Bloomingdale's *Sense and Momsense* (1986), the author describes the manipulative methods of the person who is technically powerless—the underdog, the member of the minority group—in terms that provide a paradigm of the method of women's humor. In her essay "It's All in the Game," Bloomingdale addresses the issue of power within a marriage, and proposes that "the ideal marriage . . . is one where the wife makes the husband think she is submissive when, in fact, she is calling the shots. And she doesn't do this by arguing; she does this by playing the game."[39] Just as the method of traditional American women's humor involves pretending to acquiesce to female stereotypes while actually addressing the issue of subordination, so Bloomingdale's "Yes, dear" enables the wife to buy time to manipulate herself into the role of decision-maker:

> I admit that I was brought up to be a "submissive" wife, and dutifully vowed to "obey" at my wedding. But after I had been married several years, I realized that if I took that particular vow literally, I would have, over the years, poured "concrete all over the damn yard so we wouldn't have to keep mowing it," stuffed "all that junk mail in the postman's ear," and killed "the next kid who takes my hairbrush out of the bathroom!"
>
> Obviously, even the most submissive wife must use common sense. (92-93)

In her invocation of "common sense," Bloomingdale recalls Holley's Samantha Allen, in the late nineteenth century, saying that she loves to "see folks use reason if they have got any." Like members of ethnic minorities, women recognize that their subordination is not "reasonable," and that part of their own common sense strategy involves the pretense of playing the game so that they can establish a base of power from which to manipulate the system. It is not surprising, then, that the method used by many female humorists replicates the subversive ways in which members of minority groups have claimed a measure of autonomy within the dominant culture. Outward submission disarms the dominant group and provides the freedom for subversive action and group solidarity.

Several additional factors connect women's humor to the minority-group experience. One is the observation by anthropologists and sociologists that women in all-women groups seem to feel freer to express themselves humorously than they do in groups composed of both men and women. Given the perception of humor as an aggressive behavior and the cultural restrictions on women's expression of humor, this is not surprising. Furthermore, it seems to be true not only in American culture, but generally in human populations. Mahadev L. Apte, in his cross-cultural study *Humor and Laughter*, notes that two circumstances appear to provide women with the freedom for humor: advanced age, which removes some of the pressure to behave as a "lady"—and which also reduces the risk of alienating men—and situations in which women are segregated from men. Not only are women more free to express themselves humorously when men are not present, but as Apte points out, the nature of their humor is frequently more aggressive and often more ribald than that used in mixed company:

> Some varieties of humor that are usually absent from women's expressive behavior in the public domain are present in the private domain, where the audience generally includes only women. In many preindustrial societies humor created by women individually seems confined to social situations in which only women are present; in an all-female audience women behave more freely and creatively. Common topics for humor development in such gatherings include men's physical appearance, their social behavior, their idiosyncrasies, their sexuality, their status-seeking activities, and their religious rites. These characteristics are generally presented in exaggerated and mocking fashion. (76)

Apte cites research showing that Sicilian women frequently develop a ribald humor that mocks men's sexuality to such an extent that men, who are never allowed to participate in these groups, are afraid of being their targets. Further, in some cultures, such as the Magars of Nepal, weddings are characterized by groups of women gathering at the home of the groom to parody male sexual arousal (77). In general, Apte observes, "when women act collectively, many of the behavioral constraints that they must observe as individuals can be disregarded" (78).

Folklorist Rayna Green, in an article titled "Magnolias Grow in Dirt," provides a more informal example of women's humor in all-women groups when she reminisces about her childhood visits with Southern relatives. After the men had left the dinner table, the women remained to exchange funny—often bawdy—stories, which served as a way of initiating the children into the mysteries of adult sexuality, just as they learned from "the more conventional and publicly acceptable Southern woman's store of knowledge about cooking, quilting and making do."[40] Although these women would probably not "revel in a public reputation which included being a good trashy storyteller," Green notes, in private they pride themselves on their ability to tell funny stories, and thus participate in a "hidden" tradition of women's humor. The major reason this tradition remains hidden does not escape Green: "The reason few know about Southern women's bawdy lore is that most scholars of pornography, obscenity and bawdy are male" (30), to whom it has seldom occurred to collect such material from women. "Few husbands, brothers or fathers would have sent male collectors to a female relative if the agenda was dirt. So, the dirt stays in the kitchen where men and women prefer to keep it" (30). Green further echoes Apte's findings when she notes that many of these storytellers are older women:

> I have to confess that many of the women who tell vile tales are gloriously and affirmatively old! They transcend the boundaries—not only by their station and employment—but by aging beyond the strictures that censure would lay on the young. (30)

Green notes that the butt of most of the stories and jokes she heard as a child was men—especially male pride and dominance—and she suggests that women use humor as a means of expressing to each other opinions that would not be acceptable in mixed company: "The very telling defies the rules. . . . They speak ill of all that is sacred—men, the church, marriage, home, family, parents" (33). In this sense, the humor serves as a form of warning and protest:

> The tales and sayings tell young women what they can expect in private out of the men and institutions they are taught to praise in public, and they inform them as they could never be informed in "serious" conversation. Poking fun at a man's sexual ego, for example, might never be possible in real social situations with the men who have power over their lives, but it is possible in a joke. (33)

Finally, Green points to the location of these groups of storytelling women in places traditionally associated with women's activities: "a kitchen, a porch, a parlor" (33). Today, of course, such traditional locations for women to gather in groups have been joined by—and for some women supplanted by—the office, the aerobics class, the day-care center.

That women's *bawdy* humor, in particular, is meant to stay "in the kitchen" is strikingly illuminated by Rolande Diot's recent article on Erica Jong in the *Revue Française D' Études Americaines*. Diot compares Jong to Henry Miller and addresses the issue of whether a woman can joke about sex without destroying it—and, hence, endangering the essential relationship between women and men. Is Jong's Isadora Wing a "contemporary witch/bitch"? Or is she "the modern form [of] the hysterical nymphomaniac, super-woman of the best-selling type?"[41] Diot's concern in this discussion is with the *response* to women's bawdy humor—specifically, the response of men. If, as Diot says (quoting from Miller's *The Tropic of Capricorn* to illustrate), "laughter is incompatible with erotic performances," then the woman who makes comedy of sex may commit a destructive rather than a celebratory act:

> When a woman is gifted with a sense of humor and adds to it the
> creative talent of the satirist and humorist, like Jong, and when she is
> sufficiently liberated to pratice [sic] self-debunking and
> self-disparaging humor, even sick humor; when she is bold enough
> to make fun of everything including death[,] sex, motherhood and
> the Virgin Mary, sickness and impotence—what next? What responses
> does she get from 1) her female audience 2) her male audience 3)
> her androgynous and/or homosexual audience[?]. (493)

Men may respond in two ways, according to Diot: they may be threatened or angered by humor about male sexuality, and Isadora's self-deprecation may confirm stereotypes of women as "neurotic, helpless, and schizophrenic": "it is always risky for minorities, whether they be ethnic, sexual or other, to practice this kind of self-disparaging humor" (497). But the greatest risk the female bawdy humorist takes is to usurp male dominance in sexuality and thus render herself unfit as a sexual object:

> Female humor will no longer exist as such after [Jong] if women
> exercise their power as human beings and as producers of comedy.
> They will regain power through creation and recreation, but, alack
> poor Miller!—once they have gotten rid of procreation; which means
> simply the end of the human species: if humor is at this cost, who
> said it was a problem? (499)

Another way in which women's humor resembles that of ethnic minorities is in its language, which assumes shared experience between writer and reader, speaker and listener. In several different but closely related ways, the language of women's humor reinforces the sense of separation from the dominant culture. One, which is derived from the group storytelling reported by anthropologists and sociologists, is the "just-between-us-girls" tone: the author or character speaks as if in confidence to those who will understand because of a shared cultural heritage. Frequently, the physical setting reinforces this sense of confidential sharing: Frances Whitcher's characters gossip at meetings of the all-female sewing society; Holley's Samantha Allen argues with Betsey Bobbett in her kitchen; and Anne Warner's Susan Clegg has daily conversations with her neighbor Mrs. Lathrop over the back fence.

One verbal device that appears frequently in women's humor is the phrase that links all wives, or all mothers, or indeed all women together, assuming and emphasizing common knowledge or experience. Characteristic is the opening of one of the essays in Mary Kuczkir's *My Dishtowel Flies at Half-Mast* (1980): "Like any other mother, I sometimes find it hard to understand my kids."[42] Not only do all "mothers" have commonalities, but they are distinct from "fathers," as in the following passage:

> Every mother knows that, with kids, you sometimes have to take a stand on certain issues. If you don't, kid power wins out.
> Fathers are something else. They always give up their turn by saying something like, "Go ask your mother. She knows about things like that." (130)

Similarly, Jean Kerr, in *Penny Candy*, speaks of "the ordinary man, the average husband," suggesting that this is a figure well known to her readers.[43] Such language both perpetuates traditional male-female stereotypes and, paradoxically, universalizes the woman's experience, giving it the weight of established cultural understanding.

A variation on this device is the direct address to the reader. Rather than conducting a conversation with another character, as is the case with Susan Clegg and Mrs. Lathrop or Childress's Mildred and Marge, the author includes the reader as part of the group. One of the earliest examples of this technique is in Anne Bradstreet's "Prologue," in which Bradstreet addresses those who would say her "hand a needle better fits," but also addresses those — presumably women — whose sympathy she can assume to have:

> A poet's pen all scorn I should thus wrong,
> For such despite they cast on female wits.

> If what I do prove well, it won't advance;
> They'll say it's stol'n, or else it was by chance.[44]

The "they" in this passage refers to those who deny female intelligence; the implied "you" is the sympathetic reader. By the early nineteenth century, the "you" is no longer implied. In Whitcher's *Widow Bedott Papers*, "Silly" Bedott talks directly to the reader as she attempts to establish her love for her late husband with poetry written in his memory:

> Want to hear it? Well, I'll see if I can say it ... Dident know I ever writ poetry? how you talk! used to make lots on't; haint so much in late years.[45]

The widow rambles on, as is her habit, gossiping to the reader and invoking the confidentiality of the presumed exchange "between us tew [two]": "I'll tell you why if you won't mention it, for I make a pint never to say nothin' to injure nobody" (29).

The use of the direct address to the reader has persisted into the twentieth century. Peg Bracken opens *The I Hate to Cook Book* by making clear who her intended readers are:

> This book is for those of us who hate to [cook], who have learned, through hard experience, that some activities become no less painful through repetition: childbearing, paying taxes, cooking. This book is for those of us who want to fold our big dishwater hands around a dry Martini instead of a wet flounder, come the end of a long day.[46]

Bracken thus establishes a relationship with her readers by identifying their characteristics and sets up an intimacy that justifies the chatty, confidential tone of what follows. The creation of a community of women through linguistic strategy has long been a feature of feminist humor. In the early twentieth century, for example, Alice Duer Miller titled one of her prosuffrage poems "Why We Oppose Votes for Men" — "we" clearly referring to women and establishing a sense of political solidarity. The humor of the current women's movement frequently uses this technique as well. Joan D. Uebelhoer's "We Need a Name for Bernadette Arnold," for instance, deals with women who undermine the feminist cause because of their own ignorance or fear. Subtitled "a coffeehouse monologue with audience participation," Uebelhoer's piece includes song stanzas to be sung at certain cues in the text, and is designed to bolster feminist resolve. Using both "you" and "we," Uebelhoer acknowledges the self-doubt that affects those who fight for a cause:

> Sometimes, you think you need a name for you. Because you don't like the unsisterish feelings you have. Sometimes you worry about your own feminism. Sometimes it's hard to remember we have a common enemy.[47]

One frequent use of the direct address to the reader is to give advice to readers on how to deal with the "common enemy" to which Uebelhoer refers. From the work of the mid-nineteenth century Fanny Fern to that of Deanne Stillman in the 1980's, female humorists have issued tongue-in-cheek advice to readers—most commonly on how to deal with men. Fern's "Aunt Hetty" advises young girls against matrimony, claiming that "husbands are domestic Napoleons, Neroes, Alexanders,—sighing for other hearts to conquer, after they are sure of yours."[48] Strikingly similar advice is offered in Dorothy Parker's poetry. In "To a Much Too Unfortunate Lady," for example, Parker warns of man's inconstancy. Although "he will love you presently," the lady is cautioned that this will not last:

> He will leave you white with woe,
> If you go the way you go.
> If your dreams were thread to weave
> He will pluck them from his sleeve.
> If your heart had come to rest,
> He will flick it from his breast.[49]

A similar message is conveyed in Parker's "Social Note":

> Lady, lady, should you meet
> One whose ways are all discreet,
> One who murmurs that his wife
> Is the lodestar of his life,
> One who keeps assuring you
> That he never was untrue,
> Never loved another one . . .
> Lady, lady, better run! (104)

The speaker in Parker's poems, like Fanny Fern's Aunt Hetty, speaks with the authority of common experience and assumes that other women are similarly vulnerable.

Some female humorists have employed traditional literary forms as vehicles for their advice. Josephine Daskam's *Fables for the Fair*

(1901) follow the conventional fable form with a moral at the end to provide "cautionary tales" of women who overstep the boundaries established by the culture. In "The Woman Who Had Broad Views," a woman loses "a Man who was Interested in Her" when she advocates equal sexual behavior between the sexes; and in "The Woman Who Caught the Idea," a man finds threatening a woman who abandons the "clinging vine" role and learns to "March Abreast" of him.[50] Daskam's *Fables* teach by example. These tales show women making the wrong moves in relationships with men and present the men as dominant, having the final word on what constitutes "proper behavior" for women. In the turn-of-the-century era of the "New Woman," as women tentatively explored new options for their conduct, Daskam's fables convey the sense that even when the rules change, men still make the final decisions. A few years later, Helen Rowland's *The Sayings of Mrs. Solomon* employs a mock-Biblical style to convey much the same message. The wise "Mrs. Solomon" offers advice and warnings to women, explaining how men think, react, and behave. Rowland opens the book by establishing both its purpose and an unflattering view of men:

> Hearken, my Daughter, and give ear unto my wisdom, that thou mayest understand *man* — his goings and his comings, his stayings out and his return in the morning, his words of honey and his ways of guile.[51]

By picturing men as inherently unreliable, Rowland anticipates a common theme in Parker's work, and she echoes Daskam in her depiction of the "New Woman" who was apt to alienate men with her efforts at independence and sophistication. The following excerpt is typical of Mrs. Solomon's advice, and it also embodies a reiteration of cultural restrictions on women's sense of humor:

> Oh, ye damsels of Babylon! Ye followers after fads and wearers of pearl earrings! How long will ye seek to appear *sophisticated*? How long will ye continue to pose as *cynics*, and think it chic to be satirical and piquant to be capricious?
>   Know ye not, oh foolish ones, that a man dreadeth a female cynic as a small boy dreadeth an education? (61)

By the middle of the twentieth century, women's humorous advice to other women had become far more subtle. The *persona* in the domestic humor that dominated the period after World War II merely offers her own example of failure as a muted form of cautionary tale. In recent years, more direct advice literature has reappeared, but with a method quite different from that of Daskam, Rowland, or Parker. Instead of assuming a status quo in which women must learn to maneuver in a culture with fixed rules that they violate at their peril, this new feminist advice literature mocks the rules themselves. The advice offered is sometimes deliberately outrageous, mocking the advice tradition itself—not merely humorous advice, but the popular newspaper advice column as well, from Dorothy Dix in the 1890s to today's Ann Landers. One example is the recent bestseller *Miss Manners' Guide to Excruciatingly Correct Behavior*. Judith Martin's book is an index to changing cultural mores and is not addressed exclusively to women, though a feminist consciousness underlies many of her responses, as exemplified by:

Dear Miss Manners:
     As a businessman, how do I allow a businesswoman to pay
     for my lunch?
Gentle Reader:
     With credit card or cash, as she prefers.[52]

Martin's crisp, no-nonsense answer makes apparent the sexism inherent in the question.

Deanne Stillman and Veronica Geng provide more outrageous advice, directly to women, that conveys a shared sense of the absurdity of women's subordination. Stillman parodies the advice regarding women's appearance that has permeated the American women's magazine ever since *Godey's Lady's Book* appeared in the 1830s. In "Ann Van Brothers Talks to Teens About Your Hair, Your Figure, Your Diet, Your Sweat, and Your Face," Stillman, with tongue in cheek, advises young women to wear girdles (even if they end up looking like a "human cannoli") and padded bras, match their hairstyles carefully to the shapes of their faces, and spray themselves with Lemon Pledge before dates (because it "smells so refreshing"). Stillman's section on "Filth," which advises women to take several showers a day, recalls Nora Ephron's essay on feminine hygiene deodorant products in *Crazy Salad*, in that both challenge the cultural myth that women are essentially "unclean." "The rule," Stillman says ironically, is, "Treat your body like a sink full of dirty dishes, because it can easily become one. That's what my mother used to tell me, and boy, am I ever grateful."[53] Veronica Geng directs her advice to the aspiring businesswoman, who "need no longer turn furtively to the so-called execu-cosmetology schools, which dispense little more than a bow tie and a fountain pen." While the satire on the complex codes by which men in business communicate with each other—such as the "breast-pocket-handkerchief semaphore"—is light-hearted, Geng's description of various sorts of mentors with whom women might affiliate themselves is a scathing look at men's resistance to female colleagues. The mentors who are supposed to show women the "rope" (as opposed to the "ropes," presumably so they can hang themselves) alternately laugh at their clothing, are rude to them, and ignore their ideas.[54]

Women's humorous advice literature, whether it attacks male dominance or merely cautions women about dealing with it, underscores the "we-they" dichotomy that is common in women's humor generally and also characterizes the humor of minority groups. In their use of language and the creation of stereotypes, America's female humorists convey their status as members of a group having a common relationship to another group—the division between them based on gender rather than on ethnic background. Just as male humorists speak of "women," implying that all women are alike, so women speak of "men" in the same way. Each gender emphasizes the "otherness" of the other. In *Language and Woman's Place*, Robin Lakoff points out that whereas male comedians have recently become conscious of avoiding humor that insults members of minority groups, they still feel free to single out women:

> A comedian may be very sensitive to ethnic slurs, never be caught
> dead telling Polish jokes, anti-Semitic jokes, or any of the other
> no-no's, but he will include lots of antiwomen (these days,
> anti-"women's lib") jokes in his repertoire. No one (with the
> exception of a few of those chronic female malcontents who
> obviously have no sense of humor) will be offended, and generally
> the women in the audience will laugh as loud as the men.[55]

Lakoff finds no "parallel joke types based on stereotypes of men in general" (81), but as Rayna Green and Mahadev Apte, among others, have pointed out, the sort of women's humor that stereotypes men is part of the hidden tradition.

Humorous stereotypes of men have in fact existed for a long time in women's humor, and these stereotypes are directly related to women's subordinate position in society. Men are seen as proud, boastful, messy, boisterous, and untrustworthy—all characteristics of a ruling majority that takes itself and its role very seriously—and the use of these stereotypes in women's humor seeks to undermine man's position of dominance. It is just these characteristics, for example, that make men unfit to vote, according to Alice Duer Miller in 1915. In her parody "Why We Oppose Votes for Men," Miller points out that men are too prone to violence and emotional behavior to be trusted with the vote:

> No really manly man wants to settle any question otherwise than by fighting about it. . . . Men are too emotional to vote. Their conduct at baseball games and political conventions shows this.[56]

A few years earlier, Helen Rowland, as "Mrs. Solomon," proposed that whereas women were infinitely various, men were all alike:

> Have I not known *one* man well? And verily, a woman need know but one man, in order to understand *all* men; whereas a man may know all women and understand not one of them. For men are of but one pattern whereof thou needest but to discover the secret combination; but women are as the *Yale lock*—no two of them are alike. (11)

Rowland, like Parker, emphasizes man's faithlessness and unreliability in *The Sayings of Mrs. Solomon*; these are proposed as generic characteristics, applicable to all men.

In the 1920s, after women were granted the vote and during a period in which it seemed, as it does today, that role reversals and dual-career marriages were to become the norm, Florence Guy Seabury found traditional stereotypes blurring. In the old days, she says, "we knew what men were, and we knew what women were."[57] But in the 1920s, "nothing was as it used to be in the days when one sex went to work and the other stayed at home, and life was neatly divided into two half spheres—one of which was exclusively masculine and the other feminine" (9). Seabury's vision of dramatic social change that would eradicate gender stereotypes did not come to pass in the 1920s, of course, nor has it yet. The Depression and the mid-century suburban migration had the effect of making rigid again the different roles and positions of male and female, and the traditional stereotyping persisted: female humorists viewed the "other" as domineering, remote from household concerns, and at least potentially untrustworthy because of his sense of self-importance.

Yet just as women may be viewed stereotypically in paradoxical ways—as virgin and virago, gossip and gold-digger—so there runs through women's humor a thread that is both the obverse and the inevitable result of male dominance: a condescending attitude toward men that grows out of the underdog's secret feeling of superiority. Hints of this negative stereotyping of men may be seen in the satirical portrait of Hyacinth in Fanny Fern's 1855 novel *Ruth Hall* and in Marietta Holley's conception of Josiah Allen, but these male figures are instances of particular *types* rather than representatives of the entire gender: Hyacinth is a hypocritical fop, and Josiah is a well-meaning but hopelessly traditional husband. By the early twentieth century, however, condescending sterotypes of men *as males* appear frequently. Helen Rowland's *Reflections of a Bachelor Girl* (1909), for example, includes the following "truths" about men:

> It's so hard to reform a man when he hasn't any great fault but just a little of all of them. Husbands are like Christmas gifts: you can't choose them; you've just got to sit down and wait until they arrive and then appear perfectly delighted with what you get.[58]

In 1960, Jean Kerr adopts the same tone of amused condescension in "The Ten Worst Things About a Man":

> But, charming as men are, we can't sit here and pretend they're perfect. It wouldn't be good for them, and it wouldn't be true. Marrying a man is like buying something you've been admiring for a long time in a shop window. You may love it when you get it home, but it doesn't always go with everything else in the house.[59]

The concept of the man as object extends and reinforces the sense of man as "other," and like the minority-group joke that points out the deficiencies of members of the majority, it conveys a sense of superiority to the dominant group.

A shared sense of subordination, then, emerges from the humor of American women, and demonstrates the extent to which women's experience in American culture has been the experience of a minority group. The humor employs the same subversive strategies as does the humor of racial and ethnic minorities, camouflaging with laughter the pain of the outsider who is denied access to power and must live by someone else's rules. Yet the situation of women is more complex because of their close involvement with members of the dominant group, which has blurred the boundaries between "us" and "them." In addition, the general cultural sanctioning of women's subordinate status and the attempts to deny women's sense of humor have effectively prevented a solidarity of experience and purpose, necessitating a chorus of individual voices instead of a single rallying cry.

5

Feminist Humor

"Burning dinner is not incompetence but war."
—Marge Piercy, *"What's That Smell in the Kitchen?"*

I

The traditional identification of women with piety and righteousness, rather than with relaxation and fun, has its apotheosis in the stereotypical figure of the female political activist. The temperance crusader taking an ax to a whiskey barrel, the thin-lipped women's-rights speaker of the nineteenth century, and the bra-burners of the 1960s have all been made objects of ridicule, and not only by men. Marietta Holley's feminist narrator Samantha Allen, in the late nineteenth century, chose the feminist leaders she admired on the basis of their use of what she defined as common sense. Elizabeth Cady Stanton, of whom she approved, Samantha describes as admirably strong:

> The beholder could see by the first glance onto that face, that she hadn't spent all the immortal energies of her soul in makin' clover leaf tattin', or in cuttin' calico up into little pieces, jest to sew 'em togather agin into blazin' stars and sunflower bedquilts. It was the face of an earnest noble woman, who had asked God what He wanted her to do, and then hadn't shirked out of doin' it. Who had gripped holt of life's plough, and hadn't looked back because the furrows turned over pretty hard, and the stumps was thick.[1]

But when Samantha encounters a women's-rights advocate who is "one of the wild eyed ones, that don't use no reason," she draws a verbal caricature of the woman:

> Of all the painted, and frizzled, and ruffled, and humped up, and

laced down critters I ever see, she was the cap sheaf. She had a
hump on her back bigger than any camel's I ever see to a managery,
and no three wimmen ever grew the hair that critter had piled on to
her head. (337)

Samantha's objection to this female activist derives from the woman's
lack of restraint and dignity. Corseted and bewigged, she seems to
Samantha to subvert the very cause she works for: "No wonder men
don't think that we know enough to vote when they see the way
some wimmen rig themselves out" (341).

Most of the negative reaction to outspoken feminists, however, has
come not from a sense that women should be "meegum," to use
Samantha's term, in their bid for equal rights, but from a sense that
outspoken women somehow violate the delicacy and passivity of
their "natural" selves and step out of their "proper" roles. Henry
James's portraits of Olive Chancellor and Miss Birdseye in *The Bostonians* (1886) typify the late-nineteenth-century image of the women's-rights advocate: a woman who devotes herself to a cause
rather than to a man, and in doing so loses her femininity. James's
Miss Birdseye "had been consumed by the passion of sympathy; it
had crumpled her into as many creases as an old glazed, distended
glove. She had been laughed at, but she never knew it; she was
treated as a bore, but she never cared.[2] And Olive Chancellor "was a
spinster as Shelley was a lyric poet, or as the month of August is
sultry" (14). Not only did the active feminist attack the status quo; she
also traveled, spoke in public, and engaged in other unladylike
behavior. She therefore threatened male hegemony in ways that
went beyond her political views. Marietta Holley's image of Stanton's
having "gripped holt of life's plough" is appropriately masculine.

In addition to violating culturally sanctioned standards for female
behavior, the popular image of the outspoken feminist also lacks a
sense of humor. As James says of Olive Chancellor, "she never once
laughed. Later, [Ransom] saw that she was a woman without laughter;
exhilaration, if it ever visited her, was dumb" (15). Far more recently,
in an anti-feminist book that attempts to defend the role of the housewife in contemporary American culture, Terry Hekker notes that she
once thought it was odd that the only women who wrote about
homemaking and child-raising—Jean Kerr, Erma Bombeck, Judith
Viorst—did so with humor:

Eventually it dawned on me that it wasn't odd at all—it made perfect sense, because the only women who can take motherhood in their stride are those with a well-developed sense of humor. Which may explain another phenomenon, since I've never yet read or heard anything that would make me suspect that women's libbers have a funny bone. It's no wonder they had to get away from the house and kids.[3]

On the surface, this may seem logical: those who are feeling righteous seldom laugh, and those who are angry may have better weapons than humor to use in the fight. Yet when feminists are portrayed as, or accused of, lacking a sense of humor, the cause is more complex and subtle than this, and is related to the tradition that the man tells the jokes and the woman laughs at them. This tradition is so strong that it has frequently been incorporated into women's humorous writing. For example, in her poem "This One's About Two Irishmen, or, Oliver Ames is a Raconteur," Phyllis McGinley writes:

> When meekly to Judgment I come,
>   When marital virtues are passed on,
> For comfort I'll cling to a crumb,
>   One noble attainment stand fast on.
> Though manifold duties remiss in,
>   Addicted to phoning my folks,
> I think that They'll have to put *this* in:
>   *I giggled at Oliver's jokes.*[4]

Not having to do this, on the other hand, is for Judith Viorst a sign of a secure relationship:

> Have you noticed that when you deeply love a man and he deeply loves you, and you feel completely secure in each other's love, you don't have to laugh at his jokes unless they're funny?[5]

In "Why We're Not Laughing ... Anymore," psychologist Naomi Weisstein speaks of the irony inherent in the accusation that those involved in the women's movement in the early 1970s had no sense of humor:

> When I collided with puberty in the fifties ... , the first thing I figured out was that, if I were to acquire *personality*—the key to *popularity, dates, a steady boyfriend* ...—I'd better start smiling. Laugh as much as possible, and when you can't manage a laugh, do smile. So I laughed maniacally through high school, college, graduate

school, and smiled warmly when all those chairmen of all those
psychology departments explained that women were not suited for
academic careers.

And now they tell me I have no sense of humor.[6]

What this means, Weisstein continues, is " 'You women can no longer
take a joke.' Whatsamatter, baby, don't you smile?" (51). Weisstein's
point is that freeing oneself from the conditioning of a sexist culture
involves refusing to participate in sexist humor—humor that turns
upon unflattering stereotypes of women, as so much of American
humor does.

The point is not, Weisstein argues further, that people do not commonly laugh at their own pain. There is a rich tradition, as I discussed
in the previous chapter, of the humor of oppressed groups, including women. The difference, Weisstein says, is that "if they are really
to find it funny, *they* have to have made the joke" (88). Thus, she suggests, the first step toward the creation of truly feminist humor is for
women to stop laughing at what no longer seems funny to them. Yet
to the extent that women have done just that—have stopped smiling
merely to appear charming, have stopped laughing when the joke is
on them—they have been accused of having no sense of humor.[7]
The reason feminists resent this accusation so deeply, as Weisstein
suggests, is that it hits at the heart of women's acculturated behavior:

"[H]aving a sense of humor" in the way defined for women (that is,
laughing only at those things which we are expected to laugh at) is
part of maintaining our charm. Since our charm is so tied up with
our survival, it may become a frightening accusation when people
tell us we've lost our sense of humor—it's as good as telling us
we're ugly. (89)

The sense of humor thus catches women in a double bind: while
they are not supposed to be creators of humor, inasmuch as this role
would ascribe to them power and intellectual qualities denied them
by the majority culture, they are supposed to applaud the humor of
that majority culture and, above all, not take themselves too seriously.

Not all women's humor, of course, has been feminist humor,
although much more of it has a feminist consciousness or stance than
has been acknowledged. Weisstein comes close to a definition of

feminist humor when she points out that there is inherent in women's situation an absurdity that they should use for their own purposes:

> It is quite a feat to turn what is defined as a ridiculous state of being into your own definition of the ridiculous, to take control of the *quality* of the absurdity, to turn it away from yourself. We must at the same time show that ... nobody is either WOMAN or "lady," and that all this is very funny indeed. (89-90)

Feminist humor, this suggests, would turn upon and make plain the very absurdity of the culture's views and expectations of women, and by so doing would make clear that it is not women who are ridiculous (in the sense of being easy targets for ridicule), but the culture that has subjugated them.

Perhaps the most comprehensive attempt to define feminist humor is found in Gloria Kaufman's introduction to *Pulling Our Own Strings: Feminist Humor and Satire* (1980). Distinguishing between "female" humor and "feminist" humor, Kaufman echoes Weisstein in her emphasis on the social system:

> The persistent attitude that underlies feminist humor is the attitude of social revolution—that is, we are ridiculing a social system that can be, that must be changed. *Female* humor may ridicule a person or a system from an accepting point of view ("that's life"), while the *nonacceptance* of oppression characterizes feminist humor and satire.[8]

Thus, Kaufman argues, female humor is commonly more bitter than is feminist humor, which, in its rejection of oppression, is a "humor of hope" (13). Instead of bowing to circumstances, the feminist humorist assumes that the circumstances are wrong and refuses to be bound by them.

Kaufman further states that feminist humor does not create stereotypes of men analogous to the stereotypes of women in male humor:

> Since it arises from a subculture that has no patience with stereotyping, especially in relation to sex roles, we should not be surprised at the tendency of feminist humor to avoid stereotypic characters. (14)

"Actions," she continues, "do become stereotyped in feminist humor" (14), but women have not, for example, created a father-in-law stereotype to balance or counteract the mother-in-law stereotype. The stereotype of the Male Chauvinist Pig, which was in vogue during the 1960s and the early 1970s was, Kaufman argues, more a journalistic creation than a feminist creation. Yet men expect and fear negative male stereotypes in feminist humor:

> An unwarranted expectation of stereotypes accounts, I believe, for the nervous response of many men to the term "feminist humor." They have assimilated the misogyny of male humor, and with some guilt they expect that feminist humor will return their treatment in kind. (14)

Such a response, indeed, seems to inform Harvey Mindess in the chapter "Laughter and Women's Lib" in his book *Laughter and Liberation* (1971). After speculating (to no particular conclusion) on the differences between male and female capacities for and appreciation of humor, Mindess proposes that each gender is equally at the mercy of the other and that the resulting insecurity leads to barbed wit on both sides: "Men who feel a need to ridicule the women's liberation movement may pretend to be detached, but their very compulsion to make wisecracks about it reveals the threat it poses to their security."[9] Yet Mindess chides feminists far more strongly for their part in this exchange:

> Far more than a rational attempt to insist on equality in social opportunity, [the women's liberation movement] represents, for those involved, a holy cause—a crusade designed to subdue the devils they distrust and despise. The strident quality of their proclamations expresses the intensity of their emotions. This intensity is reflected, too, in their reluctance to laugh at themselves and their mission. Proponents of women's lib often use scornful wit as a rhetorical device in their diatribes against the chauvinistic male, but good-natured humor about our common inability to appreciate and accept each other is at a minimum in their publications. (198)

Mindess here not only reveals his discomfort with feminist humor; he also redefines the women's movement, limiting it to a search for "equality in social opportunity," and says, in essence, "Why don't you women have a sense of humor?" Further, the terminology that Mindess uses—"holy cause," "crusade," "devils," "mission"—recalls the

traditional role of women as the guardians of morality: a role acceptable, apparently, unless women are fighting against, rather than for,
the status quo.

Feminist humor does not laugh at the mission itself, for to do so
would trivialize it. Instead, it laughs at the very idea of gender inequality in an attempt to render such inequality absurd and powerless.
Gloria Kaufman's definition of feminist humor as that which expresses the "nonacceptance of oppression" is adequate to describe
one type of feminist humor: that which has an overt political message. Eve Merriam's "Feminist Alphabet" provides good examples of
this kind of humor:

> D differences: as "Viva la"; more often, as in yearly average earnings
> of male and female workers.
> L lady: ludicrous label, as in lady doctor, lady governor, gentleman
> truckdriver.[10]

Just as clearly political in nature are Ellen Goodman's annual awards
for the most sexist public behavior of the year:

> The Profiles in Courage badge, once again by popular outcry, is
> awarded to a Florida state senator. The Man of the Hour is Guy
> Spicola, who ran, with ERA funds, on a pro-ERA platform only to vote
> against it. This profile is a silhouette of a chicken.[11]

Humor of this sort, though not new, has proliferated in recent years
as a result of the greater sense of group solidarity that feminists have
felt because of the women's movement.

Yet there is a more subtle sort of feminist humor that may be said
to precede the kind that Kaufman and Blakely collect in *Pulling Our
Own Strings*. In much of the humor that Kaufman says "may ridicule
a person or system from an accepting point of view," and is thus in
her terms "female" rather than feminist humor, the author or
speaker is not merely "accepting" the status quo, but is in fact calling
attention to gender inequality in ways designed to lead to its ultimate
rejection. When Shirley Jackson's narrator fails in her attempt to have
a hospital receptionist record her occupation as "writer" rather than
"housewife," she is pointing out the obduracy of bureaucratic systems in their trivialization of women. When Betty MacDonald's narrator complains about her husband's insistence that she mop the

kitchen floor daily, she reveals the tyranny of a system that makes women economically dependent on men. Marge Piercy's poem "What's That Smell in the Kitchen?" both illustrates and partially defines this kind of humor. Piercy uses the metaphor of women burning what they are cooking to stand for the anger women feel about their subordinate status and the steps they feel they can take to express that anger. The poem ends with the following lines:

> If she wants to serve him anything
> it's a dead rat with a bomb in its belly
> ticking like the heart of an insomniac.
> Her life is cooked and digested,
> Nothing but leftovers in Tupperware.
> Look, she says, once I was roast duck
> on your platter with parsley but now I am Spam.
> Burning dinner is not incompetence but war.[12]

The last line of Piercy's poem announces the subversive ways in which women have protested their condition, just as many female humorists have displayed a feminist consciousness that approaches the problem indirectly.

II

The subversive and the overt forms of feminist humor may be roughly compared to the two types of political activism that came together to form the women's movement of the 1960s, even though the two kinds of women's humor predated that movement by a century. As Jane De Hart Mathews points out in *Women's America*, two distinct groups of women with quite different political agendas ultimately joined forces to create the new feminist movement. The women's-rights advocates believed in working within the established political system to effect change: "Reform oriented, [this group] used traditional pressure group tactics to achieve changes in laws and public policy that would guarantee women equal rights." The second, somewhat younger group of women, the women's liberationists, "sought liberation from ways of thinking and behaving that they believed stunted or distorted women's growth and kept them subordinate to men." Neither group assented to the status quo, but the first accepted the existence of political and social structures, and was prepared to use them to achieve greater legal equality, whereas the second group proposed a radical transformation that was more personal and individual in its orientation. Yet what united the two groups, Mathews says, was a recognition that "the first step toward becoming feminists demanded a clear statement of women's position in society, one that called attention to the gap between the egalitarian ideal and the actual position of women in American culture."[13]

Just as these two groups of feminists have co-existed, so the two types of women's humor that may be considered feminist have co-existed in American culture for well over a century. One, operating subversively within the cultural system of subjugation, acknowledges women's subordination while protesting it in subtle and not-so-subtle ways, thus performing the necessary step of calling attention to "the actual position of women in American culture"; the other explores the fundamental absurdity of that system and calls for different ways of conceptualizing gender definition. The mid-nineteenth-century humorist Frances Whitcher, for example, would probably not have considered herself a feminist—at least, there is no evidence that she did so—and yet in portraying the husband-hunting Widow Bedott, Whitcher presents and laments the fact that the unmarried woman, whether widow or spinster, lacked social standing in a culture that viewed women only in terms of their relationships with men. Betsey Bobbet, the title character in Marietta Holley's first book, finally ends her spinsterhood with a marriage that makes her virtually a servant, but despite her desperate situation, she tells Samantha Allen, "I feel real dignified. . . . There isn't no use in a woman trying to be dignified till she is married, for she can't. I have tried it and I know" (414-15). Even in works of domestic humor such as MacDonald's *The Egg and I* and Peg Bracken's *I Didn't Come Here to Argue* (1970), the authors pose the realities of women's lives in such a way as to reveal the deep sense of frustration inherent in them. Bracken, for example, reports that she grew very tired of the way housewives were being "chucked under the chin" by the media in an effort to make them feel like "experts": "skilled business manager, . . . child psychologist, home decorator. . . . " Bracken's rebuttal exposes the actuality behind the media image:

We housewives are jugglers who, trying to keep a dozen nice big fresh eggs in the air, spend most of our time skidding in the shells. Once in a blue moon, for the fast wink of an eye, all the eggs stay up.... But for the most part, we just mouse along, putting one tennis shoe in front of the other, which is generally in the flypaper, bending over to pick up the floor mop and dropping the baby.[14]

Through the slapstick exaggeration comes the clear sense of a need for change in women's lives as well as in the way they are perceived.

The function of this type of humor is analogous to the function of the women's consciousness-raising groups that flourished in the 1960s and 1970s as women attempted to emerge from their isolation and understand their common experiences as women. As a stage in the women's movement, such groups served two functions, according to Hester Eisenstein, and one of these was to "connect the personal with the political":

Once shared in a small group with other women, individual pain and suffering appeared in a different light. It could be seen that these were not personal, idiosyncratic problems, but ones which fell into a pattern that, with variations, characterized other women's lives as well.[15]

The second function was to give validity and authority to women's experience and perceptions:

A first assumption of consciousness-raising groups was that what women had to say about the details of their daily lives, about their personal experiences and histories, mattered, it had significance, and above all it had validity.... [Further, personal failures] were not isolated phenomena, illustrating the individual failure of an individual woman within her own family to direct her own life correctly. (37)

The personal failures and chaos reported in women's humor of the 1950s and 1960s are, similarly, not merely "the individual failure of an individual woman," but rather the "symptoms of a society-wide structure of power and powerlessness" (Eisenstein, 37) that women in great numbers were beginning to realize.

The more overt feminist humor speaks directly to such issues as economic dependency, lack of political power, and open discrimination. Instead of merely *recording* women's problems with life in a sexist culture, this humor challenges the assumptions that underlie that culture and reveals their fundamental absurdity. For this reason, the humor frequently takes the form of satire or parody, both of which work to revise social realities rather than simply establishing their existence. In the late-nineteenth and early-twentieth centuries, for example, when female suffrage was the central issue for feminists, feminist humorists were fond of turning the arguments against women voting around on men. In one of the pieces in her 1872 book *Caper-Sauce*, Fanny Fern notes that women are accused of not being sufficiently "moderate"—in fashion, in managing household budgets, in hairstyles—to be capable of voting, "but," she says, "it is a poor rule that won't work both ways":

> Let him smoke "moderately." Let him drink "moderately." Let him drive "moderately." Let him stock-gamble "moderately." Let him stay out at night "moderately." . . . If "moderation" in smoking were the test of fitness for the ballot-box, how many men do you think would be able to vote?[16]

In 1915, responding to the anti-suffrage argument that polling places pose physical dangers to women, Alice Duer Miller uses the same method as does Fanny Fern, and turns the same argument back on men. Her poem "A Consistent Anti to Her Son" ends with the following lines:

> I've guarded you always, Willie,
>   Body and soul from harm;
> I'll guard your faith and honor,
>   Your innocence and charm
> From the polls and their evil spirits,
>   Politics, rum and pelf;
> Do you think I'd send my only son
>   Where I would not go myself?[17]

More recent feminist humor often uses the same methods, as the selections in *Pulling Our Own Strings* demonstrate, but it also deals with a far wider range of issues, including reproductive freedom, parenting, and discrimination in the workplace—in short, the myriad issues with which contemporary feminists are concerned. The tone of this humor is frequently angry, sometimes jubilant—the latter representing the "humor of hope" of which Gloria Kaufman speaks. The anger in overtly feminist humor is directed, not surprisingly, at men and male-created institutions, as in Flo Kennedy's comment that "any woman who still thinks marriage is a fifty-fifty proposition is only proving that she doesn't understand either men or percentages" (126). The message of such humor is that nothing has essentially changed for women. More upbeat humor, which shows women's pride in being women, is less common, and tends to be revisionist. Eve Merriam's "A Feminist Alphabet" is an example of this latter type: "J," for example, stands for "Juliet: principal character in the Shakespearian tragedy, 'Juliet and Romeo,' " and "K" for "king: most powerful court person, sometimes known familiarly as a billiejean" (174).

The distinction between the subtle and overt types of feminist humor may be made more clearly by a consideration of Umberto Eco's distinction between "humor" and "the comic" in his essay "Frames of Comic 'Freedom.' " The "frames" to which Eco refers are sets of rules or expectations for acceptable social behavior within a culture, and the comic (as opposed to the tragic) effect occurs when a frame is broken in a way that the audience (reader, listener) approves. Humor, in Eco's paradigm, is part of the comic, and involves more sympathy than does the purely comic: "In humor we smile because of the contradition between the character and the frame the character cannot comply with. But we are no longer sure that it is the character who is at fault. Maybe the frame is wrong." Further, humor reminds us that, wrong or not, the frame exists:

> Humor does not pretend, like carnival [the comic], to lead us beyond our own limits. It gives us the feeling, or better, the picture of the structure of our own limits. It is never off limits, it undermines limits from inside. It does not fish for an impossible freedom, yet it is a true movement of freedom. Humor does not promise us liberation: on the contrary, it warns us about the impossibility of global liberation, reminding us of the pressure of a law that we no longer have reason to obey. In doing so it undermines the law. It makes us feel the uneasiness of living under a law—any law.[18]

Humor, according to Eco, works "from inside," as the women's-rights advocates in the early stages of the current feminist movement sought to work within the political system to effect women's equality. Yet it "undermines the law" by breaking the "frame" of that law.

The type of humor that Gloria Kaufman terms "female humor" works in just this way. Instead of being nonfeminist, female humor that describes the conditions of women's lives is, in Eco's terms, "a true movement of freedom" because of its implicit questioning of the "law." It is this questioning of the law that Erica Jong's rebellious Isadora Wing addresses in *Parachutes and Kisses* (1984), a sequel to *Fear of Flying*:

> We are born to goodness; it is our birthright. Only sheer grit and pigheaded obstinacy make us demand the right to be bad, for we know that only by being bad can we become ourselves—not daughters and granddaughters, but individuals and possibly artists.[19]

In being "bad"—in breaking the frame—the speakers and characters in women's humor call into question the rules for female "goodness." Mary Kuczkir, in *My Dishtowel Flies at Half-Mast* (1980) reports on a meeting of "Mothers Anonymous," at which women expose their failures at perfect motherhood. One woman reports that she gives her children boiled hot dogs for breakfast even when they want blueberry pancakes. Another woman makes an even more frenzied confession:

> "I want to tell you what I did! I *need* to tell you what I did! Actually, the devil made me do it! The devil and my kids!" We all stamped our feet to spur her on. "I let one of my kids go out the door with one sneaker and one shoe on. I refused to make another Oscar Mayer bologna sandwich. Boil me in oil . . . just make sure it's Crisco!" she yelled as she slid off the stage.[20]

Having broken the rules of perfect motherhood, the women who confess their failures to each other demonstrate the "uneasiness of living under a law."

The more overtly feminist humor is analogous to what Eco speaks of as the purely comic, which involves a perception of the opposite of what is normal or acceptable. The comic is revolutionary; it inverts the rules, as Eve Merriam inverts the names of Romeo and Juliet in Shakespeare's title. In its fundamental overturning of the law or frame, the comic is analogous to a feminism that seeks change in radical ways. Instead of breaking the rules, it imagines a different set of rules. This explains why feminist humor so often involves fantasy, not only in works of speculative fiction such as Charlotte Perkins Gilman's *Herland* and Joanna Russ's *The Female Man*, but also in light verse, sketches, and the routines of stand-up comics. In *The Female Imagination*, Patricia Meyer Spacks points to the close link between the desire for freedom and the need for fantasy—fantasy that frequently leads in women's literature to imaginations of madness.[21]

Gloria Steinem's "If Men Could Menstruate" is in fact subtitled "A Political Fantasy." In this piece Steinem imagines the dramatic change in attitudes toward menstruation that would occur if it were a function of the male rather than the female body. In short, "menstruation would become an enviable, boast-worthy, masculine event":

> Men would brag about how long and how much.
> Boys would mark the onset of menses, that longed-for proof of manhood, with religious ritual and stag parties.
> Congress would fund a National Institute of Dysmenorrhea to help stamp out monthly discomforts.
> Sanitary supplies would be federally funded and free.[22]

Steinem addresses here the issue of power—the fact that "the characteristics of the powerful, whatever they may be, are thought to be better than the characteristics of the powerless" (25). Much earlier, Dorothy Sayers imagined how men would react to being in the powerless position, singled out on the basis of gender for special treatment. In "The Human-Not-Quite-Human," an essay published in 1947, Sayers wonders how a man would like being "relentlessly assessed in terms of his maleness":

> In any book on sociology he would find, after the main portion dealing with human needs and rights, a supplementary chapter devoted to "The Position of the Male in the Perfect State." His newspaper would assist him with a "Men's Corner," telling him how, by the expenditure of a good deal of money and a couple of hours a day, he could attract the girls and retain his wife's affection; and when he had succeeded in capturing a mate, his name would be taken from him, and society would present him with a special title to proclaim his achievement.[23]

Like Steinem, Sayers points to the absurdity of a cultural system based on gender inequality.

Feminist humor, then, both elucidates and challenges women's subordination and oppression. Whether detailing the tedium of a housewife's daily routine or calling for radical changes in legal or personal orientation, it assumes that women are human beings with inherent equality to men in spite of long-standing traditions and beliefs to the contrary. To assume that humor in which a female figure acknowledges injustice but does not act to change it is nonfeminist is to define feminism only in terms of activism, and to ignore the very constraints that have effectively prevented women from acting on their own behalf for most of human history—constraints such as the isolation, economic dependence, and cultural stereotyping against which feminists wage an on-going battle. As Elaine Showalter has said of the decline of feminist activity in the post-suffrage 1920s:

> Radical feminism in the 1920s was an idea whose time had not come, but we cannot blame the women for failing to create a revolution in the absence of its necessary preconditions. Almost every issue of the contemporary women's liberation movement—from job discrimination, to sex-role conditioning, to marriage contracts, to birth control—was raised in the twenties.... What was missing was a sufficiently sizable base of employed married women, experiencing firsthand the role conflict ... and a feminist analysis which could interpret the role conflict and the discrimination as a collective political phenomenon rather than as a personal problem.[24]

The sense of increased collectivity that has given rise to the current feminist movement has historically been absent from American culture. Similarly, because of underrepresentation in anthologies, histories, and critical studies, female humorists have been largely unaware of the tradition of feminist humor in America—both subtle and overt—and therefore have felt the same isolation as the suburban housewife who believes that her inability to achieve the perfection in her role promoted by the media is a problem uniquely her own.

One result of this circumstance is the misconception that feminist humor is a recent phenomenon.[25] For example, Evelyn C. White, in "Stand Up and Laugh: New Feminist Comics," states that "it has only been in the last ten years [1972-1982] that we've been able to use the term 'feminist humor.' "[26] White's specific reference is to female stand-up comics such as Lily Tomlin, Kate Clinton, and Robin Tyler, and her comment is partially justified by the relatively recent entrance of women—especially feminists—into the public arena of stand-up comedy. Yet in the somewhat safer medium of the printed page, feminist humor is by no means new. Both subtle and overt feminist humor have existed in American women's writing for at least 150 years, the former as a consistent thread and the latter emerging during periods of heightened political activity on behalf of women's liberation.

III

It is no wonder that so much of American women's humor has dealt with the domestic arena: an overwhelming majority of American women have traditionally been responsible for the care of a house-hold—a situation that is largely unchanged even when the woman has a job outside the home. In fact, as Susan Strasser points out in *Never Done: A History of American Housework*, one of the ironies of the women's movement of the 1970s, coinciding as it did with an economy that almost mandated the two-paycheck family, was that women's work was simply increased:

> The women's movement, coinciding with economic changes that made it impossible for many husbands to support their wives with one paycheck, eventually reached every woman in the United States, whether she liked it or not, and affected her life, her relationships with men, and her sense of her own career and life choices. For many, "women's liberation" became synonymous with the double burden of working full time and caring for a household, as if the movement's goal had been to make women's lives more difficult.[27]

The voices of feminist protest that arise in women's domestic humor have largely been overlooked or misunderstood, however, for at least two reasons. One is that it is easy to dismiss the fundamental seriousness of the witty statement, to assume that she who expresses herself humorously feels no pain, so that when Phyllis McGinley writes, "My life is filled with cereal," or Judith Viorst writes, "The Pop Tart crumbs are sprinkled on my soul," the surface cheer may effectively mask the message that the homemaker's life is trivialized by repetitive detail. This is, for example, the perception of Betty Friedan, who in *The Feminine Mystique* accuses what she calls the "Housewife Writers" of misleading their readers:

> "Laugh," the Housewife Writers tell the real housewife, "if you are feeling desperate, empty, bored, trapped in the bed-making, chauffering [sic] and dishwashing details. Isn't it funny? We're all in the same trap." Do real housewives then dissipate in laughter their dreams and their sense of desperation? Do they think their frustrated abilities and their limited lives are a joke?[28]

What Friedan seems to assume is that the "Housewife Writers" were laughing *at* the lives of their readers rather than pointing out women's *shared* sense of frustration; even women who are professional writers have characteristically shouldered most of the responsibility for household chores. What these humorists implicitly insist upon is that it is not they who are at fault, but instead the culture that has thwarted their dreams and restricted their lives. In Umberto Eco's words, "We are no longer sure that it is the character who is at fault. Maybe the frame is wrong."

A second reason why the feminist voice in so much of women's humor has been overlooked is the deeply ambivalent attitude toward the wife and mother in American culture. On the one hand venerated as the unifying force in the family, that most basic unit of the culture, she is at the same time subjected to harsh criticism when she slips from her pedestal. Annegret Ogden describes the situation clearly in her preface to *The Great American Housewife*:

> As the primary provider of food, comfort, and companionship, the mother has been worshipped and idolized. But throughout history her power has been challenged, her place has been restricted by choking sexual taboos and social etiquette. As the main guardian of family values, she has borne the blame whenever things have gone wrong with the American way of life. And except in retrospect through the distorting lens of nostalgia, there has never been a time when all was well for her. When American society changed from a rural religious orientation to urban consumerism, the housewife and the house she kept became a status symbol for the husband she married. And mother's work came to be judged by the product she created: the next generation of healthy and wealthy consumers. In the eyes of the family and of society at large, the housewife was held responsible for no less than the quality of American life.[29]

This heavy burden makes failure inevitable. As Ogden remarks, "her job description has always been charged with higher expectations than any normal individual could satisfy on a consistent basis" (xii). Yet because of what Ogden calls the "false idolatry" that characterizes the culture's attitude toward women, her humorous admissions of failure have been taken to mean that she, rather than the situation, is flawed. When Betty MacDonald's narrator in *The Egg and I* cannot keep her stove lit, when Jean Kerr's speaker in *The Snake Has All the Lines* cannot find anything suitable to fix for her children's lunches, when Peg Bracken speaks of her inability to follow a complicated recipe—the real message is that something is wrong with the job description, the image, the frame. In Marge Piercy's words, "Burning dinner is not incompetence but war." Even while trapped in dependent, trivializing circumstances, women use the subtle methods of the minority group to subvert the power of the majority.

Although the issues raised by the more subtle and subversive feminist humor are the same as those confronted in overtly feminist humor, the perspective is reversed: instead of constantly reminding the reader of the rules by breaking them and thus reinforcing the existence of an oppressive social structure, radical feminist humor holds nothing sacred, and denies the rules rather than merely breaking them. Frances Whitcher's Widow Bedott breaks the rules of decorum and veracity in her quest to accommodate herself to the rule that a woman needs a man to define her position; but Joanna Russ, in *The Female Man*, rejects female gender identity altogether by pointing out that if "mankind" is meant to include all people, then all people are "man," and "woman" does not exist: "for honestly now, who ever heard of Java Woman and existential Woman and the values of Western Woman and scientific Woman and alienated nineteenth-century Woman and all the rest of that dingy and antiquated ragbag?"[30] Two other examples, less widely separated in time than Whitcher and Russ, will also illustrate this difference. Peg Bracken, in *The I Hate to Cook Book*, speaks of the various strategies that a woman who hates to cook can use to save time and trouble. But she cautions that there are limits to this breaking of the rules:

> The average man doesn't care much for the frozen-food department, nor for the pizza man, nor for the chicken-pie lady. He wants to see you knead that bread and tote that bale, before you go down cellar to make the soap. This is known as Woman's Burden.[31]

Rather than thus acquiescing, however grudgingly, to the dictates of men, Flo Kennedy, in the following excerpt from *Color Me Flo* (1976), confronts sexism directly:

> When women began wearing pants there was a tremendous backlash. I can remember—I was still practicing law at that time—going to court in pants and the judge's remarking that I wasn't properly dressed, that the next time I came to court I should be dressed like a lawyer. He's sitting there in a long black dress gathered at the yoke, and I said, "Judge, if you won't talk about what I'm wearing, I won't talk about what you're wearing."[32]

The perspective in this kind of feminist humor is that of the person who knows herself to be right and who can therefore adopt an overt stance of superiority even as the culture seeks to tell her that she is breaking its rules.

The two types of feminist humor sometimes converge in the work of a single writer, in the sense that the speaker or *persona* is immersed in the traditional realities of women's domestic lives, yet is an outspoken feminist. Probably the best example of this intersection is the work of Marietta Holley, whose narrator, Samantha Allen, copes with the household chores of a rural nineteenth-century woman even as she argues for women's rights. Holley was one of the earliest female humorists to see the slapstick absurdity in women's domestic struggles that every later domestic humorist would describe. In *My Opinions and Betsey Bobbet's*, Samantha reflects on a morning's work:

> Now last Monday, no sooner did I get my hands into the suds holt of one of Josiah's dirty shirts, than the sugar would mount up in the kettle and sozzle over on the top of the furnace in the summer kitchen—or else the preserves would swell up and drizzle over the side of the pan on to the stove—or else the puddin' I was a bakin' for dinner would show signs of scorchin.' . . . (59-60)

At that point the editor of the local newspaper arrives unexpectedly to ask Samantha to take care of his twin children for a while. "Says he, 'They won't be any trouble to you, will they?' I thought of the martyrs" (60). But Samantha's comic martyrdom is not the major way in which she expresses her feminist principles: an ardent suffragist, she argues for women having the vote against the major anti-suffrage arguments of the nineteenth century,[33] showing the deep understanding of women's social and legal oppression in American culture that informed her more than twenty books between 1873 and 1914.

Another example of the intersection between subtle and overt feminist humor is the work of Judith Viorst. Unlike Samantha, who is frequently an informal platform speaker for women's rights, the speaker in Viorst's several books of light verse matures in the 1960s and struggles with the conflict between her conservative upbringing and her commitment to the women's movement. The struggle is most obvious in the poem "A Women's Liberation Movement Woman," which includes the following lines:

> And after dinner, when he talks to the company
> While I clean the broiler
> (because I am a victim of capitalism, imperialism,
>   male chauvinism, and also Playboy
>   magazine),
> And afternoons, when he invents the telephone
>   and wins the Dreyfus case and writes War
>   and Peace
> While I sort the socks
> (because I am economically oppressed, physically
>   exploited, psychologically mutilated, and also
>   very insulted),
> And after he tells me that it is genetically
>   determined that the man makes martinis and
>   the lady makes the beds
> (because he sees me as a sex object, an earth
>   mother, a domestic servant, and also dumber
>   than he is),
> Then I want to become a
> Women's Liberation Movement woman.

Yet the poem concludes with the speaker retreating from this commitment to the movement:

> And after I contemplate
> No marriage, no family, no shaving under my
>   arms,
> And no one to step on a cockroach whenever I
>   need him,
> Then I don't.[34]

Viorst's ambivalence, which mirrors that of many women in the 1960s, is expressed most clearly in her exaggerated images, such as the assumption that a truly liberated woman must be single and unshaven. Zita Dresner identifies the source of Viorst's popularity as this representation of women's ambivalence about feminism:

> Much of Viorst's appeal ... results from her ability to express
> women's anxieties about who they are and about whether or not
> who they are represents the kind of women they want or think they
> ought to be. Those females who were compelled to choose between
> a family and career and always felt cheated, as well as those who
> attempted to combine family and career but always worried that they
> were short-changing one or the other, can find in Viorst's work
> echoes of their own conflicts.[35]

Such conflicts continue to plague women, and even the most strongly feminist humorists describe their role as homemakers in terms that are interchangeable with those of the more subtly feminist writers. Barbara Holland's "The Day's Work," in *Pulling Our Own Strings*, describes a day in the life of a woman who combines family and career in a frenetic fashion. Leaving for work, she contemplates the mess she leaves behind: "The kitchen. Could I simply drop a bomb on it? Or have I already?" (46). She feels pulled apart by the demands of her children:

> They close in on me, pulling at bits of my flesh and clothing for attention. One of these days I will come apart in their hands, and each child will have a little scrap of me to shout at.
> I won't do it anymore. I can't live like this. (51)

Yet Holland's *persona* finally concludes that there is nothing in her life that she wants to give up: "Even the brown-eyed kids, even the dirty dishes. I do them for me, because I want to" (52). Her job is a source of satisfaction, an island in the midst of chaos:

> I feel so much stronger and braver at work, where I know what I'm doing. Competent, like a man, an executive, glancing at papers and crumpling them up and tossing them toward the wastebasket. Real difference between men and women, home and work: here, if I miss the wastebasket, someone else must ultimately pick the papers up. Exhilarating. (46)

She sets her own limits at work, arriving late and leaving early without apology if her life demands it, and refusing to take on extra work: "Isn't it lovely to be grown up finally, after all these years? To know what you want, to say no?" (47)

Another example of saying "no" is Erica Jong's poem "Woman Enough," in which the speaker ignores much of housekeeping in favor of her career as a writer. She remembers how her mother and grandmother, "loving houses better than themselves," spent all their time on household chores:

> Because my mother's minutes
> were sucked into the roar
> of the vacuum cleaner,
> because she waltzed with the washer-dryer
> & tore her hair waiting for repairmen —

> I send out my laundry,
> & live in a dusty house . . .

So she works at her typewriter while

> the man I love cleans up the kitchen
> grumbling only a little
> because he knows
> that after all these centuries
> it is easier for him
> than for me.[36]

As Jong's speaker says "no" to housework, she says "yes" to herself and her own needs.

A group of women central to the women's movement and increasingly so to feminist humor are lesbian feminists, who have said "yes" to themselves and their needs in quite specific and significant ways. For lesbian feminists, the issue at stake is far larger than sexual preference; it involves the ability of women to define themselves *for* themselves rather than being defined by men or their relationships with men. As Hester Eisenstein puts it in *Contemporary Feminist Thought*, "by being connected primarily to women, they escaped from, and indeed, renounced, the definition of women as secondary, derivative, or second-best to men" (52). Both personally and politically—insofar as heterosexuality reinforces male dominance, as Adrienne Rich and others have argued—lesbian feminists have encouraged women, whatever their sexual orientation, to identify themselves with other women "as a source of an alternative model for female identity" (54).

Susan J. Wolfe several years ago provided a clear definition of lesbian feminist humor, one that contrasts it to other feminist humor:

> Much of contemporary women's humor addresses itself to the roles
> and responsibilities of women in our culture and women's
> submission to or rejection of them. But the humor does not perceive
> women's roles as the result of a total *male* value system.
> Furthermore, some women's comedy is so heterosexist in its bias
> that Lesbian feminists find it offensive. Joan Rivers' jokes about her
> failure to catch a man or Phyllis Diller's about her unattractiveness to
> men are not only unfunny, but politically incorrect. . . . Joking about
> the lack of equal training and job opportunities for women due to
> discrimination against women is feminist, joking about male sexual

ineptitude is, too; but the implication that men make inadequate
lovers because they are men constitutes Lesbian humor.[37]

As Wolfe's comparisons to Rivers and Diller suggest, a large number
of lesbian feminist humorists use stand-up comedy as their medium.
Frequently, too, the occasion of emerging publicly as a comic coin-
cides with the occasion of "coming out" as a lesbian. Wolfe refers to
a time when this happened to her: "The first time I inadvertently
came out at a feminist conference by referring to Lesbians as 'we,' a
friend said, 'Better watch it. One slip of the tongue and everyone calls
you a Lesbian'" (2). For others, the conjunction of acknowledging
their comic abilities and acknowledging their homosexuality seems
to be a natural outgrowth of similar kinds of freedom. Evelyn White,
in "Stand Up and Laugh," makes this point about Seattle comic Annie
Gage:

> Comedy is a business of perpetual public risks and Gage sees a
> correlation between the courage involved in coming out as a lesbian
> and the emergence of her comic self. "It was right after I'd gotten
> into Women's Studies and come out that the comic came out in me. I
> started telling people that I had this fantasy and that was the first step
> in making it happen." Like her lesbian sexuality, her comic urges
> remained hidden until she claimed them for herself. (*Backbone 4 91*)

The fact that a woman's sexual preference and her comic ability
remain "hidden" until the proper moment of courage reinforces
once again the deep cultural resistance to women having and expressing a sense of humor.

The occasion of coming out is in fact a common topic in lesbian
feminist humor, partially because it is an event fraught with the sort
of tension best dissipated in laughter, and partially because lesbians
perceive a fundamental absurdity in the need to keep one's sexual
identity a secret. A dialogue between Susan J. Wolfe and Julia Pene-
lope, for example, focuses on colleagues' reactions to lesbians:

> JP: When I joined an English department as an uncloseted
> lesbian, women faculty members came up at the rate of one a
> day to announce that they were heterosexual.
> SJW: We decided we should post a list in the women's room
> headed THE FOLLOWING WOMEN HAVE ANNOUNCED THAT
> THEY ARE HETEROSEXUAL, so that they could sign in. Then
> we'd cross their names off and initial them.[38]

Sharon McDonald, in "What Mother Never Told Me," recalls the process of deciding to make a public lifelong commitment to her female lover. The reaction in the feminist community, she says, "broke down into three categories: The Aghast, The Amused, and The Admiring. The Aghast, of course, were radical lesbian feminists. So were the Amused. So were The Admiring."[39] While the women of the couple's families were generally supportive, the men, who were not invited to the ceremony, "reacted to this with customary outrage, half of them 'threatening' not to come, the other half threatening to come" (135).

The major goal of the lesbian feminist comics, however, is to extol women's virtues rather than presenting them as victims of male-originated stereotypes. Kate Clinton, one of the most popular of this group of comics, is well aware that she has a mission to perform: to educate women about feminist issues and to help them value themselves in a culture that denigrates them. Evelyn C. White quotes one of Clinton's favorite one-liners: "Being a lesbian is making a commitment to joy in your life, and let me tell you, Joy is not an easy woman to please" ("Stand Up and Laugh" 93). Like so many other female humorists, Clinton was raised to believe that for women, "humor was not valid" (92), so that claiming her identity as a humorist has been in many ways analogous to claiming her identity as a lesbian. She is also aware that many women—including many feminists—are put off by lesbianism, and, as White comments, she attempts to deal with their fears:

> As a stand-up comic she is able to influence such women quickly, to change her routine if it is not working so as to engage the audience in a manner that is not threatening, but rather supportive and *fun*. She is like an "unbound feminist edition"—not limited by the permanence of the printed word. (93)

Lesbian feminist humor represents a stage in the development of feminist humor that seems far removed from the domestic humor of the 1950s. In its emphasis on women's positive qualities and its insistence on women loving other women, it appears to negate the pressures of the heterosexual world that give rise to domestic humor. Further, it has an "in-group" quality that is quite conscious and that sometimes makes the humor inaccessible to those outside the group. Susan J. Wolfe has pointed out that straight women frequently do not understand the import of the line "I called my friend Julia a clone and she said 'thank you'" as arising from the lesbian's desire to be created by something other than heterosexual activity.[40] Yet the impulse for all feminist humor is the fundamental absurdity of one gender oppressing the other, whether this perception is stated subversively or is expressed as part of a radical critique of gender relations.

IV

Two issues remain to be explored in this discussion of feminist humor. One is the extent to which feminists can indeed laugh at themselves and their "mission," and the other is the way in which contemporary women's humor mirrors changes in women's lives and attitudes as a result of the women's movement of the 1960s and 1970s. The two issues are related in the sense that both speak to the maturity and effectiveness of women's struggle for liberation. The image of the grim-faced feminist arose in part because of the terrible seriousness of her task; with some success in that task should come a greater ability to relax and to see one's own absurdities when they arise. Similarly, if the women's movement has had a significant effect on attitudes as well as policies, women's humor should have changed to reflect that effect.

Susan J. Wolfe speaks to the first of these issues from the perspective of lesbian feminists when she notes that "many of us are ... becoming secure enough in our own politics to start spoofing them." For one thing, she says, a radical socio-political agenda sets up myriad rules that even the faithful may transgress:

> Jokes about political correctness have become commonplace among Lesbian feminists. In a group which opposes sexism, racism, heterosexism, the oppression of the physically challenged, antisemitism, capitalism, ageism, looksism, pollution, nuclear weapons and warfare, child and animal abuse, the irresponsible consumption of drugs and meat and sugar, and hierarchical social structures and political organizations, it is *fairly* easy to fall into political error in word and deed. (3)

In her introduction to *Backbone 4: Humor by Northwest Women*

(1982), Barbara Wilson extends Wolfe's point to include women's ability to laugh at things other than their own circumstances:

> Yes, Virginia, it is possible to be politically correct (at heart) and funny. This hasn't stopped feminists and lesbian-feminists from learning to laugh at themselves, however. While it's still common (and necessary) for women humorists to take well-aimed shots at men and male institutions ... *Backbone 4* is good news that feminist humor doesn't need to depend only on the satiric recognition of our continuing financial and political oppression. (5-6)

Wilson's first statement, that one can be simultaneously "politically correct" and "funny," refers once more to the tradition that feminists do not—should not—have a sense of humor.

But even in the earlier years of the contemporary women's movement, feminists were able to see the humor in the movement itself and some of their own actions within it. Felicia Lamport's poem "Paradigm," written shortly after the publication of Friedan's *The Feminine Mystique*, speculates on the dangers facing women who decide to abandon the "mystique":

> The lady who, in pique,
>   Determines to forsake
> The feminine mystique
>   Is likeliest to make
> The masculine mystaque.[41]

A short while later, Nora Ephron wrote several essays that reflect amusingly on the behavior of women and men at the height of the movement. Always supportive of the goals of the movement, Ephron nonetheless appraises some of its manifestations with a less-than-worshipful attitude. One of these manifestations is the consciousness-raising group. While Ephron acknowledges that for many women these groups have been effective and even crucial, she suggests that for others they became merely a forum for unchanging gripes about men, "a running soap opera, with new episodes on the same theme every week":

> Barbara and Peter, Episode 13 of the Barbara is Uninhibited and Peter is a Drag Show ... Joanna and Dave, Episode 19 of the Will

Joanna Ever Get Dave to Share the Household Duties Show ... Claire
and Herbie in the Claire Has Sexual Boredom but Loves her
Husband Show.[42]

Ephron also comments on the divisions within the women's movement itself, a movement which, she says, "makes the American Com-
munist Party of the 1930s look like a monolith":

> I have even heard a woman defend her affection for cooking to an
> incredulous group who believed that to cook at all—much less to
> like it—was to swallow the worst sort of cultural conditioning. Once
> I tried to explain to a fellow feminist why I liked wearing makeup;
> she replied by explaining why she does not. Neither of us
> understood a word the other said. ("On Never Having Been a Prom
> Queen," 20)

More recently, Deanne Stillman has written about the feminist revision of male-centered language by taking it to some logical—and
absurd—extremes. In her "Feminish Dictionary," Stillman proposes
such changes as "opeople" for "omen" and "midspouses" for "mid-
wives."[43]

What all of these writers seem to point out is the need for Samantha Allen's "meegum" behavior. And yet, a reading of contemporary
humor by both women and men serves as one among many indica-
tors that the women's movement has done little to change women's
lives, despite repeated attempts at fundamental revisions of political
and social policies and attitudes. Even the titles of recent books indi-
cate the gulf that still exists between genders: Roy Blount Jr.'s 1984
What Men Don't Tell Women perpetuates the traditional concept of
separate male and female cultures, while Mary Kuczkir's *My Dishtowel Flies at Half-Mast* (1980) and Teresa Bloomingdale's *Sense and
Momsense* (1986) accomplish the same thing by continuing the
genre of domestic humor into the 1980s. Blount's humor reveals an
uneasiness about feminism, especially in the "Blue Yodels" sections
of the book. "Blue Yodel 4," for example, begins as follows:

> I don't understand guys who say they're feminists. That's like the
> time Hubert Humphrey, running for President, told a black audience
> that he was a soul brother.
> And say you fall in love with somebody and it turns out she's *not* a
> feminist. It happens. You've kind of painted yourself into a corner,

haven't you? What are you going to say—you've always believed in feminism but you'll give it up for her? How's she going to take that?[44]

Such passsages reinforce the concept of woman as "other," and also approach feminism as though it were equivalent to being a Democrat or a Methodist—an affiliation to be changed at will—both of which represent a continuing cultural resistance to the principle of gender equality. The continuation of domestic humor similarly testifies to the persistence of woman's primary gender-identity as homemaker and to her feelings of isolation in the home. Bloomingdale and Kuczkir reinforce traditional female stereotypes: Bloomingdale tells us that she is not a good driver and cannot balance her checkbook, and Kuczkir has problems with her kitchen appliances and buys a car on the basis of its color. In the work of these writers, time almost seems to have stood still since the 1950s.

Further, feminist humor—particularly that which is overtly political—is by no means mainstream humor. With few exceptions (one of them being *Ms.* magazine), it is published by small presses or is not published at all until an anthology such as *Pulling Our Own Strings* makes it available to the public. Feminist humor seems to have made its greatest inroads in stand-up comedy and in cartoons,[45] both of which are relatively ephemeral as compared to prose and poetry. The "women's culture with its own character, its fighting humor, its defiant celebration of our worth" that Naomi Weisstein called for in 1973 ("Why We're not Laughing" 90) has not come about in any full-scale sense, even though the tradition of such humor is longer and richer than is generally thought.

The very need for and existence of what Weisstein terms women's "fighting humor" is, of course, a symptom of the fact that there is something to fight—for or against. Like the humor of ethnic and racial minorities, feminist humor assumes an oppressor, whether the oppression is confronted subversively or openly. In a situation of true gender equality, would feminist humor disappear? Or would *all* humor be feminist in the sense that it would *assume* gender equality? Women's—and men's—humor of the 1980s suggests that these questions will not require answers anytime soon. In 1936, Agnes Repplier, in *In Pursuit of Laughter*, noted that Americans do not use the insights of their humorists as the basis for social change:

We have outgrown several layers of civilization, we have outlived repeated degradations of public service. It is not hard for us to recognize absurdities, but we are content with recognition. We cannot be made to understand their danger.[46]

More than fifty years later, the same seems to be true.

6

The Tradition and Beyond: Contemporary Women's Humor and the Canon of American Literature

"you got to laugh"
—*Molly Ivins*

I

Frances Whitcher's rather plaintive statement in the mid-nineteenth century that "it is a very serious thing to be a funny woman" referred specifically to the circumstances of her own personal and professional life. But her comment can now be understood on several different levels. America's cultural bias against women as humorists has meant that women have had to exercise both courage and subterfuge in order to express themselves humorously, and that they have frequently been unaware of a female humorous tradition that might well have emboldened them. Despite the efforts of Kate Sanborn in 1885 and Martha Bruère and Mary Beard in 1934 to preserve in their anthologies substantial amounts of women's written humor, women in the 1980s still feel as though they are pioneers, unaware that others have not only gone before, but also expressed in their humor many of the same concerns about women's lives in America. In addition, the issues with which women's humor has typically been concerned are of vital importance to women's status, position, and role in American culture. Fanny Fern's humorous sketches about women's economic dependence upon men in the 1850s, Dorothy Parker's ironic laments about the sexual double standard in the 1920s, and Nora Ephron's satiric description of the manufacturers of feminine hygiene products in the 1970s all expose fundamental elements of women's subordination—issues that have been central concerns of successive groups of feminists since the mid-nineteenth century. Perhaps most significantly, women's humor is serious in the sense that it reinforces our emerging realization of the extent of women's essential powerlessness over time and, simultaneously, belies the assumptions of nonintellectuality and essential passivity that have been used to justify women's subordinate status.

The study of women's humor therefore must, as is the case with the study of women's literature generally, respond to two seemingly contradictory factors: from a literary standpoint, the extent to which the female voice and the uniqueness of women's gender experience is revealed in the works; and from a cultural standpoint, the way in which the humor of both women *and* men, taken together, demonstrates changes in values, attitudes, institutions, and tastes in the culture itself in a more comprehensive fashion than can the humor of either gender considered alone. The tension between exclusivity and inclusivity—between the celebration of women's art on its own terms as a product of peculiarly female inspiration and experience, and the need to balance the canon of art in terms of gender as well as race and class—is central to the women's movement, to feminist scholarship, and to women's humor itself. To consider women's humor as a separate, discrete tradition may be to again place it in a literary and cultural ghetto; to include it in the canon without a new vision of the American humorous tradition may be to bury it or make it a mere token. The latter tendency has been pervasive among critics and editors of humor anthologies. Typical of this tendency of the last 150 years is the comment of Marshall P. Wilder, who in 1908 edited a ten-volume *Wit and Humor of America*. In his foreword, Wilder notes:

> In these volumes are selections from the pen of all whom I have mentioned, as well as many more, including a number by the clever women humorists, of whom America is justly proud.[1]

Wilder's tone suggests that "clever women" are an interesting oddity; and the fact that America has not, in fact, been "justly proud" of its female humorists has been far more recently demonstrated by the devotion of a mere two pages to the history of women's humor in Walter Blair and Hamlin Hill's *America's Humor: From Poor Richard to Doonesbury* (1978).

The result of such patronizing and omission has been to obscure a tradition that is central to our understanding of woman's perception of self in relation to American society. The humorist—or the "serious" writer who uses humor as a device—occupies a unique position as interpreter of cultural values. Just as the joker or trickster figure in preindustrial cultures has privileged status for his capacity to mock the sacred, so the humorous writer reveals perceptions that are often at odds with official cultural rhetoric and practice. Yet whereas Mark Twain's pointed satire on the evils of slavery in *Huck Finn* has been an enduring part of American literary and cultural history, Marietta Holley's equally pointed satire on opposition to female suffrage in *My Opinions and Betsey Bobbet's* has been, until recently, unavailable as a resource for understanding late-nineteenth-century attitudes and values. Reclaiming the female humorous perspective not only adds a new dimension to American cultural history, but also revises assumptions about women's attitudes toward a passive, subordinate role: instead of meek acquiescence, the female humorist displays a fundamental understanding and rejection of her status and the absurdity of its premises.

Contemporary women's humor continues to provide a critique of the culture in ways that both continue the tradition of the past and reveal a gradually evolving sense of equality and self-worth. A comparison of two issues of *Ms.* magazine—one published in 1973 and the other in 1987—provides one index of the directions that women's humor has taken in recent years. The cover of the November 1973 issue is a cartoon drawing of a man and a woman. The man asks, "Do you know the women's movement has no sense of humor?" and the woman responds, "No . . . but hum a few bars and I'll fake it."[2] It is in this same issue that Naomi Weisstein, in "Why we aren't laughing . . . anymore," laments both the lack of a tradition of women's humor and the pressure women feel to laugh at men's humor. The July/August, 1987, 15th anniversary issue, in contrast, contains Dallas *Times Herald* columnist Molly Ivins's "There Will Always Be a Texas," a satire on Texas sexism which concludes with the statement that to deal with such absurdity "you got to laugh." Catharine Stimpson's article "The 'F' Word," in the same issue, features satiric sketches of several types of people who refuse to identify themselves as feminists, and ends on a note similar to that of Ivins: "We need even more audacity, more humor, when we speak of feminism. We are strong enough to know that self-satire does not signify self-contempt."[3] Both writers exemplify the tradition that Weisstein sought in 1973, when it seemed that humor about feminism was "politically incorrect."

Perhaps the most dramatic changes have occurred in the field of stand-up comedy. The 15th anniversary issue of *Ms.* also includes an article about comic Roseanne Barr, who takes the *persona* of the disgruntled housewife a step further than did the writers of the 1950s and 1960s: she rejects the demands with which earlier humorous *personae* struggled to comply. Barr's routine includes such remarks as, "I figure when my husband comes home from work, if the kids are still alive, then I've done my job"; and, "I will clean house when Sears comes out with a riding vacuum cleaner." Barr, like other contemporary female humorists, began as a comic without any consciousness of a female tradition:

> I realized that I had to create a whole new kind of comedy called "funny womanness." . . . But there wasn't any language to name women's experience and make it funny to men and women—very paranoid women, I might add. I felt like I had to invent the language.[4]

Numerous other women are finding what they believe to be a new comic language. George Schlatter, the producer of television's "Rowan and Martin's Laugh-In," estimates that there are at least 300 female comics currently performing, and forty percent of the comics on his new television series, "The Laugh Machine," will be women.[5]

The perception that to laugh at one's own foibles need not diminish either oneself or other women seems to be shared by many contemporary female humorists. While the women's movement that began in the 1960s has by no means accomplished its major objectives, it has succeeded in fostering the sense among many women that their problems are not personal and unique, but essentially political and certainly widely shared, and that there exists a group of people—an audience, a readership—who are sympathetic not only to the circumstances of women's lives but also to the fact that women can laugh about them without trivializing either the circumstances or women themselves.

Although women's domestic humor continues to be written and published, it is no longer dominant, as it was in the 1950s and 1960s. As women have assumed an increasingly larger role in the world outside the home, women's humor has reflected this transition, and consequently it deals with a wide variety of cultural issues. The work of such writers as Fran Lebowitz, Veronica Geng, Mary Bess Whidden, and Molly Ivins offers a commentary on contemporary American culture—politics, fads, annoyances, relationships—that is remarkably similar to that of male humorists such as Woody Allen and Garrison Keillor. Women's humor that does not depend upon gender-identity—that is, in which gender-identity is not central to either the thematic or stylistic texture of the work—could result from one of two phenomena: either the author has submerged gender-specific perspective and references to write humor that will be published and widely appreciated, or she simply perceives her culture from the angle of one who is affected by it as neither primarily male or female, but simply human. Some feminist theorists would deny that the latter is possible and would insist that the female voice is always present. In most works of literature this is certainly true, but in some forms of humor, such as parody and word play, it is not. The following excerpts from parodies of college catalogs, for example, do not intrinsically involve the gender of either author:

MAKING IT WITHOUT MATH. Cylvia Cypher, instructor. Too often we are compelled to think of the world numerically. This course teaches effective ways of living in the modern age without doing even simple calculations, and students will learn the futility of mathematical concepts and formulations. A reading knowledge of English is not required but might come in handy.[6]

The New Mathematics: Standard mathematics has recently been rendered obsolete by the discovery that for years we have been writing the numeral five backward. This has led to a reevaluation of counting as a method of getting from one to ten. Students are taught advanced concepts of Boolean Algebra, and formerly unsolvable equations are dealt with by threats of reprisals.[7]

The first passage is from *Provincial Matters*, by Mary Bess Whidden; the second from Woody Allen's *Getting Even*. Those who are aware of the fact that more women than men suffer from math anxiety might suggest that Whidden's tongue-in-cheek dismissal of mathematical equations marks her work as that of a woman, or that Allen's phrase "threats of reprisal" identifies his passage as masculine, but it is likely that most readers would be unaware of these distinctions. The purpose of both selections is to mock the pomposity and aridity of the average college catalog by rendering it absurd; neither has a clear male or female perspective.

Humor that lacks gender-specific references is by no means a new phenomenon, whether written by women or by men. Whereas the tall tale is a form both rooted in and expressive of a male culture, and the domestic saga involving small children, cooking, and cleaning emerges clearly from female experience, light verse involving the sort of word-play favored by Ogden Nash and Felicia Lamport is not necessarily referential to either a male or a female perspective. The fact that women have consistently written literary parody and nonsense verse as well as satires on male hegemony and ironic accounts of their own suppression testifies to the fact that women have been capable of transcending the limitations of the "separate sphere" to observe cultural absurdities and revel in the possibilities of language. However, as the lives of educated, middle-class women have increasingly been centered in the workplace rather than the home, women's humor has begun to occupy the spaces and feature the themes that had previously been the province of male humor: politics, bureaucracies, professional stresses, and the minor annoyances that characterize daily life.

For example, one of the most sophisticated satires on the enormous popularity of Lt. Col. Oliver North when he testified to House and Senate committees investigating the Iran/Contra scandal in July of 1987 was written by Veronica Geng, whose book *Partners* (1984) includes several pieces that satirize contemporary American politics. Until recently, women's political humor has concerned issues of particular interest to women; here, Geng writes about a phenomenon that affects *all* Americans, and the only hint that this piece might have been written by a woman is that it has as its core the abandonment of a woman by a man. Inspired by an opinion poll in which respondents were asked to say whether the phrase "someone I would want to marry my daughter" describes Col. North (26% said yes), Geng creates a monologue in which the speaker identifies North as the man who had pretended to marry and then left the speaker's sister in "Cocoahole," Florida, a few years earlier. The speaker several times interrupts the narrative to conduct his/her own opinion polls:

(Do you have the feeling that I'm basically an honest person? I know

you can't answer that for certain, but do you get a general sense of
probity and forthrightness from the way I express myself?
                              YES   NO
  Don't forget to put a check mark or, preferably, your initials in the
appropriate space, then clip and send to CBS News Poll, New York,
New York 10019.)

Such interjections make fun of the American obsession with opinion
polls, while the speaker's voice seems at some points almost to be
that of North himself—"Now, the rest of what I know I only learned
after it was over"—or of one of his Congressional questioners—
"Even if you feel you've already answered the question"—so that
Geng also parodies the language of Congressional hearings and
questions their effectiveness in determining the truth, "as the shifting
winds and erosions of public opinion alter your perception of
reality."[8]

Some earlier female humorists had careers quite apart from writing humor—e.g., Cornelia Otis Skinner was an actress, Jean Kerr was
a playwright—and wrote about their experiences as professionals,
but even in these pieces they write from a distinctly female stance.
Skinner, for example, describes the nervousness that assails an actor
during the day before opening night by using gynecological references. Early in the sketch, she remarks, "Some weeks ago, I had an
opening (the obstetrical phraseology is apposite)." Later, as she is
trying to relax before her performance, several well-meaning friends
visit her: "They stood about the bed in a manner that made me feel
the anesthetist would come along shortly and we'd all go together to
the delivery room."[9] In 1950, when this piece was published in Skinner's book *Nuts in May*, the act of giving birth seemed a natural metaphor for a woman writing about the opening night of a play. Similarly, Jean Kerr, in 1960, writes about going to an out-of-town
opening of one of her plays with relief at knowing that "somebody
else back in Larchmont will have to find the storm windows." In the
days when she was "still in love with room service," she looked upon
such trips as vacations from her life as a wife and mother:

> I felt, like any other red-blooded American housewife, that a whole
> day spent rewriting the first act was a small price to pay for the
> privilege of having someone else make my breakfast and bring it up
> to me on a tray.[10]

In contrast to the gender-specific references of these pieces, Veronica Geng's "Poll" is narrated in a voice that is neither clearly male or female.

Molly Ivins's columns in the Dallas *Times Herald* deal with the politics and culture of what she terms the "wonderfully awful" state of Texas in a bold, breezy style that is anything but stereotypically feminine. Although Ivins is a staunch feminist who is deeply concerned about women's issues, she writes from the perspective of an intelligent, alert observer who, like Holley's Samantha Allen in the late nineteenth century, would like to see people be reasonable, yet finds herself surrounded by absurdity. On the antics of a Texas congressman, for example, she writes:

> When people start calling you from around the state, and indeed the nation, in conditions ranging from helpless laughter to extreme indignation to hysterics, saying, "There is a Texas congressman in Afghanistan killing Russians and he's got a former Miss World with him. She is a sloe-eyed beauty and he is wearing black monogrammed cowboy boots!" then, my friends, there is only one thing to say: "Must be Charlie Wilson."[11]

In another column, Ivins muses about the "common-sense directive" that she would like to issue to all bureaucrats: "No rule or regulation of this department is ever to be followed if it flies directly in the face of common sense." But, she concludes, if this were done, "it probably would tie our civilization in a knot for the rest of recorded history trying to define common sense."[12] By casting herself in the role of the comically outraged gadfly, Ivins recalls not only Samantha Allen's indignant common sense, but also the male wise-innocent figures of the nineteenth century such as Seba Smith's Jack Downing.

Such androgynous humor is common among contemporary female humorous writers. In *Light Metres* (1982), Felicia Lamport parodies T. S. Eliot's "The Love Song of J. Alfred Prufrock" in "The Love Song of R. Milhous Nixon," which includes the lines:

> I keep cool .... I keep cool ....
> I shall have another thousand days to rule.
> Shall I let my tapes unroll? Shall I dare
>   them to impeach?
> I shall triumph thanks to Rose Mary's
>   extraordinary reach.

I have heard my staffers peaching each on each.
I do not think that they will peach on me.[13]

In *Provincial Matters* (1985), Mary Bess Whidden writes humorous essays that deal with junk mail, career changes, dress-for-success manuals, and other realities that affect both women and men in contemporary America. Whidden's feminist orientation emerges occasionally, as in her spoof of advice columnists titled "Dear Nanny," when a little girl writes to request a list of names of all the female governors and senators from New Mexico, and Nanny responds flatly, "DEAR LITTLE: No. Space does not permit."[14] But for the most part, there is little gender-identification in Whidden's work; the voice is that of an independent person reminding us of the absurdities that permeate our daily lives.

Fran Lebowitz's *Social Studies* (1981) takes on contemporary urban life: apartment-hunting, pretentious restaurants, and fads. Lebowitz's rather brittle, world-weary tone is more reminiscent of that of S. J. Perelman, the ultimate cosmopolite, than it is of Dorothy Parker, who manages at every turn to remind us that she is a woman and—despite her cleverness—quite a vulnerable one. Lebowitz expresses the urbanite's preference for the artificial over the natural, preferring windfall profits to windfall apples and linguini with clam sauce to almost anything. Like many New Yorkers, she finds California, especially Los Angeles, alien, and offers a guide to it as though to a foreign country:

CHIEF PRODUCTS
The chief products of Los Angeles are novelizations, salad,
game-show hosts, points, muscle tone, mini-series and rewrites. They
export all of these items with the twin exceptions of muscle tone and
points, neither of which seem to travel well.[15]

Most earlier female humorists wrote about dieting and other forms of physical self-improvement as particularly female activities: ordeals that women endured to make themselves more attractive to men. By describing women's failures to achieve whatever ideal body was in vogue at the moment, these writers attempted to subvert the concept of a culturally sanctioned, media-promoted physical ideal for women, just as they similarly subverted the formulations of ideal wife and mother. More recent humorists, however, tend to present such issues as dieting merely as characteristics of contemporary

American life, and to mock the human search for perfection. In "The Fran Lebowitz High Stress Diet and Exercise Program," for example, Lebowitz makes fun of the concept of the perfect diet while at the same time speaking to the pervasive stress of contemporary life. She suggests that a high stress level will counteract the effects of even the most fattening foods, and that stressful interruptions at mealtimes can effectively kill the appetite. Even a mid-morning snack of dough-nuts and sugar-laden coffee loses its threat if one follows Lebowitz's recommended procedure:

a. Take first sip of coffee
b. Open mail and find disconnect notice from telephone company, threatening letter from spouse of new flame and a note from a friend informing you that you have been recently plagiarized on network television. (Tones up fist area.) (*Social Studies* 119)

Lebowitz acknowledges that women are as subject to the stresses of professional life as are men, and in fact her parody of fad diets does not make reference to gender except by the author's name in its title.

Yet this tendency toward an androgynous humor does not mean that women who write humor in the 1980s reveal no consciousness of themselves as female. Some pieces by each of these contemporary humorists have specific relevance to women's experience and con-cerns, and others include references to the fact that the author or speaker is a woman. But, in contrast to earlier women's humor, these are not the perspectives of women as failures and victims, addressing subversively a culture that demeans them; rather, they are the confi-dent voices of women who comment on contemporary American life.

Politics is a common theme in the work of these writers. Mary Bess Whidden, for example, takes a subtle poke at President Ronald Rea-gan's economic policies — policies that have a particularly devastating effect on women — in one of her "Dear Nanny" exchanges:

DEAR NANNY: I can't get work and can't support my children. Where can I go for help?

SINGLE MOTHER
DEAR SINGLE: The private sector will take care of you. If you find its address, please let Nanny know.

(*Provincial Matters* 145)

In *Partners*, Veronica Geng deals with a number of political issues, from the tapes incriminating President Richard Nixon in the Watergate scandal to unsolicited campaign literature from political candidates. In "Supreme Court Roundup," she parodies reports of Supreme Court decisions, including one in which the court upholds the right of a twelve-year-old girl to audition for the male lead in a Hollywood western, not on grounds of sex discrimination, but on the First Amendment right of freedom of expression. "The Court thus affirmed for the first time the constitutional right to a screen test."[16] In "My Mao," Geng satirizes the tendency for women to write exposés of their affairs with famous men, and in the process comments on the Cultural Revolution in China:

> I was beginning to find [Mao's] demeanor a little stylized. But what right did I have to demand emotion? The Cultural Revolution had just started, and ideas of the highest type were surely forming themselves inside his skull.
>
> He said, "I want to be sure you understand that you won't see me very often."
>
> "That's insulting," I said. "Did you suppose I thought China was across the street?"
>
> "It's just that you mustn't expect me to solve your problems," he said. "I already have eight hundred million failures at home, and the last thing I need is another one over here." (19)

The narrative voice in "My Mao" is that of a woman, but the humor is directed at a culture that hungers for news of the personal lives of famous people.

When the contemporary female humorist deals with issues of specific relevance to women's lives, she typically adopts a stance of superiority to the sources of discrimination. Deanne Stillman's parody "Ann Van Brothers Talks to Teens . . . ," for example, uses hyperbole to mock not only the advice-column format but also the assumption that women must use artifice to survive in the competition for male approval. Adopting the breezily confidential style of advice literature, Stillman reminds teenage women that "if your hairdo is not right for the shape of your face, you could be in big trouble,"[17] and tempers the extremes of her advice by saying, "who ever said that beauty would be a breeze? Beauty is *not* a breeze, and I don't care who says different" (37). In the mock dedication of this parody, Stillman identifies the sources of women's anxieties about their appearance as marketers and advertisers, not women themselves:

With special thanks to the American Girdle and Brassiere Council,
The American Council for a Germ-Free America, The American
Depilatory and Deodorant Council, and The American Frozen Pizza
Lobby. (32)

Veronica Geng targets the film industry as a source of distorted
images of women. In "Ten Movies That Take Women Seriously," she
parodies the plots of well-known films to demonstrate how films perpetuate stereotypes of women. Geng imagines a remake of "Dressed
to Kill" in which a gas-company employee enters the bathroom of a
woman who is taking a shower and accuses her of being "a gro-
tesquely oversexed, middle-aged bourgeois bitch," whereupon "she
realizes this is true and cancels her shrink appointment to stay home
and preheat the oven according to his guidelines." The "Gas Man"
then continues "on his search for the ideal woman—a professor of
quantum physics (Diane Keaton) who is upper-class, young, and
moderately sexed" (27).

The freedom to laugh at oneself and also make ridiculous the cultural sources of women's oppression is also evident in contemporary
lesbian humor. Gail Sausser's *Lesbian Etiquette*, for example, challenges the concept of "proper" behavior for women as it points to
the particular problems that lesbians face—not only coming out, but
also confronting parents, marriage, and the medical establishment.
Sausser is able to laugh at herself—her crushes, her insecurities, her
bad habits—but she is most effective when she addresses homopho-
bia and reveals its absurdity. In "Hello, I Am Lesbian," Sausser writes
about her role as an educator, telling classes and groups about the
gay experience. She is commonly asked why people choose to be
gay, "As if one morning each of us stood in front of the mirror and
said, 'I think I'll become a persecuted minority today'."[18] In "Gays
Need Better P.R.," Sausser speaks of this persecution: "We have been
blamed for it *all*, from child abuse to the moral deterioration of the
country. . . . I look in the mirror some mornings and say, 'Can this
person really be the corruptor of mankind?'" (52) Yet much of what
Gail Sausser writes about affects *all* women, not just gay women: the
insensitivity of many male gynecologists, the difficulty of living with
someone whose personal habits are in conflict with one's own, and
efforts to escape women's socialization to be shy, passive, and dependent.

Women's humor of the 1980s demonstrates that although the women's movement has not accomplished its major goals, such as passage of the Equal Rights Amendment, it has provided many women with the courage and the sense of community to claim in their writing the stance of superiority that the humorist requires if she is to confront and transcend cultural restrictions. The humorous domestic saga of the isolated housewife, such as Teresa Bloomingdale's *Sense and Momsense*, seems almost anachronistic in a field populated by such writers as Molly Ivins and Veronica Geng; yet it serves as a reminder that for many women the trivializing routine of the domestic life continues unchanged.

II

In *Humor and Social Change* (1979), Joseph Boskin notes that art and humor are related in the sense that "each attempts to create a perspective within which humans can define their individual and cultural existence."[19] For women, the task of defining both individual and cultural existence has been especially problematic. When Constance Rourke says of the mid-nineteenth century that "the lady ... was lost in the culture and the presiding masculine genius stood apart from it,"[20] she suggests the central paradox of women's self-definition, for to be "lost" in the culture is to be defined by it, to be one of its phenomena rather than one of its shapers. The "presiding masculine genius" placed woman in comedy in such a way as to codify her allowable roles and influences: she is the silly status-seeking matron in Royall Tyler's *The Contrast*; she is Rip Van Winkle's nagging wife; she is the morbidly sentimental Emmeline Grangerford in *Huck Finn*.

For women to use humor as a means of defining self in relation to culture, therefore, they had first to do battle with these images, to work from within a thicket of established stereotypes that denigrated their intellectual capacities and denied their autonomy. America's early female humorists established a tradition that clearly acknowledges these confining images and profoundly rejects them. The twentieth century merely contributed a new set of stereotypes to be fought—among them the dumb blonde, the lovelorn woman, the inept housewife. The overtly feminist and the androgynous humor of recent years have a tradition of their own that parallels closely the ebb and flow of the women's movement; their flowering now, in what has been called a "post-feminist" era, suggests that in some fundamental ways the relation of women to humor—and thus to American culture—may have been altered. While it is clear that stereotypes of women still exist and have force (and some, such as the stereotype of the lesbian, have *renewed* force), women have begun to stand more frequently apart from the culture and exercise, to paraphrase Rourke, a "female genius."

In what ways do these perceptions alter our conception of American humor? Is women's humorous literature during the past century and a half simply one more example of the general pattern in which women's art is ignored or regarded as trivial, or does it offer new insights into the relationship of Americans to their culture? The concept of a "national character" was abandoned, and with good reason, several decades after Constance Rourke's study of American humor was published in 1931; America is a coalition of numerous ethnic and racial groups, socio-economic classes, and value systems, tied loosely by a set of laws and an official rhetoric. It has long been the task of the humorist to call that rhetoric into question, and women's humor does this. But the official messages of concern to women have been substantially different from those that the male humorist has questioned: they have dictated not her public life but her private life—the manner in which she talks to her husband, cleans the house, raises her children, and conducts herself socially.

Reformulating the canon of American humorous literature so that it represents both male and female humor would compel us to acknowledge that the American humorous tradition, and therefore some important aspects of American culture itself, arises from at least two central conflicts that have heretofore been considered peripheral: the conflict between genders and the conflict between public and private spheres of experience. Frances Whitcher's gossipy sewing-circle ladies and Erma Bombeck's distraught housewives may seem to have little to do with the broad social movements and issues of public policy that have been long identified as the essence of American humor, but in fact they reveal a great deal about American social organization, with its emphasis on family, the home, and strict gender-role definition. As long as humor was considered a male-defined activity, and male humor identical with American humor, such issues as female economic dependence, child-raising practices, and the effects of technology on housekeeping—all of which are basic to social attitudes and values—were denied their centrality in the American social fabric.

For Louis D. Rubin, as for many others, the "approved American mode of humor" is "that in which cultural and social pretension are made to appear ridiculous and artificial."[21] The humorist, this suggests, prefers the ordinary to the elaborate, the commonplace to the celebrated. Yet ironically, it is precisely the commonplace, the routine, and the ordinary that women's humor has depicted, at least until recently, rather than the formal, official transaction. But because it has done so, it has been seen as reflecting the experience of a private minority rather than dealing with fundamental conflicts that are reflected in the public sphere: male dominance over women in the domestic setting mirrors the submerging of the individual by bureaucratic hierarchies of all sorts; the struggle to achieve ideal performance in an assigned role characterizes not only women's experience, but also that of every group of immigrants that has sought acceptance and assimilation into the mainstream of American life.

Perhaps most important, women's humor challenges the basic assumptions about women that have justified their public and private subordination. Instead of passive, emotional beings, women in their humorous writing show themselves to be assertive and insightful, alert to the absurdities that affect not only their lives but the values of American culture in a larger sense. The tradition of women's humor is a record of women's conscious denial of inferiority and subordination and a testament to their spirit of survival in a sexist culture.

Notes

Notes

INTRODUCTION

1. Nancy Boyd [Edna St. Vincent Millay], *Distressing Dialogues*. New York: Harper & Brothers, 1924, 281.

2. Edna St. Vincent Millay, *Letters of Edna St. Vincent Millay*, ed. Allan Ross Macdougall. Camden, Maine: Down East Books, 1952, 165-66. Subsequent references will be page numbers in the text.

3. The fact that the writing of humor is a common avocation of the "serious" writer came to me most forcefully when Eleanor Bender asked me in 1983 to be guest editor of a special issue of *Open Places* devoted to the humorous work of well-known contemporary writers. The resulting Spring 1985 issue of *Open Places*, which contained humorous prose and poetry by writers that included Cynthia Ozick, Marilyn Hacker, X. J. Kennedy, Amy Clampitt, June Jordan, Rita Dove, William Stafford, and many others, is a testament to the humorous spirit of both male and female American writers. (*Open Places* 38/39 [Spring 1985].)

4. Deanne Stillman, introduction to *Getting Back at Dad*. N.p.: Wideview Books, 1981, 5. Subsequent references will be page numbers in the text.

5. Erma Bombeck, *At Wit's End*. New York: Doubleday, 1967, 10.

6. Erma Bombeck, "At Wit's End," *Columbia (MO) Daily Tribune*, 9 Feb. 1982, 8.

7. Erma Bombeck, "Fear of Buying," *Aunt Erma's Cope Book: How To Get From Monday to Friday . . . In 12 Days*. New York: McGraw-Hill, 1979, 33.

1. THE FEMALE HUMORIST IN AMERICA

1. Francis M. Whicher, *The Widow Bedott Papers*, ed. Alice B. Neal. New York: J. C. Derby, 1856, ix. This is how the author's name is spelled on the title page of this edition, but most references spell it Frances Whitcher. I will use this latter spelling in the text. Subsequent references will be page numbers in the text.

2. Other forces were at work to counter sentimentality even as Roche's novel was published. Judith Sargent Murray (1751-1820), a crusader for women's education just after the Revolutionary War, believed that women should avoid sentimentality and fashion and turn their attention to useful occupations—including, but not limited to, homemaking. Murray's essays and stories were collected in three volumes titled *The*

Gleaner in, coincidentally, 1798, and it is worth noting that several of Murray's *Gleaner* pieces are written in a decidedly humorous style, sometimes employing dialect. For more about Murray's career, see Madelon Cheek, " 'An Inestimable Prize,' Educating Women in the New Republic: The Writings of Judith Sargent Murray," *Journal of Thought*, 20, 3 (Fall 1985): 250-62. For more about the conflict between wit and sentimentality, see Nancy Walker, "Wit, Sentimentality and the Image of Women in the Nineteenth Century," *American Studies*, 22, 2 (Fall 1981): 5-22.

3. The collected Widow Bedott and Aunt Maguire sketches, first published in 1855, sold more than 100,000 copies in the first decade after publication, and the character of the Widow Bedott was kept alive into the 1880s by Neil Burgess, a female impersonator who acted in a stage version of the Widow's adventures written by David R. Locke.

4. Linda Ann Finton Morris, "Women Vernacular Humorists in Nineteenth-Century America: Ann Stephens, Frances Whitcher, and Marietta Holley." Diss., Univ. of California-Berkeley, 1978, 139-40.

5. Walter Blair and Hamlin Hill, *America's Humor: From Poor Richard to Doonesbury*. New York: Oxford Univ. Press, 1978, 186. Despite the comprehensive-sounding title of the book, Blair and Hill largely ignore women's humor in American culture.

6. Whitcher's intention has been shared by a number of America's female humorists, one of whom, Josephine Daskam, made this explicit by titling her 1901 publication *Fables for the Fair: Cautionary Tales for Damsels Not Yet in Distress*, by One of Them.

7. Frances M. Whitcher, *Widow Spriggins, Mary Elmer, and Other Sketches*, ed. Mrs. M. L. Ward Whitcher. New York: Carleton, 1867, 44.

8. *The Widow Bedott Papers*, 316.

9. Constance Rourke, *American Humor: A Study of the National Character*. New York: Harcourt, Brace, 1931, 118-19. Subsequent references will be page numbers in the text.

10. *The Complete Poems of Emily Dickinson*, ed. Thomas H. Johnson. Boston: Little, Brown, 1955, #288.

11. Neil Schmitz, *Of Huck and Alice: Humorous Writing in American Literature*. Minneapolis: University of Minnesota Press, 1983, 6.

12. Dorothy Parker, introduction to *The Most of S. J. Perelman*. New York: Simon and Schuster, 1958, xii.

13. Sigmund Freud, "Humour," *The Complete Psychological Works of Sigmund Freud*, trans. James Strachey, 24 vols.. London: The Hogarth Press, 1961, 21: 162.

14. Joseph Boskin, *Humor and Social Change in Twentieth-Century America*. Boston: Trustees of the Public Library of the City of Boston, 1979, 11.

15. Mahadev L. Apte, *Humor and Laughter: An Anthropological Approach*. Ithaca, NY: Cornell Univ. Press, 1985, 16-17. Subsequent references will be page numbers in the text.

16. Mary Douglas, "Jokes," *Implicit Meanings: Essays in Anthropology*. London: Routledge and Kegan Paul, 1975, 107.

17. Freud, "Humour," 166. Freud's comments should be understood in the context of the clearly parental role he saw the super-ego as having in relation to the other parts of consciousness. However, that role reinforces the sense of superiority that humor requires.

18. Anne Bradstreet, *The Works of Anne Bradstreet*, ed. Jeannine Hensley. Cambridge: Belknap Press of Harvard Univ. Press, 1967, 16.

19. Bradstreet, *Works*, 198.

20. Barbara Welter, "Anti-Intellectualism and the American Woman: 1800-1860," *Mid-America*, 48 (Oct. 1966): 258.

21. Ann Beatts, "Why More Women Aren't Funny," *New Woman* (March-April 1976): 22.

22. Deanne Stillman, *Getting Back at Dad*. N.p.: Wideview Books, 1981, 5.

23. Josiah Allen's Wife [Marietta Holley], *My Opinions and Betsey Bobbet's*. Hartford: American Publishing Company, 1882, 95. *My Opinions* was first published in 1873 and was reprinted several times during the next twenty years.

24. Dorothy Parker, "Indian Summer," *The Penguin Dorothy Parker*. London: Penguin Books, 1977, 107. The irony of the title of this poem should not be lost on us, however. As an Indian summer is fleeting, so may be this speaker's decision not to change herself to please men.

25 Phyllis McGinley, *A Short Walk from the Station*. New York: Viking, 1951, 10.

26. Martha Bensley Bruère and Mary Ritter Beard, *Laughing Their Way: Women's Humor in America*. New York: Macmillan, 1934, viii.

27. Interview with Erma Bombeck, May 10, 1981, Columbia, Missouri.

28. The anthologies to which I refer are Kate Sanborn's *The Wit of Women*, published in 1885; Bruère and Beard's *Laughing Their Way*, published in 1934; and *Pulling Our Own Strings: Feminist Humor and Satire*, ed. Gloria Kaufman and Mary Kay Blakely, 1980.

29. Dorothy Parker, "Big Blonde," in *Here Lies: The Collected Stories of Dorothy Parker*. New York: The Literary Guild of America, 1939, 214.

30. Betty MacDonald, *The Egg and I*. Philadelphia: Lippincott, 1945, 71.

31. Josephine Daskam, "The Woman Who Took Things Literally," *Fables for the Fair: Cautionary Tales for Damsels Not Yet in Distress*. New York: Holt, Rinehart, 1967, 65-66.

32. Dorothy Parker, "The Waltz," *Here Lies: The Collected Stories of Dorothy Parker*. New York: The Literary Guild of America, 1939, 171-78.

33. Shirley Jackson, *Life Among the Savages*. New York: Farrar, Straus and Young, 1953, 67-73.

34. Teresa Bloomingdale, *Sense and Momsense*. Garden City, NY: Doubleday, 1986, 16.

35. Louis D. Rubin, "Introduction: 'The Great American Joke,'" *The Comic Imagination in American Literature*. New Brunswick: Rutgers University Press, 1973, 12.

36. *My Opinions and Betsey Bobbet's*, 62. 1934,

2. THE MALE TRADITION AND THE FEMALE TRADITION

1. Several books have demonstrated that New England Puritan culture was not entirely without humor. One of the earliest was Carl Holliday, *The Wit and Humor of Colonial Days, 1607-1800*. Philadelphia, 1912; more recent is W. Howland Kenney, *Laughter in the Wilderness: Early American Humor to 1783*. Kent, OH: Kent State Univ. Press, 1976.

2. E. B. and Katharine S. White, *A Subtreasury of American Humor*. New York: Modern Library, 1948, xviii. E. B. White acknowledges that he has written this intro-

duction himself, but Katharine was a fully participating editor. She was also a great appreciator of humor and deserves some of the credit for Phyllis McGinley choosing a career as a humorous writer. At least, McGinley reported that when Katharine accepted an early poem of hers for *The New Yorker*, she wrote, "we are buying your poem, but why do you sing the same sad songs all lady poets sing?"

3. Rev. H. R. Haweis, M.A., *American Humorists*. New York: Funk & Wagnalls, 1882, 12-13.

4. Haweis, 180.

5. Walter Blair, *Native American Humor*. San Francisco: Chandler, 1960, 3-10. [First published as *Native American Humor (1800-1900)*. Hartford: American Book Company, 1937.]

6. Louis D. Rubin, Jr., " 'The Barber Kept on Shaving': The Two Perspectives of American Humor," *The Comic Imagination in American Literature*, ed. Louis D. Rubin, Jr. New Brunswick: Rutgers Univ. Press, 1973, 385-86.

7. For a more complete discussion of this role for women in Twain's *Huck Finn*, see Nancy Walker, "Reformers and Young Maidens: Women and Virtue in *Adventures of Huckleberry Finn*," *One Hundred Years of Huckleberry Finn: The Boy, His Book, and American Culture*, ed. Robert Sattelmeyer and J. Donald Crowley. Columbia: Univ. of Missouri Press, 1985, 171-185.

8. Mary Ellen Goad, "The Image and the Woman in the Life and Writings of Mark Twain," *Emporia State Research Studies*, 19, 3 (March 1971): 5.

9. Alfred Habegger, *Gender, Fantasy, and Realism in American Literature*. New York: Columbia Univ. Press, 1982, 117, 124-25.

10. Mrs. Mitty wins more clearly than does Dame Van Winkle, because at the end of the story she has once again penetrated Mitty's fantasy life—and, significantly, she has the last word. But Rip Van Winkle returns from *his* fantasy to find a completely unfamiliar world. For an interesting analysis of "The Secret Life of Walter Mitty," especially as it relates to its era (1939) and to Thurber's own views, see Walter Blair and Hamlin Hill, *America's Humor: From Poor Richard to Doonesbury*. New York: Oxford Univ. Press, 1978, 448-59.

11. In *Never Done: A History of American Housework*, Susan Strasser points out that the concept of "separate spheres" was more ideology than reality, since men and women both occupied the same household for many hours of the week, but she notes that the ideology that the home was woman's particular sphere entered popular literature in the 1820s, followed closely by those—such as Lydia Maria Child and Catharine Beecher—who sought to make housework a profession. See esp. Ch. 10: "Redeeming Woman's Profession." New York: Pantheon, 1982.

12. The few poems of Emily Dickinson's that were published during her lifetime were published in the *Springfield* (MA) *Republican*, and such publication was common before the growth of the "little magazines" near the end of the century. Women seeking to publish their poetry in local newspapers were frequently the targets of satire in women's humor of the period, sometimes because of the poor quality and sentimentality of the verse and sometimes because the women's motives were not altogether literary—e.g., in Marietta Holley's *My Opinions and Betsey Bobbet's*, the husband-hunting Betsey hopes that by directing her poetry to the editor of the local paper she may snare this recently widowed prospect.

13. For an analysis of the popularity of America's dialect humor, see the introduction to *The Mirth of a Nation: America's Great Dialect Humor*, Walter Blair and Raven I. McDavid, Jr., eds, Minneapolis: Univ. of Minnesota Press, 1983, ix-xxvii.

14. "Of All Things," *The New Yorker*, 21 (February 1925): 2. The Spring 1984 issue of *Studies in American Humor* (Vol. 3 [New Series], No. 1) is a special issue devoted to the origins and development of *New Yorker* humor.

15. Such trends in humor are, of course, never consistent in a diverse society. Dialect humor—in this case, the dialect of immigrants—reappeared in the 1930s in such works as Leo C. Rosten's *The Education of Hyman Kaplan*, and regional dialect and even the tall tale have been revived more recently in the work of Garrison Keillor, both in his "Prairie Home Companion" monologues and the pieces in *Happy to Be Here* (New York: Penguin, 1983), most of which were originally published in *The New Yorker*.

16. Samuel S. Cox. *Why We Laugh*. New York: Harper and Brothers, 1876; New York: Benjamin Blom, 1969, 97.

17. Mrs. Mary Clavers [Caroline Matilda Kirkland], *A New Home—Who'll Follow? Glimpses of Western Life*, ed. William S. Osborne (1839; rpt. New Haven, CT, 1965), 105-106.

18. Clavers, 112. Mrs. Doubleday, the dumbfounded mother, is presented by the author as the stereotypical nag and model housekeeper: "She is possessed with a neat devil; I have known many such cases; her floor is scoured every night, after all are in bed but the unlucky scrubber, Betsey, the maid of all work" (108). The frequency with which female humorists make use of unflattering portraits of obsessively neat housewives suggests that the figure of the "ideal" housewife is a particularly threatening one.

19. Fanny Fern [Sara Willis Parton], "Aunt Hetty on Matrimony," *Ruth Hall and Other Writings*, ed. Joyce W. Warren, American Women Writers Series. New Brunswick: Rutgers Univ. Press, 1986, 220-21. Subsequent references will be page numbers in the text.

20. Florence Guy Seabury, *The Delicatessen Husband and Other Essays*. New York: Harcourt, Brace, 1926, 28-29.

21. Betty MacDonald [Anne Elizabeth Campbell Bard], *The Egg and I*. Philadelphia: J. B. Lippincott, 1945, 11. Subsequent references will be page numbers in the text.

22. Martha Bensley Bruère and Mary Ritter Beard, *Laughing Their Way: Women's Humor in America*. New York: Macmillan, 1934, 239-40.

23. Many of Sara Willis Parton's short columns for the *True Flag*, the *New York Ledger*, and other newspapers were collected in two volumes titled *Fern Leaves from Fanny's Portfolio*, published in 1853 and 1854. Joyce W. Warren has included a number of these in *Ruth Hall and Other Writings*.

24. E. B. White, "The Door," *Poems and Sketches of E. B. White*. New York: Harper and Row, 1981, 37.

25. S. J. Perelman, "Frou-Frou, or, the Future of Vertigo," *The Most of S. J. Perelman*. New York: Simon and Schuster, 1958, 53.

26. Woody Allen, "My Speech to the Graduates," in *Side Effects*. New York: Ballantine, 1980, 81. Several of the selections in *Side Effects* were originally published in *The New Yorker*.

27. Fanny Fern, *Ruth Hall and Other Writings*, 341.

28. Fanny Fern, 253.

29. Nancy Boyd [Edna St. Vincent Millay], "Tea for the Muse," *Distressing Dialogues*. New York: Harper and Brothers, 1924, 205-6.

30. Cornelia Otis Skinner, "Municipal Efficiency," *Laughing Their Way*, 261-62.

31. Ann J. Lane, introduction to Charlotte Perkins Gilman, *Herland*. 1915; New York: Pantheon, 1979, xiv.

32. Gilman, *Herland*, 45-46. Subsequent references will be page numbers in the text.

33. Charlotte Perkins Gilman, "If I Were a Man," in *The Charlotte Perkins Gilman Reader*, ed. Ann J. Lane. New York: Pantheon, 1980, 35. Subsequent references will be page numbers in the text.

34. Joanna Russ, *The Female Man*. London: The Women's Press, 1985, 140. Subsequent references will be page numbers in the text. Explaining her choice of genre, Russ has written:

> When I became aware (in college) of my "wrong" [i.e., female] experience, I chose fantasy. Convinced that I had no real experience of life, since my own obviously wasn't part of Great Literature, I decided consciously that I'd write of things nobody knew anything about, dammit. So I wrote realism disguised as fantasy, that is, science fiction. (*How to Suppress Women's Writing*. Austin: Univ. of Texas Press, 1983, p. 127.)

35. Natalie M. Rosinsky, "A Female Man? The 'Medusan' Humor of Joanna Russ," *Extrapolation*, 23, 1 (1982): 32-33.

36. Both humor and the all-female or genderless society are common in women's speculative fiction. Hortense Calisher's *Journal From Ellipsia* (1965) details the frequently comic misadventures of a genderless being from the planet Ellipsia who comes to Earth to learn to become human as part of an apparent exchange program between the two planets. To do so, s/he must learn the concept of "I-ness," having experienced only "we-ness" on Ellipsia. As the being becomes acquainted with human society, s/he muses on the concept of the differences between individuals implied by the concept of "I":

> Difference, we'd been taught, led to a purposelessness which in the end could only destroy; together with birth, this is the second of the three great subjects of our seasonal laughter.... I had an idea you had not our style of humor. (Boston: Little, Brown, 1965, 241-42)

37. Julia Klein, "The New Stand-up Comics," *Ms.*, October 1984: 116-26. The answer to the question asked by the subtitle is "yes," in Klein's view.

38. Florence Guy Seabury, *The Delicatessen Husband and Other Essays*. New York: Harcourt, Brace, 1926, 35.

39. Josiah Allen's Wife [Marietta Holley], *My Opinions and Betsey Bobbet's*, Hartford: American Publishing Company, 1882, 27-28.

40. Holley, 414-15.

41. Dorothy Parker, "For a Favorite Granddaughter," *The Penguin Dorothy Parker*. New York: Viking, 1973, 232-33.

42. *The Penguin Dorothy Parker*, 242.

43. Baird Leonard, "Metropolitan Monotypes," *Laughing Their Way: Women's Humor in America*, 225-26.

44. Shirley Jackson, *Life Among the Savages*. New York: Farrar, Straus and Young, 1953, 41.

45. Lawrence W. Levine, in *Black Culture and Black Consciousness*, identifies a similar use of stereotypes in the humor of American blacks. By making use of white-created stereotypes of blacks in their humor, Levine says, blacks did not reveal low self-esteem, but instead turned the tables on whites: "No other mechanism in Afro-American expressive culture was more effective than humor in exposing the absurdity of the American racial system and in releasing pent-up black aggression toward it. . . . Blacks used the majority's stereotypes in their humor in order to rob them of their power to hurt and humiliate." *Black Culture and Black Consciousness: Afro-American Folk Thought from Slavery to Freedom*. New York: Oxford Univ. Press, 1977, 335-36.

46. Jackson, 67-68.

47. Gertrude Stein, *Fernhurst, Q.E.D., and Other Early Writings*. New York, 1971, 58.

48. Neil Schmitz, *Of Huck and Alice: Humorous Writing in American Literature*. Minneapolis: Univ. of Minnesota Press, 1983, 96.

49. Linda Ann Finton Morris, "Women Vernacular Humorists in Nineteenth-Century America: Ann Stephens, Frances Whitcher, and Marietta Holley," Diss. Univ. of California-Berkeley, 1978, 8.

50. *The Egg and I*, 50, 136.

51. Phyllis McGinley, "Confessions of a Reluctant Optimist," *Times Three: Selected Verse from Three Decades*. New York: Viking, 1961, 149-50.

52. Phyllis McGinley, Introduction to *A Short Walk From the Station*. New York: Viking, 1951, 21.

53. Nora Ephron, "Dealing with the, uh, Problem," *Crazy Salad: Some Things About Women*. New York: Bantam, 1976, 80. Subsequent references will be page numbers in the text.

54. Pat Mainardi, "The Politics of Housework," *Sisterhood is Powerful* (1970); Gloria Kaufman and Mary Kay Blakely, *Pulling Our Own Strings: Feminist Humor and Satire*. Bloomington: Indiana Univ. Press, 1980, 129-30.

55. Deanne Stillman, "The Feminish Dictionary: A Guide to Defining Ourselves," *Getting Back at Dad*. N.p.: Wideview Books, 1981, 68-72.

56. Judy Little, *Comedy and the Woman Writer: Woolf, Spark, and Feminism*. Lincoln: Univ. of Nebraska Press, 1983, 6.

57. Russ, *How to Suppress Women's Writing*, 76.

58. Lawrence W. Levine makes a similar argument about white response to the humor of blacks in *Black Culture and Black Consciousness*. See especially "Laughing at the Man," 300-20. At just the time when scholars are re-examining the life and work of Dorothy Parker, Mordecai Richler explains his omission of her work from his recent anthology in the following terms:

> The legendary Miss Parker gave me endless trouble. I'm afraid I found her comic stories brittle, short on substance, and, to come clean, no longer very funny; and I can't help wondering how many of her devoted admirers have read her recently. (*The Best of Modern Humor*. New York: Knopf, 1983, xviii.)

Richler's use of the term "Miss" signals the condescending tone of the comment.

59. Jane Curry, "Women as Subjects and Writers of Nineteenth Century American Humor." Diss. University of Michigan, 1975; Linda Ann Finton Morris, "Women Vernacular Humorists in Nineteenth-Century America: Ann Stephens, Frances Whitcher, and

Marietta Holley," Diss. University of California-Berkeley, 1978; Zita Zatkin Dresner, "Twentieth Century American Women Humorists." Diss. University of Maryland, 1982.

60. Marietta Holley, *Samantha Rastles the Woman Question*, ed. Jane Curry. Urbana: Univ. of Illinois Press, 1983; Fanny Fern, *Ruth Hall and Other Writings*.

3. HUMOR, INTELLECT, FEMININITY

1. Alice Wellington Rollins, "Woman's Sense of Humor," *The Critic and Good Literature*, I (new series), no. 13 (29 March 1884), 145-46; "The Humor of Women," I, no. 26 (28 June 1884), 301-2.

2. Kate Sanborn, *The Wit of Women*. New York: Funk & Wagnalls, 1885, 14. Subsequent references will be page numbers in the text.

3. Anna Cora Mowatt, *Fashion*, in *Plays by American Women: The Early Years*, ed. Judith E. Barlow. New York: Avon, 1981, 5-6.

4. W. A. Jones, "The Ladies' Library," *Graham's Magazine*, 21 (1842): 333. Alfred Habegger quotes this and other, similar comments about women's humorlessness as part of his argument that one of the essential ingredients in American humor has been the idealization of woman as the reformer of the male jokester. *Gender, Fantasy, and Realism in American Literature*. New York: Columbia Univ. Press, 1982. See especially Ch. 12, "Easygoing Men and Dressy Ladies."

5. Kate H. Winter, *Marietta Holley: Life with "Josiah Allen's Wife."* Syracuse: Syracuse Univ. Press, 1984, 79.

6. Fanny Fern, *Ruth Hall and Other Writings*, ed. Joyce W. Warren. American Women Writers Series. New Brunswick, NJ: Rutgers Univ. Press, 1986, xxxvi-xxxvii. It was undoubtedly this "masculine" writing that occasioned Nathaniel Hawthorne's comment about *Ruth Hall*—"The woman writes as if the devil was in her"—a compliment that set her apart from the "scribbling women" whose popularity he deplored.

7. Arthur B. Maurice, "Feminine Humorists," *Good Housekeeping* 50 (January 1910): 34.

8. Thomas L. Masson, "Dorothy Parker," *Our American Humorists*. New York: Moffat, Yard, 1922, 276.

9. Margaretta Newell, "Are Women Humorous?" *Outlook and Independent* 14 Oct. 1931: 206. Subsequent references will be page numbers in the text.

10. Elizabeth Stanley Trotter, "Humor with a Gender," *The Atlantic Monthly*, Dec. 1922: 784.

11. Mary Austin, "The Sense of Humor in Women," *The New Republic*, 41, 1, 26 Nov. 1924: 11. Subsequent references will be page numbers in the text.

12. Martha Bensley Bruère and Mary Ritter Beard, foreword to *Laughing Their Way: Women's Humor in America*. New York: Macmillan, 1934, vii.

13. Deanne Stillman, *Getting Back at Dad*. N.p.: Wideview Books, 1981, 5.

14. Kathy Witkowsky, "Cartoon Verite," *Vogue*, February 1986: 222.

15. Siriol Hugh-Jones, "We Witless Women," *Twentieth Century*, July 1961: 16-17.

16. Ann Beatts, "Why More Women Aren't Funny," *New Woman*, March-April 1976: 22-28.

17. Julia Klein, "The New Stand-Up Comics," *Ms.* October 1984: 126.

18. Barbara Welter, "Anti-Intellectualism and the American Woman: 1800-1860," *Mid-America*, 48 (October 1966): 258. Subsequent references will be page numbers in the text.

19. Interestingly, in Fanny Fern's *Ruth Hall*, when Ruth's benefactor, John Walter, insists that she have a phrenological examination, the phrenologist finds that she has "great powers of sarcasm" and a "keen sense of the ludicrous," qualities that set Fern's heroine apart from the common image of mid-nineteenth century womanhood. 170.

20. Susan P. Conrad, *Perish the Thought: Intellectual Women in Romantic America, 1830-1860*. Secaucus, NJ: Citadel Press, 1978, 24. Subsequent references will be page numbers in the text.

21. Josiah Allen's Wife [Marietta Holley], *My Opinions and Betsey Bobbet's*. Hartford, CT: American Publishing Company, 1882, 92. Subsequent references will be page numbers in the text.

22. Alice James, *The Diary of Alice James*, ed. Leon Edel. New York: Penguin, 1964, 95, 61.

23. A. Winterstein, "Contributions to the Problem of Humor," *The Psychoanalytic Quarterly*, 3 (1934): 303. It is interesting to note that 1934 was the same year in which the second anthology of American women's humor, *Laughing Their Way*, was published.

24. David Zippin, "Sex Differences and the Sense of Humor," *Psychoanalytic Review*, 53 (1966): 50.

25. The age range results from the fact that most psychologists doing such studies are in academic settings and derive their subjects from the available student populations.

26. Alice Sheppard [Klak], "Sex-Role Attitudes, Sex Differences, and Comedian's Sex," paper presented at the International Conference on Humour and Laughter, Cardiff, Wales, July 1976, 3. See also Alice [Sheppard] Klak, "Joking and Appreciation of Humor in Nursery School Children," *Child Development* 45 (1974): 1098-1102; Alice Sheppard [Klak], "Humor and Sex-Role Stereotypes," paper presented at Pioneers for Century III, Conference on the Power of Women and Men, Cincinnati, April 1975; Louise Omwake, "A Study of the Sense of Humor: Its Relation to Sex, Age and Personal Characteristics," *Journal of Applied Psychology* 21 (1937): 688-704.

27. Greer Litton Fox, " 'Nice Girl': Social Control of Women through a Value Construct," *Signs*, 2, 4 (Summer 1977): 805. Subsequent references will be page numbers in the text.

28. Alice B. Neal, ed. *The Widow Bedott Papers* by Frances M. Whitcher. New York: J. C. Derby, 1856, ix.

29. Mahadev L. Apte, *Humor and Laughter: An Anthropological Approach*. Ithaca: Cornell Univ. Press, 1985, 73. Subsequent references will be page numbers in the text.

30. Carol Mitchell, "Some Differences in Male and Female Joke Telling," *Women's Folklore, Women's Culture*, ed. Rosan A. Jordan and Susan J. Kalcik. Philadelphia: Univ. of Pennsylvania Press, 1985, 168. Subsequent references will be page numbers in the text.

31. Robin Lakoff, *Language and Woman's Place*. New York: Harper and Row, 1975, 4. Subsequent references will be page numbers in the text.

32. Hélène Cixous, "The Laugh of the Medusa," trans. Keith and Paula Cohen, *Signs*, 1, 4 (Summer 1976): 885, 879.

33. Alice Duer Miller, *Are Women People? A Book of Rhymes for Suffrage Times*. New York: George H. Doran, 1915, 59. Subsequent references will be page numbers in the text.

34. Josephine Daskam, *Fables for the Fair: Cautionary Tales for Damsels Not Yet in Distress*. 1901; New York: Holt, Rinehart, 1967, 15-16. Subsequent references will be page numbers in the text.

35. Louisa May Alcott, "Transcendental Wild Oats," *Silver Pitchers and Independence*. London: Sampson, Low, Marston & Co., 1876, 76. Subsequent references will be page numbers in the text.

36. Mrs. Mary Clavers [Caroline Mathilda Kirkland], *A New Home — Who'll Follow? or Glimpses of Western Life*, ed. William S. Osborne. 1839; New Haven: Yale University Press, 1965, 109, 144.

37. Fanny Fern [Sara Willis Parton], *Fern Leaves from Fanny's Port-Folio*. Caxton Edition. Chicago: Donohue, Henneberry, 1890, 372. Subsequent references will be to this edition.

38. Anita Loos, *Gentlemen Prefer Blondes*. New York: Liveright, 1925, 12-13. Subsequent references will be page numbers in the text.

39. Zita Zatkin Dresner, "Twentieth Century American Women Humorists." Diss. Univ. of Maryland, 1982, 64-65. Subsequent references will be page numbers in the text.

40. Dorothy Parker, "Big Blonde," in *Here Lies: The Collected Stories of Dorothy Parker*. New York: The Literary Guild of America, 1939, 213. Subsequent references will be page numbers in the text.

41. Jean Kerr, "Tales Out of School: The Sandwich Crisis," in *How I Got to be Perfect*. Gerden City, NY: Doubleday, 1978, 102. This essay was orginally published in *Ladies Home Journal* in 1959.

42. Peg Bracken, *The I Hate to Cook Book*. New York: Fawcett Crest, 1960, 29.

43. Erma Bombeck, *Aunt Erma's Cope Book*. New York: McGraw-Hill, 1979, 31-32.

44. Phyllis McGinley, "Apology for Husbands," *Times Three: Selected Verse from Three Decades*. New York: Viking, 1961, 261.

45. Phyllis McGinley, "Trial and Error," *A Short Walk from the Station*. New York: Viking, 1951, 130.

46. Shirley Jackson, *Life Among the Savages*. New York: Farrar, Straus and Young, 1953, 148.

47. Phyllis McGinley, "Collector's Items," *Times Three*, 182.

48. Jean Kerr, "The Children's Hour After Hour After Hour," *How I Got to be Perfect*, 236.

49. Judith Viorst, "Where is it Written," *It's Hard to be Hip Over Thirty and other Tragedies of Married Life*. New York: New American Library, 1968, 55.

4. THE HUMOR OF THE "MINORITY"

1. Langston Hughes, "A Note on Humor," *The Book of Negro Humor*. New York: Dodd, Mead, 1966, vii.

2. Martha Bensley Bruère and Mary Ritter Beard, foreword to *Laughing Their Way: Women's Humor in America*. New York: Macmillan, 1934, viii.

3. The terminology here is admittedly tricky. Obviously, a "white" woman can be a member of a distinct ethnic minority. I use the term to refer to women of at least the

middle class whose ethnic origins are sufficiently indistinct that they have not suffered overt ethnic prejudice in American culture, though their ancestors (e.g., Irish) may have.

4. William H. Chafe, *Women and Equality: Changing Patterns in American Culture*. New York: Oxford Univ. Press, 1977, 4. Subsequent references will be page numbers in the text. See also the much earlier study by Helen Mayer Hacker, "Women as a Minority Group," *Social Forces* 30 (October 1951): 60-69.

5. Louis Wirth, "The Problem of Minority Groups," *The Science of Man in the World Crisis*, ed. Ralph Linton. New York, 1945, 347-50.

6. Carolyn Heilbrun, "Woman as Outsider," *Reinventing Womanhood*. New York: W. W. Norton, 1979, 42.

7. Nina Auerbach, *Communities of Women: An Idea in Fiction*. Cambridge: Harvard Univ. Press, 1978, 5. Subsequent references will be page numbers in the text.

8. "Literature and Ethnicity," ed. Stephan Thernstrom, *Harvard Encyclopedia of American Ethnic Groups*, Cambridge: Harvard Univ. Press, 1980, 648.

9. New York: Oxford University Press, 1986, 16-17. Subsequent references will be page numbers in the text.

10. Reported in Lawrence W. Levine, *Black Culture and Black Consciousness: Afro-American Folk Thought from Slavery to Freedom*. New York: Oxford Univ. Press, 1977, 315. Subsequent references will be page numbers in the text.

11. Alice Childress, *Like One of the Family . . . Conversations from a Domestic's Life*. 1956; Boston: Beacon Press, 1986, 1-3. Subsequent references will be page numbers in the text.

12. *The Book of Negro Humor*, 160-61.

13. Food is a common ethnic linkage, and Mattie's longing for black-eyed peas represents her desire for the comfort of a group with which she feels comfortable. Similar is the situation of the immigrant mother in Anzia Yezierska's 1920 story "The Fat of the Land," who rejects American food and yearns for the herring and onions of her days on the Lower East Side while living in a Riverside Drive apartment with servants.

14. Zora Neale Hurston, *Dust Tracks on a Road: An Autobiography*, ed. Robert E. Hemenway. 2nd ed. Urbana: Univ. of Illinois Press, 1984, 13. Subsequent references will be page numbers in the text.

15. John Lowe, "Hurston, Humor, and the Harlem Renaissance," in *The Harlem Renaissance Re-examined*, ed. Victor Kramer. New York: AMS Press, 1987, 286.

16. John Keats, *You Might as Well Live: The Life and Times of Dorothy Parker*. 1970; New York: Paragon House, 1986, 87.

17. Fredrik Barth, Introduction to *Ethnic Groups and Boundaries: The Social Organization of Culture Difference*, ed. Fredrik Barth. Boston: Little, Brown, 1969, 9-38.

18. Wsevolod W. Isajiw, "Definitions of Ethnicity," *Ethnicity*, 1 (1974): 122.

19. Werner Sollors, *Beyond Ethnicity: Consent and Descent in American Culture*. New York: Oxford, 1986, 132-41. Sollors in fact argues that all American literature is "ethnic" literature because of the immigrant status of virtually all Americans; those such as white Anglo-Saxon Protestants who are supposed to have no "ethnic" identity have in fact the same kind of group cultural linkages — religion, food, language, etc. — as do members of any other group commonly referred to as "ethnic."

20. W. Howland Kenney, *Laughter in the Wilderness: Early American Humor to 1783*. Kent, OH: Kent State Univ. Press, 1976, 5.

21. Allen Guttmann, "Jewish Humor," *The Comic Imagination in American Literature*, ed. Louis D. Rubin, Jr. New Brunswick, NJ: Rutgers Univ. Press, 1973, 330.

22. *The Book of Negro Humor*, 25.

23. Reprinted in Mahadev L. Apte, *Humor and Laughter: An Anthropological Approach*. Ithaca, NY: Cornell Univ. Press, 1985, 116. Subsequent references will be page numbers in the text.

24. Tey Diana Rebolledo, "Walking the Thin Line: Humor in Chicana Literature," in *Beyond Stereotypes: The Critical Analysis of Chicana Literature*, ed. María Harrera-Sobek. Binghamton, NY: Bilingual Press, 1985, 94. Subsequent references will be page numbers in the text.

25. An exception to this trend is Leslie Tonner's *Nothing But the Best: The Luck of the Jewish Princess*, which describes the lives of the pampered daughters of upwardly mobile American Jewish families. (New York: Ballantine, 1975)

26. Judith Viorst, *People & Other Aggravations*. New York: Harper & Row, 1971, 61. Subsequent references will be page numbers in the text.

27. Nora Ephron, "*Gourmet* Magazine," *Scribble Scribble: Notes on the Media*. New York: Knopf, 1978, 120.

28. Fran Lebowitz, "When Smoke Gets in Your Eyes . . . Shut Them," *Social Studies*. New York: Random House, 1981, 104.

29. Naomi Weisstein, "Why We Aren't Laughing . . . Anymore," *Ms.*, November 1973: 90.

30. Sharon Weinstein, "Don't Women Have a Sense of Comedy They Can Call Their Own?" *American Humor: An Interdisciplinary Newsletter*, 1, 2 (Fall 1974): 9.

31. Josiah Allen's Wife [Marietta Holley], *My Opinions and Betsey Bobbet's*. Hartford: American Publishing Co., 1882, 236.

32. *Samantha Rastles the Woman Question*, ed. Jane Curry. Urbana: Univ. of Illinois Press, 1983, 167.

33. Betty MacDonald, *The Egg and I*. Philadelphia: Lippincott, 1945, 108.

34. Regenia Gagnier, in a study of British women's autobiographies of the nineteenth and early twentieth centuries, has come to much the same conclusion. In "Between Women: A Cross-Class Analysis of Anarchic Humor," a paper delivered at the December 1986 meeting of the Modern Language Association, Gagnier asserts that "Victorian women used humor neither for disparagement nor temporary release, but rather as an anarchic assault against the codes constricting them" (5).

35. Neil Schmitz, *Of Huck and Alice: Humorous Writing in American Literature*. Minneapolis: Univ. of Minnesota Press, 1983, 135.

36. Joseph M. Peck, M.D., *Life with Women and How to Survive It*. Englewood Cliffs, NJ: Prentice-Hall, 1961, xi-xii.

37. From the jacket blurb for *Dithers and Jitters*. New York: Dodd, Mead, 1938.

38. *Dithers and Jitters*, 117. Subsequent references will be page numbers in the text.

39. Teresa Bloomingdale, "It's All in the Game," *Sense and Momsense*. New York: Doubleday, 1986, 92-93. Subsequent references will be page numbers in the text.

40. Rayna Green, "Magnolias Grow in Dirt: The Bawdy Lore of Southern Women," *Southern Exposure*, 4 (1977): 29. Subsequent references will be page numbers in the text.

41. Rolande Diot, "Sexus, Nexus and Taboos versus Female Humor: The Case of Erica Jong," *Revue Française D' Études Americaines*, 30 (November 1986), 492. Subsequent references will be page numbers in the text.

42. Mary Kuczkir, *My Dishtowel Flies at Half-Mast*. New York: Ballantine, 1980, 133. Subsequent references will be page numbers in the text.

43. Jean Kerr, *Penny Candy*. Garden City, NY: Doubleday, 1970, 52.

44. Anne Bradstreet, *The Works of Anne Bradstreet*, ed. Jeannine Hensley. Cambridge: Belknap Press of Harvard Univ. Press, 1967, 16.

45. Frances Whitcher. *The Widow Bedott Papers*. New York: J. C. Derby, 1856, 26. Subsequent references will be page numbers in the text.

46. Peg Bracken. *The I Hate to Cook Book*. New York: Fawcett, 1960, vii.

47. Joan D. Uebelhoer, "We Need a Name for Bernadette Arnold," *Pulling Our Own Strings: Feminist Humor and Satire*, ed. Gloria Kaufman and Mary Kay Blakely. Bloomington: Indiana Univ. Press, 1980, 97.

48. Fanny Fern [Sara Willis Parton], "Aunt Hetty on Matrimony," *Fern Leaves from Fanny's Port-Folio*. Chicago: Donohue, Henneberry, 1890, 377. Subsequent references will be page numbers in the text.

49. Dorothy Parker, "To a Much Too Unfortunate Lady," *The Portable Dorothy Parker*, Rev. ed. New York: Viking, 1973, 84. Subsequent references will be page numbers in the text.

50. Josephine Daskam, *Fables for the Fair: Cautionary Tales for Damsels Not Yet in Distress*. 1901; New York: Holt, Rinehart, 1967.

51. Helen Rowland, *The Sayings of Mrs. Solomon*. New York: Dodge, 1913, 11. Subsequent references will be page numbers in the text.

52. Judith Martin, *Miss Manners' Guide to Excruciatingly Correct Behavior*. New York: Atheneum, 1982, 409. Traditionally, women have been more frequent seekers of advice from newspaper columnists than men, and have typically been the ones to purchase, consult, and be guided by etiquette books, so in that sense Martin could be appealing primarily to a female readership.

53. Deanne Stillman, "Ann Van Brothers Talks to Teens about Your Hair, Your Figure, Your Diet, Your Sweat, and Your Face," *Getting Back at Dad*. N.p.: Wideview Books, 1975, 32-40.

54. Veronica Geng, "Petticoat Power," *Partners*. New York: Harper and Row, 1984, 52-58.

55. Robin Lakoff, *Language and Woman's Place*. New York: Harper and Row, 1975, 82. Subsequent references will be page numbers in the text.

56. Alice Duer Miller, *Are Women People? A Book of Rhymes for Suffrage Times*. New York: George H. Doran, 1915, 50.

57. Florence Guy Seabury, *The Delicatessen Husband and Other Essays*. New York: Harcourt, Brace, 1926, 3. Subsequent references will be page numbers in the text.

58. Helen Rowland, *Reflections of a Bachelor Girl*. New York: Dodge, 1909, 33, 12.

59. Jean Kerr, "The Ten Worst Things About a Man," *The Snake Has All the Lines*. Garden City, NY: Doubleday, 1960, 121.

5. FEMINIST HUMOR

1. Josiah Allen's Wife [Marietta Holley], *My Opinions and Betsey Bobbet's*. Hartford: American Publishing Co., 1872, 313-14. Subsequent references will be page numbers in the text.

2. Henry James, *The Bostonians*. 1886. Rpt. New York: Dial Press, 1945, 31. Subsequent references will be page numbers in the text.

3. Terry Hekker, *Ever Since Adam and Eve*. New York: Fawcett Crest, 1980, 138. Hekker's defense of the profession of homemaking is ultimately unconvincing, because she continually undercuts it with comments that reveal her own discomfort and dependency. As the most blatant example, she dedicates the book to her mother and grandmother, but then says in a footnote that she had thought of dedicating it to her husband, but had noticed "how many women dedicated first books to their supportive and understanding husbands and the husbands subsequently decided to support and understand a younger woman. Why tempt fate?" Later in the book, arguing that careers do not give women economic independence because they are never assured of keeping their jobs, she rationalizes her own economic dependence:

> I do have one edge that has historically been a weighty advantage (forgive me Gloria Steinem); I sleep with the boss. I also know the date of his mother's birthday and the name of the only starch that doesn't give him hives. And how much Tabasco goes into his bloody marys. (184)

4. Phyllis McGinley, *Stones from a Glass House: New Poems*. New York: Viking, 1946, 73.

5. Judith Viorst, *Love & Guilt & The Meaning of Life, Etc.* New York: Simon and Schuster, 1979, 7.

6. Naomi Weisstein, "Why We're Not Laughing . . . Anymore," *Ms.*, November 1973: 51. Subsequent references will be page numbers in the text.

7. In Fay Weldon's satiric novel *Down Among the Women*, her character Scarlet, deciding to take charge of her own life, breaks up with the man with whom she has been having an affair. Angered, he says to her, "You have no sense of humor." " 'Get out,' says Scarlet, made more furious by this than by any other insult he has offered her." 1972; Chicago: Academy Chicago Publishers, 1984, 182.

8. Gloria Kaufman and Mary Kay Blakely, eds. *Pulling Our Own Strings: Feminist Humor and Satire*. Bloomington: Indiana Univ. Press, 1980, 13. Subsequent references will be page numbers in the text.

9. Harvey Mindess, *Laughter and Liberation*. Los Angeles: Nash Publishing, 1971, 199. Subsequent references will be page numbers in the text.

10. *Pulling Our Own Strings*, 174.

11. *Pulling Our Own Strings*, 70.

12. Marge Piercy, "What's That Smell in the Kitchen?" *The Norton Book of Light Verse*, ed. Russell Baker. New York: W. W. Norton, 1986, 397-98. Originally published in *Circles on the Water*, 1982.

13. Jane De Hart Mathews, "The New Feminism and the Dynamics of Social Change," *Women's America: Refocusing the Past*, ed. Linda K. Kerber and Jane De Hart Mathews. New York: Oxford Univ. Press, 1982, 406.

14. Peg Bracken, *I Didn't Come Here to Argue*. New York: Harcourt, Brace & World, 1969, 12.

15. Hester Eisenstein, *Contemporary Feminist Thought*. Boston: G. K. Hall, 1983, 36. Subsequent references will be page numbers in the text.

16. Reprinted in *Pulling Our Own Strings*, 85.

17. Alice Duer Miller, *Are Women People? A Book of Rhymes for Suffrage Times*. New York: George H. Doran, 1915, 12.

18. Umberto Eco, "Frames of Comic 'Freedom,'" *Carnival!*, ed. Thomas A. Sebeok. Berlin: Mouton Publishers, 1984, 8. Subsequent references will be page numbers in the text.

19. Erica Jong, *Parachutes and Kisses*. New York: New American Library, 1984, 40.

20. Mary Kuczkir, *My Dishtowel Flies at Half-Mast*. New York: Ballantine, 1980, 227.

21. Patricia Meyer Spacks, *The Female Imagination*. New York: Alfred A. Knopf, 1972. See especially Ch. 8: "Free Women."

22. Gloria Steinem, "If Men Could Menstruate," *Ms.*, October 1978: 25.

23. Dorothy L. Sayers, "The Human-Not-Quite-Human," *Unpopular Opinions*, 1947; *Are Women Human?* Grand Rapids, MI: William B. Eerdmans, 1971, 40.

24. Elaine Showalter, introduction to *These Modern Women: Autobiographical Essays from the Twenties*. Old Westbury, NY: The Feminist Press, 1978, 26.

25. For an earlier refutation of this perception, see Nancy Walker, "Do Feminists Ever Laugh? Women's Humor and Women's Rights," *International Journal of Women's Studies*, 4, 1 (January/February 1981): 1-9.

26. Evelyn C. White, "Stand Up and Laugh: New Feminist Comics," *Backbone 4: Humor by Northwest Women*, ed. Barbara Wilson and Rachel Da Silva. Seattle: The Seal Press, 1982, 88.

27. Susan Strasser, *Never Done: A History of American Housework*. New York: Pantheon, 1982, 307-308.

28. Betty Friedan, *The Feminine Mystique*. New York: W. W. Norton, 1963, 57.

29. Annegret S. Ogden, *The Great American Housewife: From Helpmate to Wage Earner, 1776-1986*. Westport, CT: Greenwood Press, 1986, xii-xiii. Subsequent references will be page numbers in the text.

30. Joanna Russ, *The Female Man*, 1975. London: The Women's Press, 1985, 140.

31. Peg Bracken, *The I Hate to Cook Book*. New York: Fawcett, 1960, 24.

32. Reprinted in *Pulling Our Own Strings*, 67.

33. For an excellent brief analysis of these arguments and Samantha's typical responses, see Jane Curry's introduction to *Samantha Rastles the Women Question*, Urbana: Univ. of Illinois Press, 1983. Holley promoted her feminist principles only through her character Samantha, refusing invitations by leading feminists of her day to more publicly espouse the cause. See Kate H. Winter, *Marietta Holley: Life with "Josiah Allen's Wife."* Syracuse: Syracuse Univ. Press, 1984, esp. 65-68. In looking back at her life, Holley did not even acknowledge her use of humor as a political weapon, stating instead that humor was a useful coping mechanism: "our daily life which we must needs all endure—has so many disagreeable and sad happenings that it may be well to turn from them as often as may be and think of pleasanter things." Marietta Holley, "About My Books and Interesting People I have Met," undated, handwritten ms., Univ. of Illinois Rare Book Room, Champaign-Urbana, IL.

34. Judith Viorst, "A Women's Liberation Movement Woman," *It's Hard to Be Hip Over Thirty and other Tragedies of Married Life*. New York: New American Library, 1968, 17.

35. Zita Zatkin Dresner, "Twentieth Century American Women Humorists." Diss., Univ. of Maryland, 1982, 269-70.

36. Erica Jong, "Woman Enough," *At the Edge of the Body*. New York: Holt, Rinehart and Winston, 1979, 70-71.

37. Susan J. Wolfe, "Ingroup Lesbian Feminist Political Humor." Paper delivered at the Midwest Modern Language Association, Minneapolis, November, 1980, 1-2. Subsequent references will be page numbers in the text.

38. "Crooked and Straight in Academia," *Pulling Our Own Strings*, 119.

39. *Pulling Our Own Strings*, 134.

40. "Ingroup Lesbian Feminist Political Humor," 2-3.

41. Felicia Lamport, "Paradigm," *Cultural Slag*. Boston: Houghton Mifflin, 1966, 134.

42. Nora Ephron, "On Consciousness-Raising," *Crazy Salad: Some Things About Women*. New York: Alfred A. Knopf, 1975, 72. Subsequent references will be page numbers in the text.

43. Deanne Stillman, "The Feminish Dictionary: A Guide to Defining Ourselves," *Getting Back at Dad*. N.p.: Wideview Books, 1981, 68-72.

44. Roy Blount, Jr., *What Men Don't Tell Women*. New York: Penguin, 1984, 31. The shallowness of male commitment to feminism is the message of the last section of Erica Jong's "Seventeen Warnings in Search of a Feminist Poem," which recalls the long tradiiton of women's advice humor: "Beware of the man who praises liberated women: he is planning to quit his job" (*Half-Lives*. New York: Holt, Rinehart and Winston, 1973, 13).

45. Feminist cartooning seems to flourish particularly in England, which has several active feminist presses. Two recent collections of feminist cartoons are *Sourcream 2* London: Sheba Feminist Publishers, 1981, and Christine Roche's *I'm Not a Feminist but . . .* London: Virago Press, 1985.

46. Agnes Repplier, *In Pursuit of Laughter*. Boston: Houghton Mifflin, 1936, 221.

6. THE TRADITION AND BEYOND

1. Marshall P. Wilder, ed. *The Wit and Humor of America*. 10 vols. New York: Funk & Wagnalls, 1908, 1, vii.

2. *Ms.*, 2, 5 (November 1983). Cover drawing by Marie Severin.

3. Catharine R. Stimpson, "The 'F' Word," *Ms.* 16, 1/2 (July/August 1987): 196.

4. Susan Dworkin, "Roseanne Barr: The Disgruntled Housewife as Stand-up Comedian," *Ms.* 16, 1/2 (July/August 1987): 106-8.

5. Pat Sellers, "Funny Ladies: Stand-up's Newest Standouts," *Cosmopolitan*. Sept. 1987: 291.

6. Mary Bess Whidden, "Course Offerings," *Provincial Matters*. Albuquerque: Univ. of New Mexico Press, 1985, 23-24. Subsequent references will be page numbers in the text.

7. Woody Allen, "Spring Bulletin," *More Tales Out of School*, eds. Helen S. Weiss and M. Jerry Weiss. New York: Bantam, 1980, 114.

8. Victoria Geng, "Poll," *The New Yorker*, 3 August 1987: 21.

9. Cornelia Otis Skinner, "Opening Night," *Nuts in May*. New York: Dodd, Mead, 1950, 103-12.

10. Jean Kerr, "Out of Town with a Show," *How I Got to be Perfect*. Garden City, NY: Doubleday, 1978, 161. This piece was originally published in *Harper's Magazine* in 1960.

11. Molly Ivins, "Wilson is one of a kind—even in Afghanistan," Dallas *Times Herald*, 27 Feb. 1986, A-21.

12. Molly Ivins, "Bureaucrats should be issued common-sense directive," Dallas *Times Herald*, 26 Jan. 1986, A-25.

13. Felicia Lamport, "The Love Song of R. Milhous Nixon," *Light Metres*. New York: Perigree Books, 1982, 121.

14. *Provincial Matters*, 144.

15. Fran Lebowitz, "Lesson One," *Social Studies*. New York: Random House, 1981, 83. Subsequent references will be page numbers in the text.

16. Veronica Geng, *Partners*. New York: Harper & Row, 1984, 169. Subsequent references will be page numbers in the text.

17. Deanne Stillman, "Ann Van Brothers Talks to Teens About Your Hair, Your Figure, Your Diet, Your Sweat, and Your Face," *Getting Back at Dad*. N.p.: Wideview Books, 1981, 34. Subsequent references will be page numbers in text.

18. Gail Sausser, *Lesbian Etiquette*. Freedom, CA: The Crossing Press, 1986, 55. Subsequent references will be page numbers in the text.

19. Joseph Boskin, *Humor and Social Change in Twentieth Century America*. Boston: Trustees of the Public Library of the City of Boston, 1969, 3.

20. Constance Rourke, *American Humor: A Study of the National Character*. New York: Harcourt, Brace, 1931, 119.

21. Louis D. Rubin, Jr., "'The Barber Kept on Shaving': The Two Perspectives of American Humor," *The Comic Imagination in American Literature*. New Brunswick, NJ: Rutgers Univ. Press, 1973, 386.

Bibliography

Selected Bibliography

Alcott, Louisa May. "Transcendental Wild Oats." In *Silver Pitchers and Independence*. London: Sampson, Low, Marston & Co., 1876. 66-83.

Allen, Woody. *Side Effects*. New York: Ballantine, 1980.

Apte, Mahadev L. *Humor and Laughter: An Anthropological Approach*. Ithaca, NY: Cornell UP, 1985.

Auerbach, Nina. *Communities of Women: An Idea in Fiction*. Cambridge: Harvard UP, 1978.

Austin, Mary. "The Sense of Humor in Women." *The New Republic* 26 November 1924: 10-13.

Baker, Russell, ed. *The Norton Book of Light Verse*. New York: Norton, 1986.

Barth, Frederik, ed. *Ethnic Groups and Boundaries: The Social Organization of Culture Difference*. Boston: Little, Brown, 1969.

Beatts, Ann. "Why More Women Aren't Funny." *New Woman* March/April 1976: 22-28.

———. "Can a Woman Get a Laugh and a Man Too?" *Mademoiselle* Nov. 1975: 140 + .

Bier, Jesse. *The Rise and Fall of American Humor*. Ames: Iowa State UP, 1968.

Blair, Walter. *Native American Humor*. 1937. San Francisco: Chandler, 1960.

Blair, Walter, and Hamlin Hill. *America's Humor: From Poor Richard to Doonesbury*. New York: Oxford UP, 1978.

Blair, Walter, and Raven I. McDavid, Jr. *The Mirth of a Nation: America's Great Dialect Humor*. Minneapolis: U of Minnesota Press, 1983.

Blicksilver, Edith. "Literature as Social Criticism: The Ethnic Woman Writer." *Modern Language Studies* 5 (Fall 1975): 46-54.

Bloomingdale, Teresa. *Sense and Momsense*. Garden City, NY: Doubleday, 1986.

Blount, Roy, Jr. *What Men Don't Tell Women*. New York: Penguin, 1984.

Bombeck, Erma. *At Wit's End*. New York: Doubleday, 1967.

———. *Aunt Erma's Cope Book: How To Get From Monday to Friday . . . In 12 Days*. New York: McGraw-Hill, 1979.

Boskin, Joseph. *Humor and Social Change in Twentieth-Century America*. Boston: Trustees of the Public Library of the City of Boston, 1979.

Boyd, Nancy [Edna St. Vincent Millay]. *Distressing Dialogues*. New York: Harper and Brothers, 1924.

Bracken, Peg. *I Didn't Come Here to Argue*. New York: Harcourt, Brace & World, 1969.

_____. *The I Hate to Cook Book*. New York: Fawcett Crest, 1960.

Bradstreet, Anne. *The Works of Anne Bradstreet*. Ed. Jeannine Hensley. Cambridge: Belknap Press of Harvard UP, 1967.

Bruère, Martha Bensley, and Mary Ritter Beard. *Laughing Their Way: Women's Humor in America*. New York: Macmillan, 1934.

Burma, John H. "Humor as a Technique in Race Conflict." *American Sociological Review* 11.6 (Dec. 1946): 710-15.

Calisher, Hortense. *Journal From Ellipsia*. Boston: Little, Brown, 1965.

Chafe, William H. *Women and Equality: Changing Patterns in American Culture*. New York: Oxford UP, 1977.

Childress, Alice. *Like One of the Family . . . Conversations from a Domestic's Life*. 1956. Boston: Beacon Press, 1986.

Cheek, Madelon. " 'An Inestimable Prize,' Educating Women in the New Republic: The Writings of Judith Sargent Murray." *Journal of Thought* 20.3 (Fall 1985): 250-62.

Cixous, Hélène. "The Laugh of the Medusa." Trans. Keith and Paula Cohen. *Signs* 1.4 (Summer 1976): 875-93.

Clavers, Mrs. Mary [Caroline Matilda Kirkland]. *A New Home—Who'll Follow? Glimpses of Western Life*. Ed. William S. Osborne. 1839. New Haven, CT: Yale UP, 1965.

Cohen, Sandy. "Racial and Ethnic Humor in the United States." *Amerikastudien* 30 (1985): 203-11.

Conrad, Susan P. *Perish the Thought: Intellectual Women in Romantic America, 1830-1860. Secaucus, NJ: Citadel Press, 1978.*

Cox, Samuel S. *Why We Laugh*. 1876. Boston: Benjamin Blom, 1969.

Curry, Jane, ed. *Samantha Rastles the Woman Question*. Urbana: U of Illinois Press, 1983.

Curry, Jane. "Women as Subjects and Writers of Nineteenth Century American Humor." Diss. U of Michigan, 1975.

Daskam, Josephine Dodge. *Fables for the Fair: Cautionary Tales for Damsels Not Yet in Distress*. 1901. New York: Holt, Rinehart, 1967.

Dearborn, Mary V. *Pocahontas's Daughters: Gender and Ethnicity in American Culture*. New York: Oxford UP, 1986.

Dickinson, Emily. *The Complete Poems of Emily Dickinson*. Ed. Thomas H. Johnson. Boston: Little, Brown, 1955.

Diot, Rolande. "Sexus, Nexus and Taboos versus Female Humor: The Case of Erica Jong." *Revue Française D'Études Americaines* 30 (November 1986): 491-99.

Douglas, Mary. "Jokes." In *Implicit Meanings: Essays in Anthropology*. London: Routledge and Kegan Paul, 1975. 90-114.

Dresner, Zita Zatkin. "Twentieth Century American Women Humorists." Diss. U of Maryland, 1982.

Dworkin, Susan. "Roseanne Barr: The Disgruntled Housewife as Stand-up Comedian." *Ms.* 16:½ (July/August 1987): 106-8 + .

Eco, Umberto. "Frames of Comic 'Freedom.'" In *Carnival!* Ed. Thomas A. Sebeok. Berlin: Mouton, 1984. 1-9.

Eimerl, Sarel. "Can Women Be Funny? Humor Has Nothing to Do with Sex . . . Or Does It?" *Mademoiselle* Nov. 1962: 151 + .

Eisenstein, Hester. *Contemporary Feminist Thought*. Boston: G. K. Hall, 1983.

Ephron, Nora. *Crazy Salad: Some Things About Women*. New York: Knopf, 1975.

_____. *Scribble Scribble: Notes on the Media*. New York: Knopf, 1978.

Selected Bibliography

Fern, Fanny [Sara Willis Parton]. *Fern Leaves from Fanny's Port-Folio*. 1853. Chicago: Donohue, Henneberry, 1890.

――――. *Ruth Hall and Other Writings*. Ed. Joyce W. Warren. New Brunswick, NJ: Rutgers UP, 1986.

Fox, Greer Litton. "'Nice Girl': Social Control of Women through a Value Construct." *Signs*. 2.4 (Summer 1977): 805-17.

Freud, Sigmund. "Humor." In *The Complete Psychological Works of Sigmund Freud*. Trans. James Strachey. 24 vols. London: Hogarth Press, 1961. Vol. 21. 159-66.

Friedan, Betty. *The Feminine Mystique*. New York: Norton, 1963.

Gagnier, Regenia. "Between Women: A Cross-Class Analysis of Anarchic Humor." Paper delivered at the Modern Language Association. New York, December 1986.

Geng, Veronica. *Partners*. New York: Harper and Row, 1984.

――――. "Poll." *The New Yorker* 3 August 1987: 21.

Gilman, Charlotte Perkins. *Herland*. 1915. New York: Pantheon, 1979.

Goad, Mary Ellen. "The Image and the Woman in the Life and Writings of Mark Twain." *Emporia State Research Studies* 19.3 (March 1971).

Goodchilds, Jacqueline D., and Ewart E. Smith. "The Wit and His Group." *Human Relations* 17.1 (1964): 23-31.

Green, Rayna. "Magnolias Grow in Dirt: The Bawdy Lore of Southern Women." *Southern Exposure* 4 (1977): 29-33.

Habegger, Alfred. *Gender, Fantasy, and Realism in American Literature*. New York: Columbia UP, 1982.

Hacker, Helen Mayer. "Women as a Minority Group." *Social Forces* 30 (October 1951): 60-69.

Haweis, Rev. H. R. *American Humorists*. New York: Funk & Wagnalls, 1882.

Heilbrun, Carolyn. "Woman as Outsider." In *Reinventing Womanhood*. New York: Norton, 1979. 37-70.

Hekker, Terry. *Ever Since Adam and Eve*. New York: Fawcett Crest, 1980.

Holley, Marietta. "About My Books and Interesting People I Have Met." Undated handwritten ms. Rare Book Room, U of Illinois Library, Champaign-Urbana, IL.

Holliday, Carl. *The Wit and Humor of Colonial Days, 1607-1800*. Philadelphia, 1912. Williamstown, MA: Corner House, 1975.

Hugh-Jones, Siriol. "We Witless Women." *Twentieth Century* (July 1961): 16-25.

Hughes, Langston. *The Book of Negro Humor*. New York: Dodd, Mead, 1966.

Hurston, Zora Neale. *Dust Tracks on a Road: An Autobiography*. Ed. Robert E. Hemenway. 2nd ed. Urbana: U of Illinois Press, 1984.

Isajiw, Wsevolod W. "Definitions of Ethnicity." *Ethnicity* 1 (1974): 111-24.

Ivins, Molly. "Bureaucrats Should Be Issued Common-Sense Directive." Dallas *Times Herald* 26 Jan. 1986: A25.

――――. "There Will Always Be a Texas." *Ms.* 15.½ (July/August 1987): 82-84.

――――. "Wilson Is One of a Kind—Even in Texas." Dallas *Times Herald* 27 Feb. 1986: A21.

Jackson, Shirley. *Life Among the Savages*. New York: Farrar, Straus and Young, 1953.

James, Alice. *The Diary of Alice James*. Ed. Leon Edel. 1964. New York: Penguin, 1982.

James, Henry. *The Bostonians*. 1886. New York: Dial Press, 1945.

Jones, W. A. "The Ladies' Library." *Graham's Magazine* 21 (1842): 333.

Jong, Erica. *At the Edge of the Body*. New York: Holt, Rinehart and Winston, 1979.

――――. *Half-Lives*. New York: Holt, Rinehart and Winston, 1973.

_____. *Parachutes and Kisses*. New York: New American Library, 1984.

Josiah Allen's Wife [Marietta Holley]. *My Opinions and Betsey Bobbet's*. 1873. Hartford, CT: American Publishing Co., 1882.

Kaufman, Gloria, and Mary Kay Blakely. *Pulling Our Own Strings: Feminist Humor and Satire*. Bloomington: Indiana UP, 1980.

Keats, John. *You Might as Well Live: The Life and Times of Dorothy Parker*. 1970. New York: Paragon House, 1986.

Keillor, Garrison. *Happy to Be Here*. New York: Penguin, 1983.

Kenney, W. Howland. *Laughter in the Wilderness: Early American Humor to 1783*. Kent, OH: Kent State UP, 1976.

Kerr, Jean. *How I Got to Be Perfect*. Garden City, NY: Doubleday, 1978.

_____. *Penny Candy*. Garden City, NY: Doubleday, 1970.

_____. *The Snake Has All the Lines*. Garden City, NY: Doubleday, 1960.

Klein, Julia. "The New Stand-up Comics." *Ms.* (October 1984): 116-26.

Kuczkir, Mary. *My Dishtowel Flies at Half-Mast*. New York: Ballantine, 1980.

Lakoff, Robin. *Language and Woman's Place*. New York: Harper and Row, 1975.

Lamport, Felicia. *Cultural Slag*. Boston: Houghton Mifflin, 1966.

_____. *Light Metres*. New York: Perigree Books, 1982.

Lebowitz, Fran. *Social Studies*. New York: Random House, 1981.

Levine, Lawrence W. *Black Culture and Black Consciousness: Afro-American Folk Thought from Slavery to Freedom*. New York: Oxford UP, 1977.

Little, Judy. *Comedy and the Woman Writer: Woolf, Spark, and Feminism*. Lincoln: U of Nebraska Press, 1983.

Loos, Anita. *Gentlemen Prefer Blondes*. New York: Liveright, 1925.

Lowe, John. "Hurston, Humor, and the Harlem Renaissance." In *The Harlem Renaissance Re-examined*. Ed. Victor Kramer. New York: AMS Press, 1987. 283-313.

McCullough, Joseph B. "Shades of Red and Black: A Consideration of Modern Humor by Women." *Amerikastudien* 30.2 (1985): 191-201.

MacDonald, Betty [Anne Elizabeth Campbell Bard]. *The Egg and I*. Philadelphia: Lippincott, 1945.

McGhee, Paul E. "Sex Differences in Children's Humor." *Journal of Communication* 26 (1976): 176-89.

McGinley, Phyllis. *On the Contrary*. Garden City, NY: Doubleday, Doran, 1934.

_____. *A Short Walk from the Station*. New York: Viking, 1957.

_____. *Times Three: Selected Verse from Three Decades*. New York: Viking, 1971.

Martin, Judith. *Miss Manners' Guide to Excruciatingly Correct Behavior*. New York: Atheneum, 1982.

Mathews, Jane DeHart. "The New Feminism and the Dynamics of Social Change." In *Women's America: Refocusing the Past*. Ed. Linda K. Kerber and Jane DeHart Mathews. New York: Oxford UP, 1982.

Maurice, Arthur B. "Feminine Humorists." *Good Housekeeping* 50 (January 1910): 34-39.

Millay, Edna St. Vincent. *Letters of Edna St. Vincent Millay*. Ed. Allan Ross Macdougall. Camden, ME: Down East Books, 1952.

Miller, Alice Duer. *Are Women People? A Book of Rhymes for Suffrage Times*. New York: George H. Doran, 1915.

Mindess, Harvey. *Laughter and Liberation*. Los Angeles: Nash, 1971.

Selected Bibliography

Mitchell, Carol. "Hostility and Aggression Toward Males in Female Joke Telling." *Frontiers* 3.3 (Fall 1978): 19-23.

———. "The Sexual Perspective in the Appreciation and Interpretation of Jokes." *Western Folklore* 36 (1977): 303-29.

———. "Some Differences in Male and Female Joke Telling." In *Women's Folklore, Women's Culture*. Ed. Rosen A. Jordan and Susan J. Kalcik. Philadelphia: U of Pennsylvania Press, 1985. 163-86.

Morris, Linda Ann Finton. "Women Vernacular Humorists in Nineteenth-Century America: Ann Stephens, Frances Whitcher, and Marietta Holley." Diss. U of California-Berkeley, 1978.

Mowatt, Anna Cora. *Fashion*. In *Plays by American Women: The Early Years*. Ed. Judith E. Barlow. New York: Avon, 1981.

Newell, Margaretta. "Are Women Humorous?" *Outlook and Independent* 14 October 1931: 206-7+.

Ogden, Annegret S. *The Great American Housewife: From Helpmate to Wage Earner, 1776-1986*. Westport, CT: Greenwood Press, 1986.

Omwake, Louise. "A Study of the Sense of Humor: Its Relation to Sex, Age, and Personal Characteristics." *Journal of Applied Psychology* 21 (1937): 688-704.

Open Places 38/39 (Spring 1985). Special Issue: *Humor in America: The View from Open Places*.

Parker, Dorothy. *Here Lies: The Collected Stories of Dorothy Parker*. New York: Literary Guild of America, 1939.

———. Introduction. *The Most of S. J. Perelman*. New York: Simon and Schuster, 1958. xi-xiv.

———. *The Penguin Dorothy Parker*. London: Penguin, 1977.

———. *The Portable Dorothy Parker*. Rev. ed. New York: Viking, 1973.

Peck, Joseph M. *Life with Women and How to Survive It*. Englewood Cliffs, NJ: Prentice-Hall, 1961.

Perelman, S. J. *The Most of S. J. Perelman*. New York: Simon and Schuster, 1958.

Rather, Lois. "Were Women Funny? Some 19th Century Humorists." *American Book Collector* 21.5 (1971): 5-10.

Rebolledo, Tey Diana. "Walking the Thin Line: Humor in Chicana Literature." In *Beyond Stereotypes: The Critical Analysis of Chicana Literature*. Ed. María Herrera-Sobek. Binghamton, NY: Bilingual Press, 1985. 91-107.

Repplier, Agnes. *In Pursuit of Laughter*. Boston: Houghton Mifflin, 1936.

Richler, Mordecai. *The Best of Modern Humor*. New York: Knopf, 1983.

Rinder, Irwin D. "A Note on Humor as an Index of Minority Group Morale." *Phylon: The Atlanta University Review of Race and Culture* 26.2 (Summer 1965): 117-21.

Roche, Christine. *I'm Not a Feminist but . . .* London: Virago Press, 1985.

Rollins, Alice Wellington. "The Humor of Women." *The Critic and Good Literature* 1 (new series) 26 (28 June 1884): 301-2.

———. "Woman's Sense of Humor." *The Critic and Good Literature* 1 (new series) 13 (29 March 1884): 145-46.

Rosinsky, Natalie M. "A Female Man? The 'Medusan' Humor of Joanna Russ." *Extrapolation* 23.1 (1982): 31-36.

Ross, Harold. "Of All Things." *The New Yorker* 21 February 1925: 2.

Rourke, Constance. *American Humor: A Study of the National Character*. New York: Harcourt, Brace, 1931.

Selected Bibliography

Rowland, Helen. *Reflections of a Bachelor Girl*. New York: Dodge, 1909.

———. *The Sayings of Mrs. Solomon*. New York: Dodge, 1913.

Rubin, Louis D. ed. *The Comic Imagination in American Literature*. New Brunswick, NJ: Rutgers UP, 1973.

Russ, Joanna. *The Female Man*. 1975. London: The Women's Press, 1985.

———. *How to Suppress Women's Writing*. Austin: U of Texas Press, 1983.

Sanborn, Kate. *The Wit of Women*. New York: Funk & Wagnalls, 1885.

Sausser, Gail. *Lesbian Etiquette*. Freedom, CA: The Crossing Press, 1986.

Sayers, Dorothy L. "The Human-Not-Quite-Human." In *Unpopular Opinions*, 1947, rpt. in *Are Women Human?* Grand Rapids, MI: William B. Eerdmans, 1971.

Schmitz, Neil. *Of Huck and Alice: Humorous Writing in American Literature*. Minneapolis: U of Minnesota Press, 1983.

Seabury, Florence Guy. *The Delicatessen Husband and Other Essays*. New York: Harcourt, Brace, 1926.

Sellers, Pat. "Funny Ladies: Stand-up's Newest Standouts." *Cosmopolitan* Sept. 1987: 290-93 +.

Sheppard, Alice. "Humor and Sex-Role Stereotypes." Paper presented at Pioneers for Century III, Conference on the Power of Women and Men, Cincinnati, Ohio, April 1975.

———. "Joking and Appreciation of Humor in Nursery School Children." *Child Development* 45 (1974): 1098-1102.

———. "Sex-Role Attitudes, Sex Differences, and Comedian's Sex." Paper presented at the International Conference on Humor and Laughter, Cardiff, Wales, July 1976.

———. "There Were Ladies Present: American Women Cartoonists and Comic Artists in the Early Twentieth Century." *Journal of American Culture* 7 (Fall 1974): 38-48.

Showalter, Elaine, ed. *These Modern Women: Autobiographical Essays from the Twenties*. Old Westbury, NY: Feminist Press, 1978.

Skinner, Cornelia Otis. *Dithers and Jitters*. New York: Dodd, Mead, 1938.

———. *Nuts in May*. New York: Dodd, Mead, 1950.

Slater, E., and F. H. Freshfield. "The Sense of Humor in Men." *Cornhill* 6 (third series) (1899): 347-52.

Sollors, Werner. "Literature and Ethnicity." In *Harvard Encyclopedia of American Ethnic Groups*. Ed. Stephan Thernstrom. Cambridge: Harvard UP, 1980. 647-65.

———. *Beyond Ethnicity: Consent and Descent in American Culture*. New York: Oxford UP, 1986.

Sourcream 2. London: Sheba Feminist Publishers, 1981.

Spacks, Patricia Meyer. *The Female Imagination*. New York: Knopf, 1972.

Stein, Gertrude. *Fernhurst, Q.E.D., and other early writings*. New York: Liveright, 1971.

Steinem, Gloria. "If Men Could Menstruate." *Ms.* (October 1978): 110.

Stillman, Deanne. *Getting Back at Dad*. N.p.: Wideview Books, 1981.

Stimpson, Catharine R. "The 'F' Word." *Ms.* 16.1/2 (July/August 1987): 80 +.

Strasser, Susan. *Never Done: A History of American Housework*. New York: Pantheon, 1982.

Studies in American Humor. 3 (new series) 1 (Spring 1984).

Tonner, Leslie. *Nothing But the Best: The Luck of the Jewish Princess*. New York: Ballantine, 1975.

Toth, Emily. "Female Wits." *Massachusetts Review* 22.4 (Winter 1981): 783-93.

_____. "A Laughter of Their Own: Women's Humor in the United States." In *Critical Essays on American Humor*, ed. William Bedford Clark and W. Craig Turner. Boston: G. K. Hall, 1984. 199-215.

Trotter, Elizabeth Stanley. "Humor with a Gender." *The Atlantic Monthly* (Dec. 1922): 784-87.

Viorst, Judith. *It's Hard to Be Hip Over Thirty and Other Tragedies of Married Life*. New York: New American Library, 1968.

_____. *Love & Guilt & The Meaning of Life, Etc*. New York: Simon and Schuster, 1979.

_____. *People & Other Aggravations*. New York: Harper & Row, 1971.

Walker, Nancy. "Do Feminists Ever Laugh? Women's Humor and Women's Rights." *International Journal of Women's Studies* 4.1 (January/February 1981): 1-9.

_____. "Reformers and Young Maidens: Women and Virtue in *Adventures of Huckleberry Finn*." In *One Hundred Years of Huckleberry Finn: The Boy, His Book, and American Culture*. Ed. Robert Sattelmeyer and J. Donald Crowley. Columbia: U of Missouri Press, 1985. 171-85.

_____. "Wit, Sentimentality, and the Image of Women in the Nineteenth Century." *American Studies* 22.2 (Fall 1981): 5-22.

Weinstein, Sharon. "Don't Women Have a Sense of Comedy They Can Call Their Own?" *American Humor: An Interdisciplinary Newsletter* 1.2 (Fall 1974): 9-12.

Weiss, Helen S., and M. Jerry Weiss. *More Tales Out of School*. New York: Bantam, 1980.

Weisstein, Naomi. "Why We Aren't Laughing ... Anymore." *Ms.* (November 1973): 49-51 +.

Weldon, Fay. *Down Among the Women*. 1972. Chicago: Academy Chicago Publishers, 1984.

Welter, Barbara. "Anti-Intellectualism and the American Woman: 1800-1860." *Mid-America* 48 (October 1966): 258-70.

Whidden, Mary Bess. *Provincial Matters*. Albuquerque: U of New Mexico Press, 1985.

Whitcher, Frances M. *The Widow Bedott Papers*. Ed. Alice B. Neal. New York: J. C. Derby, 1856.

_____. *Widow Spriggins, Mary Elmer, and Other Sketches*. Ed. Mrs. M. L. Ward Whitcher. New York: Carleton, 1867.

White, E. B. *Poems and Sketches of E. B. White*. New York: Harper and Row, 1981.

White, E. B., and Katharine S. White. *A Subtreasury of American Humor*. New York: Modern Library, 1948.

Wilder, Marshall P., ed. *The Wit and Humor of America*. 10 vols. New York: Funk & Wagnalls, 1908.

Wilson, Barbara, and Rachel Da Silva, eds. *Backbone 4: Humor by Northwest Women*. Seattle: Seal Press, 1982.

Winter, Kate H. *Marietta Holley: Life with "Josiah Allen's Wife."* Syracuse: Syracuse UP, 1984.

Winterstein, A. "Contributions to the Problem of Humor." *The Psychoanalytic Quarterly* 3 (1934): 303-15.

Wirth, Louis. "The Problem of Minority Groups." In *The Science of Man in the World Crisis*. Ed. Ralph Linton. New York: Columbia UP, 1945. 347-72.

Witkowsky, Kathy. "Cartoon Verite: She Strips to Conquer—Nicole Hollander's 'Sylvia.'" *Vogue* (February 1986): 222 +.

Selected Bibliography

Wolfe, Susan J. "Ingroup Lesbian Feminist Political Humor." Paper delivered at the Midwest Modern Language Association, Minneapolis, MN, November, 1980.

Zippin, David. "Sex Differences and the Sense of Humor." *Psychoanalytic Review* 53 (1966): 45-55.

Selected List of Humor by American Women

The following list is not intended to be a complete bibliography of American women's humorous writing; rather, its purpose is to suggest the quantity, range, and variety of women's humorous expression from the early eighteenth century to the present. The list of individual works is arranged chronologically by date of the author's first published work.

COLLECTIONS

Kate Sanborn, ed. *The Wit of Women* (1885).
Martha Bensley Bruère and Mary Ritter Beard, eds. *Laughing Their Way: Women's Humor in America* (1934).
Deanne Stillman and Anne Beatts, eds. *Titters: The First Collection of Humor by Women* (1976).
Gloria Kaufman and Mary Kay Blakely, eds. *Pulling Our Own Strings: Feminist Humor and Satire* (1980).
Nancy Walker and Zita Dresner, eds. *Redressing the Balance: American Women's Humor from the Colonies to the 1980s* (1988).

INDIVIDUAL WORKS

Sarah Kemble Knight
  The Journal of Madame Knight (1704)
Judith Sargent Murray
  The Gleaner (1798)

Tabitha Tenney
  Female Quixotism (1801)
Mrs. Mary Clavers [Caroline Kirkland]
  A New Home—Who'll Follow? Glimpses of Western Life (1839)
Anna Cora Mowatt
  Fashion (1845)
Fanny Fern [Sara Willis Parton]
  Fern Leaves from Fanny's Port-Folio (1853)
  Fern Leaves: Second Series (1854)
Phoebe Cary
  Poems and Parodies (1854)
Ann Stephens
  High Life in New York by Jonathan Slick, Esq. (1854)
Frances Whitcher
  The Widow Bedott Papers (1856)
  Widow Spriggins, Mary Elmer, and Other Sketches (1867)
Harriet Beecher Stowe
  Oldtown Folks (1869)
  Sam Lawson's Oldtown Fireside Stories (1872)
Josiah Allen's Wife [Marietta Holley]
  My Opinions and Betsey Bobbet's (1873)
  Samantha at Saratoga (1887)
  Samantha at the World's Fair (1893)
  Samantha in Europe (1896)
  Samantha on the Woman Question (1913)
Gail Hamilton [Mary Abigail Dodge]
  Twelve Miles from a Lemon (1874)
Carolyn Wells
  Idle Idyls (1900)
  Folly for the Wise (1904)
  The Rubaiyat of a Motor Car (1906)
  Baubles (1917)
  Ptomaine Street: The Tale of Warble Petticoat
Josephine Daskam
  Fables for the Fair: Cautionary Tales for Damsels Not Yet in Distress (1901)

Agnes Repplier
  Compromises (1904)
  Points of Friction (1920)
Ann Warner
  Susan Clegg and Her Friend Mrs. Lathrop (1904)
  Susan Clegg and Her Love Affairs (1906)
  Susan Clegg and Her Neighbors' Affairs (1906)
  Susan Clegg and a Man in the House (1907)
Mary Roberts Rinehart
  The Amazing Adventures of Letitia Carberry (1911)
  Tish (1916)
  More Tish (1921)
  Tish Plays the Game (1926)
  The Book of Tish (1931)
  Tish Marches On (1937)
Charlotte Perkins Gilman
  Herland (1915)
Alice Duer Miller
  *Are Women People? A Book of Rhymes for Suffrage
    Times* (1915)
  Women are People! (1917)
Dorothy Parker
  Men I'm Not Married To (1922)
  Enough Rope (1926)
  Sunset Gun (1928)
  Laments for the Living (1930)
  Death and Taxes (1931)
  After Such Pleasures (1933)
  Here Lies (1939)
Nancy Boyd [Edna St. Vincent Millay]
  Distressing Dialogues (1924)
Anita Loos
  Gentlemen Prefer Blondes (1925)
  But Gentlemen Marry Brunettes (1928)
Florence Guy Seabury
  The Delicatessen Husband and Other Essays (1926)
Margaret Fishback
  I Feel Better Now (1932)

Out of my Head (1933)
I Take It Back (1935)
One to a Customer (1937)

Cornelia Otis Skinner
Tiny Garments (1932)
Dithers and Jitters (1938)
Soap Behind the Ears (1941)
Nuts in May (1950)

Phyllis McGinley
On the Contrary (1934)
One More Manhattan (1937)
A Pocketful of Wry (1940)
Husbands Are Difficult; or, The Book of Oliver Ames (1941)
Stones from a Glass House (1946)
A Short Walk from the Station (1951)
Times Three: Selected Verse from Three Decades (1960)

Margaret Halsey
With Malice Toward Some (1938)
Some of My Best Friends Are Soldiers (1944)
This Demi-Paradise: A Westchester Diary (1960)

Betty MacDonald [Anne Elizabeth Campbell Bard]
The Egg and I (1945)
The Plague and I (1948)
Anybody Can Do Anything (1950)
Onions in the Stew (1955)

Shirley Jackson
Life Among the Savages (1953)
Raising Demons (1957)

Alice Childress
Like One of the Family . . . Conversations from a Domestic's Life (1956)

Emily Hahn
Spousery (1956)

Jean Kerr
Please Don't Eat the Daisies (1957)
The Snake Has All the Lines (1960)
Penny Candy (1970)
How I Got to Be Perfect (1978)

Selected List

Peg Bracken
The I Hate to Cook Book (1960)
The I Hate to Housekeep Book (1962)
I Try to Behave Myself (1964)
Felicia Lamport
Scrap Irony (1961)
Cultural Slag (1966)
Light Metres (1982)
Judith Viorst
The Village Square (1965)
It's Hard to Be Hip Over Thirty and Other Tragedies of Married Life (1968)
People and Other Aggravations (1971)
Yes, Married: A Saga of Love and Complaint (1972)
How Did I Get to Be Forty and Other Atrocities (1976)
Love & Guilt & the Meaning of Life, Etc. (1979)
Erma Bombeck
At Wit's End (1967)
I Lost Everything in the Post-Natal Depression (1972)
The Grass Is Always Greener Over the Septic Tank (1976)
If Life Is a Bowl of Cherries—What Am I Doing in the Pits? (1978)
Phyllis Diller
Phyllis Diller's Marriage Manual (1967)
Nora Ephron
Wallflower at the Orgy (1970)
Crazy Salad: Some Things About Women (1973)
Scribble Scribble: Notes on the Media (1978)
Heartburn (1983)
Gail Parent
Sheila Levine Is Dead and Living in New York (1972)
Rita Mae Brown
Rubyfruit Jungle (1973)
Southern Discomfort (1982)
Erica Jong
Fear of Flying (1973)
How to Save Your Own Life (1977)
Parachutes and Kisses (1984)

Leslie Tonner
  Nothing But the Best: The Luck of the Jewish Princess (1975)
Cyra McFadden
  The Serial (1977)
Fran Lebowitz
  Metropolitan Life (1978)
  Social Studies (1981)
Ellen Goodman
  Close to Home (1979)
Terry Hekker
  Ever Since Adam and Eve (1980)
Mary Kuczkir
  My Dishtowel Flies at Half-Mast (1980)
Teresa Bloomingdale
  Up a Family Tree (1981)
  Sense and Momsense (1986)
Deanne Stillman
  Getting Back at Dad (1981)
Judith Martin
  Miss Manners' Guide to Excruciatingly Correct Behavior (1982)
Veronica Geng
  Partners (1984)
Joan Rivers
  The Life and Hard Times of Heidi Abramowitz (1984)
Mary Bess Whidden
  Provincial Matters (1985)
Gail Sausser
  Lesbian Etiquette (1986)

Index

Index

Index

Index

Index

69, 151; "If I Were a Man," 59-60;
Moving the Mountain, 57; *With Her
in Ourland*, 57; *Women and
Economics*, 57; "The Yellow
Wallpaper," 57, 82
Gleaner, The, 167-88*n*2
Godey's Lady's Book, 7, 8, 17, 18, 19, 46,
134
Golden, Harry, 115
Good Housekeeping magazine, 71
Goodman, Ellen, 7, 35, 45, 145
"Great American Joke, The," 36
Greenwood, Grace, 74

Haliburton, Thomas: Sam Slick, 19, 41
Halsey, Margaret, 107
Harte, Bret, 40: "The Luck of Roaring
Camp," 41
Hawthorne, Nathaniel: "scribbling
women," 9, 46
Hazel (television series), 109
Hekker, Terry: *Ever Since Adam and
Eve*, 140-41
Here Lies, 35
Herland, 57-59, 61, 69, 151
Hero Ain't Nothin' But a Sandwich, A,
107
Holland, Barbara: "The Day's Work,"
159
Hollander, Nicole: "Sylvia," 78
Holley, Marietta, 8, 11, 41, 46, 72, 74,
87, 120, 130: Betsey Bobbet, 63-64,
66, 89, 147; on Elizabeth Cady
Stanton, 139; Josiah Allen, 137; *My
Opinions and Betsey Bobbet's*, 37,
171; Samantha Allen, 28, 30, 35, 81,
126, 157; use of pseudonyms, 74-75.
See also Allen, Samantha; Josiah
Allen's Wife
Hurston, Zora Neale, 107, 114: *Dust
Tracks on a Road*, 111, 112-13;
Harlem Renaissance, 113; *Moses,
Man of the Mountain*, 111; *Their
Eyes Were Watching God*, 111
Holmes, Oliver Wendell, 40
How I Got to be Perfect, 95-96, 98
Huck Finn, 18, 36-37, 171, 181: and
images of women, 124

Hughes, Langston, 113: *The Book of
Negro Humor*, 101-2, 106, 116
Humor: definitions of, xi-xii
Humor (Freud), 23, 25
"Hungry Husbands," 53

I Didn't Come Here to Argue, 147-48
I Hate to Cook Book, The, 95-96, 131,
156
"If I Were a Man," 59-60
"If Men Could Menstruate," 152
In Pursuit of Laughter, 166-67
"Indian Summer," 28
Interview magazine, 7
Irving, Washington, 40: "Rip Van
Winkle," 43-44
Ivins, Molly, 7, 171, 173, 181: *Times
Herald* (Dallas), 176

Jackson, Shirley, 4, 91, 107, 145: image
of the housewife, 125; *Life Among
the Savages*, xi, 31, 33-34, 35, 48-49,
65, 66, 95, 97; *Raising Demons*, xi
James, Alice, 82
James, Henry: *The Bostonians*, 140
Jewett, Sarah Orne, 74
Jong, Erica, 202*n*44: compared to Henry
Miller, 128-29; *Parachutes and
Kisses*, 151; "Woman Enough,"
159-60
Josiah Allen's Wife, 120-22. *See also*
Holley, Marietta
Journal from Ellipsia, 192*n*36
"Just a Little One," 64-65, 66

Kaufman, Gloria: definition of feminist
humor, 143-44, 145
Kaufman, Gloria, and Mary Kay Blakely:
*Pulling Our Own Strings: Feminist
Humor and Satire*, x, 145
Keillor, Garrison: *Happy to Be Here*,
191*n*15
Kennedy, Flo, 149-50: *Color Me Flo*, 156
Kerr, Jean, 4, 47, 91, 107, 140, 175: *How
I Got to be Perfect*, 95-96, 98; image
of the housewife, 125; *Penny
Candy*, 130; *Please Don't Eat the
Daisies*, ix, 48; *The Snake Has All the*

Index

Nancy Walker received her Ph.D. in American Literature from Kent State University in 1971 and has taught American Literature/American Studies since then at Stephens College in Columbia, Missouri, where she is now department chair of languages and literature. She has served as president of the Midcontinent American Studies Association (1984-85) and as chair of the bibliography committee of the American Studies Association (1987-88), and is currently on the editorial boards for *American Studies* and *Tulsa Studies in Women's Literature*. Walker is co-editor, with Zita Dresner, of *Redressing the Balance: American Women's Humor from the Colonies to the 1980s,* an anthology published in 1988 by the University Press of Mississippi. She contributes to *International Journal of Women's Studies, Southern Quarterly, Studies in American Fiction, American Quarterly,* and *Denver Quarterly.*